Grammar Sense 1

SECOND EDITION

TEACHER'S BOOK

AUTHOR
Susan Iannuzzi

OXFORD

UNIVERSITY PRESS

OXFORD
UNIVERSITY PRESS

198 Madison Avenue
New York, NY 10016 USA

Great Clarendon Street, Oxford, OX2 6DP, United Kingdom

Oxford University Press is a department of the University of Oxford.
It furthers the University's objective of excellence in research, scholarship,
and education by publishing worldwide. Oxford is a registered trade
mark of Oxford University Press in the UK and in certain other countries

First published in 2012

2016 2015 2014 2013 2012

10 9 8 7 6 5 4 3 2 1

General Manager, American ELT: Laura Pearson
Publisher: Stephanie Karras
Associate Publishing Manager: Sharon Sargent
Managing Editor: Alex Ragan
Director, ADP: Susan Sanguily
Executive Design Manager: Maj-Britt Hagsted
Electronic Production Manager: Julie Armstrong
Sr. Designer: Yin Ling Wong
Image Manager: Trisha Masterson

Publishing and Editorial Management: hyphen S.A.

ISBN: 978 0 19 448938 6 Teacher's Book 1 with Online Practice pack
ISBN: 978 0 19 448942 3 Teacher's Book 1 as pack component
ISBN: 978 0 19 448928 7 Online Practice as pack component

Printed in China

This book is printed on paper from certified and well-managed sources

Contents

Welcome to Grammar Sense

A Sensible Solution to Learning Grammar

Grammar Sense Second Edition gives learners a true understanding of how grammar is used in authentic contexts.

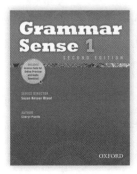 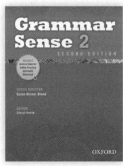  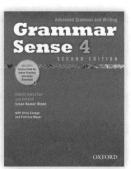

With Grammar Sense Online Practice

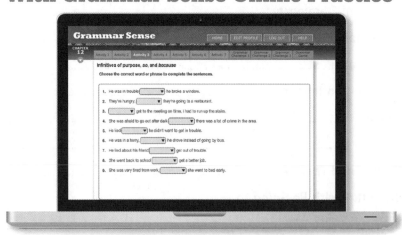

- **Student Solutions:** a **focus on Critical Thinking** for improved application of grammatical knowledge.

- **Writing Solutions:** a **Writing section in every chapter** encourages students to see the relevance of grammar in their writing.

- **Technology Solutions:** *Grammar Sense Online Practice* provides additional practice in an easy-to-use **online workbook**.

- **Assessment Solutions:** the Part Tests at the end of every section and the Grammar Sense Test Generators allow **ongoing assessment**.

Each chapter in *Grammar Sense Second Edition* **follows** this format.

The Grammar in Discourse section introduces the target grammar in its natural context via high-interest readings.

> **Pre- and post-reading tasks** help students understand the text.

A GRAMMAR IN DISCOURSE

What Kind of Learner Are You?

A1 Before You Read

Discuss these questions.

Do you like to listen to lectures? Do you prefer to look at pictures and diagrams? Do you like to do experiments? Do you think everyone learns in the same way?

A2 Read

 CD1 T43 Read the article from a science magazine on the following page. What kind of learner are you?

A3 After You Read

Write *T* for true or *F* for false for each statement.

_T_ **1.** Teachers like good listeners.

___ **2.** Good listeners don't always follow instructions.

___ **3.** Julie Hong does well in school.

___ **4.** Larry

___ **5.** Hands-

___ **6.** Pete D

> Exposure to **authentic readings** encourages awareness of the grammar in daily life: in textbooks, magazines, newspapers, websites, and so on.

▶ SCIENCE MAGAZINE

What Kind of Learner Are You?

Researchers say that there are at least three different types of learners.

Some learners are good listeners. Teachers like them because they always
5 follow instructions. Julie Hong is a student like this. She gets A's in all her classes at Deerfield High School in
10 Connecticut. She loves school, and her teachers love her because she always pays attention in class. "I pay attention because I don't want to miss important information," she says.

15 Some people learn from pictures and diagrams. They are very creative but don't like details.
20 Larry Dawson is a good example of this kind of learner. He is studying graphic design at Warfield Community College in Ohio. He is usually

25 very good with ideas and concepts but sometimes has problems with details. "New ideas are exciting, but I often get bored at the end of a big project," Larry admits.

Some learners
30 rarely learn from books or pictures. They are "hands-on" learners. They learn from
35 experience. Pete Donaldson is a good example of a hands-on learner. Pete is studying computer science at the University of Florida. Pete never reads
40 computer manuals and seldom looks at diagrams. He just spends hours on the computer. "That's the best way for me to learn," he says.

So, what kind of learner are you?
45 Do you always learn the same way? Or do you learn one way in some classes and another way in others?

The Form section(s) provides clear presentation of the target grammar, detailed notes, and thorough practice exercises.

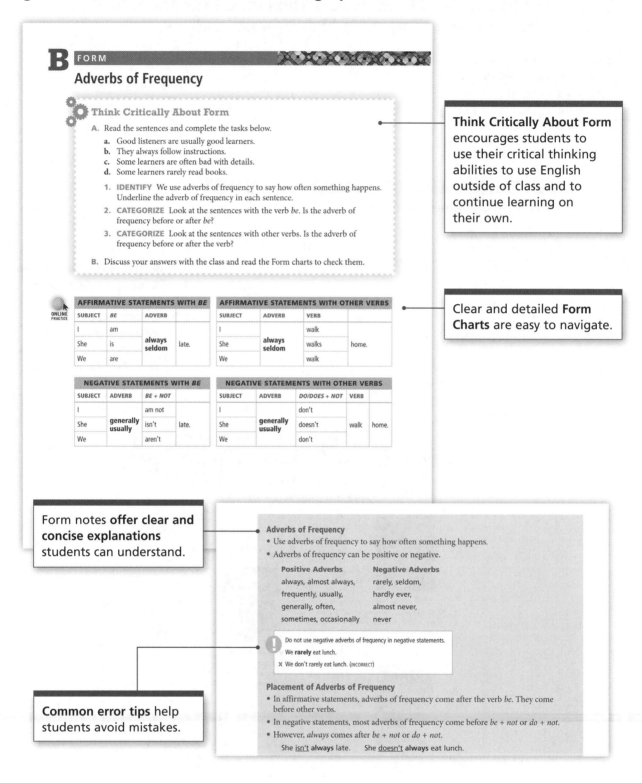

B FORM

Adverbs of Frequency

Think Critically About Form

A. Read the sentences and complete the tasks below.
  a. Good listeners are usually good learners.
  b. They always follow instructions.
  c. Some learners are often bad with details.
  d. Some learners rarely read books.

1. **IDENTIFY** We use adverbs of frequency to say how often something happens. Underline the adverb of frequency in each sentence.

2. **CATEGORIZE** Look at the sentences with the verb *be*. Is the adverb of frequency before or after *be*?

3. **CATEGORIZE** Look at the sentences with other verbs. Is the adverb of frequency before or after the verb?

B. Discuss your answers with the class and read the Form charts to check them.

Think Critically About Form encourages students to use their critical thinking abilities to use English outside of class and to continue learning on their own.

ONLINE PRACTICE

AFFIRMATIVE STATEMENTS WITH *BE*

SUBJECT	BE	ADVERB	
I	am	**always seldom**	late.
She	is		
We	are		

AFFIRMATIVE STATEMENTS WITH OTHER VERBS

SUBJECT	ADVERB	VERB	
I	**always seldom**	walk	home.
She		walks	
We		walk	

NEGATIVE STATEMENTS WITH *BE*

SUBJECT	ADVERB	BE + NOT	
I	**generally usually**	am not	late.
She		isn't	
We		aren't	

NEGATIVE STATEMENTS WITH OTHER VERBS

SUBJECT	ADVERB	DO/DOES + NOT	VERB	
I	**generally usually**	don't	walk	home.
She		doesn't		
We		don't		

Clear and detailed **Form Charts** are easy to navigate.

Form notes offer clear and concise explanations students can understand.

Adverbs of Frequency
• Use adverbs of frequency to say how often something happens.
• Adverbs of frequency can be positive or negative.

Positive Adverbs	**Negative Adverbs**
always, almost always,	rarely, seldom,
frequently, usually,	hardly ever,
generally, often,	almost never,
sometimes, occasionally	never

❗ Do not use negative adverbs of frequency in negative statements.
  We **rarely** eat lunch.
  ✗ We don't rarely eat lunch. (INCORRECT)

Placement of Adverbs of Frequency
• In affirmative statements, adverbs of frequency come after the verb *be*. They come before other verbs.
• In negative statements, most adverbs of frequency come before *be* + *not* or *do* + *not*.
• However, *always* comes after *be* + *not* or *do* + *not*.
  She <u>isn't</u> **always** late.   She <u>doesn't</u> **always** eat lunch.

Common error tips help students avoid mistakes.

The Meaning and Use section(s) offers clear and comprehensive explanations of how the target structure is used, and exercises to practice using it appropriately.

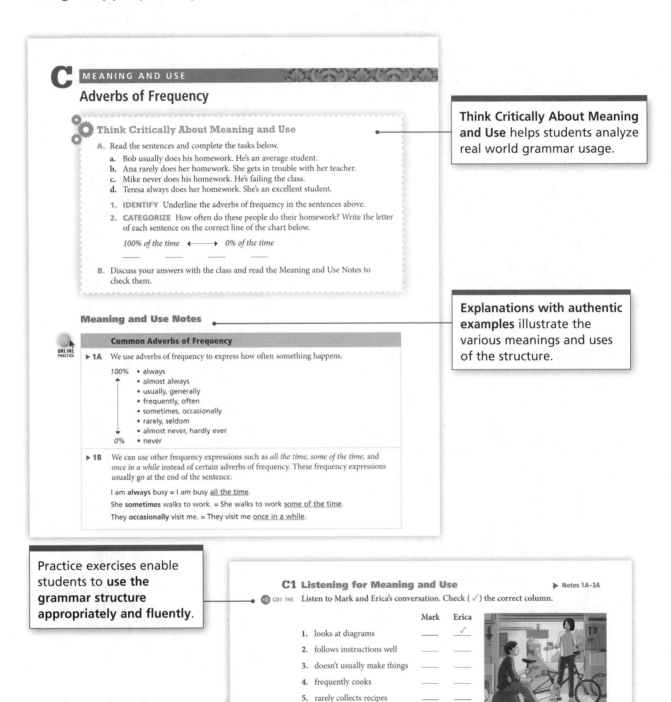

C MEANING AND USE

Adverbs of Frequency

⚙ **Think Critically About Meaning and Use**

A. Read the sentences and complete the tasks below.

a. Bob usually does his homework. He's an average student.
b. Ana rarely does her homework. She gets in trouble with her teacher.
c. Mike never does his homework. He's failing the class.
d. Teresa always does her homework. She's an excellent student.

1. **IDENTIFY** Underline the adverbs of frequency in the sentences above.

2. **CATEGORIZE** How often do these people do their homework? Write the letter of each sentence on the correct line of the chart below.

100% of the time ◄——► 0% of the time

_____   _____   _____   _____

B. Discuss your answers with the class and read the Meaning and Use Notes to check them.

Think Critically About Meaning and Use helps students analyze real world grammar usage.

Meaning and Use Notes

ONLINE
PRACTICE

Common Adverbs of Frequency

▶ **1A** We use adverbs of frequency to express how often something happens.

100% • always
↑   • almost always
       • usually, generally
       • frequently, often
       • sometimes, occasionally
       • rarely, seldom
↓   • almost never, hardly ever
0%   • never

▶ **1B** We can use other frequency expressions such as *all the time, some of the time,* and *once in a while* instead of certain adverbs of frequency. These frequency expressions usually go at the end of the sentence.

I am **always** busy = I am busy <u>all the time</u>.

She **sometimes** walks to work. = She walks to work <u>some of the time</u>.

They **occasionally** visit me. = They visit me <u>once in a while</u>.

Explanations with authentic examples illustrate the various meanings and uses of the structure.

Practice exercises enable students to **use the grammar structure appropriately and fluently.**

C1 Listening for Meaning and Use   ▶ Notes 1A–3A

🔊 CD1 T45   Listen to Mark and Erica's conversation. Check (✓) the correct column.

	Mark	Erica
1. looks at diagrams	____	✓
2. follows instructions well	____	____
3. doesn't usually make things	____	____
4. frequently cooks	____	____
5. rarely collects recipes	____	____
6. usually fixes things.	____	____

Special sections appear throughout the chapters with clear explanations, authentic examples, and follow-up exercises.

Beyond the Sentence demonstrates how structures function differently in extended discourses.

Informally Speaking clarifies the differences between written and spoken language.

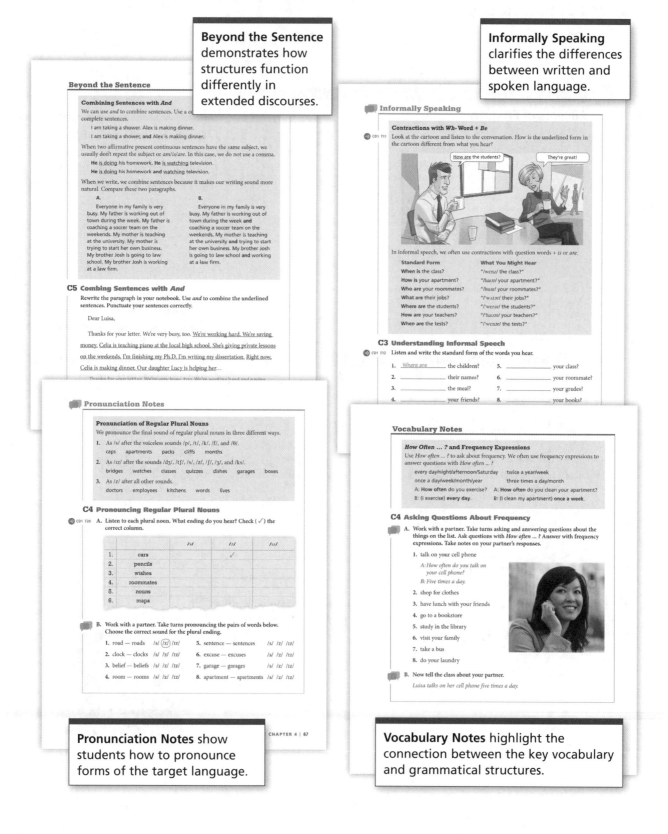

Beyond the Sentence

Combining Sentences with *And*

We can use *and* to combine sentences. Use a c[...] complete sentences.

I am taking a shower. Alex is making dinner.

I am taking a shower, **and** Alex is making dinner.

When two affirmative present continuous sentences have the same subject, we usually don't repeat the subject or *am/is/are*. In this case, we do not use a comma.

He is doing his homework. He is watching television.

He is doing his homework **and** watching television.

When we write, we combine sentences because it makes our writing sound more natural. Compare these two paragraphs.

A.
Everyone in my family is very busy. My father is working out of town during the week. My father is coaching a soccer team on the weekends. My mother is teaching at the university. My mother is trying to start her own business. My brother Josh is going to law school. My brother Josh is working at a law firm.

B.
Everyone in my family is very busy. My father is working out of town during the week **and** coaching a soccer team on the weekends. My mother is teaching at the university **and** trying to start her own business. My brother Josh is going to law school **and** working at a law firm.

C5 Combining Sentences with *And*

Rewrite the paragraph in your notebook. Use *and* to combine the underlined sentences. Punctuate your sentences correctly.

Dear Luisa,

Thanks for your letter. We're very busy, too. We're working hard. We're saving money. Celia is teaching piano at the local high school. She's giving private lessons on the weekends. I'm finishing my Ph.D. I'm writing my dissertation. Right now, Celia is making dinner. Our daughter Lucy is helping her…

Pronunciation Notes

Pronunciation of Regular Plural Nouns

We pronounce the final sound of regular plural nouns in three different ways.

1. As /s/ after the voiceless sounds /p/, /t/, /k/, /f/, and /θ/.
   caps   apartments   packs   cliffs   months

2. As /ɪz/ after the sounds /dʒ/, /tʃ/, /s/, /z/, /ʃ/, /ʒ/, and /ks/.
   bridges   watches   classes   quizzes   dishes   garages   boxes

3. As /z/ after all other sounds.
   doctors   employees   kitchens   words   lives

C4 Pronouncing Regular Plural Nouns

A. Listen to each plural noun. What ending do you hear? Check (✓) the correct column.

		/s/	/z/	/ɪz/
1.	cars		✓	
2.	pencils			
3.	wishes			
4.	roommates			
5.	nouns			
6.	maps			

B. Work with a partner. Take turns pronouncing the pairs of words below. Choose the correct sound for the plural ending.

1. road — roads   /s/ /z/ /ɪz/
2. clock — clocks   /s/ /z/ /ɪz/
3. belief — beliefs   /s/ /z/ /ɪz/
4. room — rooms   /s/ /z/ /ɪz/
5. sentence — sentences   /s/ /z/ /ɪz/
6. excuse — excuses   /s/ /z/ /ɪz/
7. garage — garages   /s/ /z/ /ɪz/
8. apartment — apartments   /s/ /z/ /ɪz/

Pronunciation Notes show students how to pronounce forms of the target language.

Informally Speaking

Contractions with *Wh-* Word + *Be*

CD1 T11 Look at the cartoon and listen to the conversation. How is the underlined form in the cartoon different from what you hear?

> How are the students?

> They're great!

In informal speech, we often use contractions with question words + *is* or *are*.

Standard Form	What You Might Hear
When is the class?	"/wɛnz/ the class?"
How is your apartment?	"/haʊz/ your apartment?"
Who are your roommates?	"/huər/ your roommates?"
What are their jobs?	"/wʌtər/ their jobs?"
Where are the students?	"/wɛrər/ the students?"
How are your teachers?	"/haʊər/ your teachers?"
When are the tests?	"/wɛnər/ the tests?"

C3 Understanding Informal Speech

CD1 T12 Listen and write the standard form of the words you hear.

1. _Where are_ the children?
2. _____ their names?
3. _____ the meal?
4. _____ your friends?
5. _____ your class?
6. _____ your roommate?
7. _____ your grades?
8. _____ your books?

Vocabulary Notes

How Often … ? and Frequency Expressions

Use *How often … ?* to ask about frequency. We often use frequency expressions to answer questions with *How often … ?*

every day/night/afternoon/Saturday	twice a year/week
once a day/week/month/year	three times a day/month
A: **How often** do you exercise?	A: **How often** do you clean your apartment?
B: (I exercise) **every day.**	B: (I clean my apartment) **once a week.**

C4 Asking Questions About Frequency

A. Work with a partner. Take turns asking and answering questions about the things on the list. Ask questions with *How often … ?* Answer with frequency expressions. Take notes on your partner's responses.

1. talk on your cell phone
   A: *How often do you talk on your cell phone?*
   B: *Five times a day.*
2. shop for clothes
3. have lunch with your friends
4. go to a bookstore
5. study in the library
6. visit your family
7. take a bus
8. do your laundry

B. Now tell the class about your partner.

Luisa talks on her cell phone five times a day.

Vocabulary Notes highlight the connection between the key vocabulary and grammatical structures.

The Writing section guides students through the process of applying grammatical knowledge to compositions.

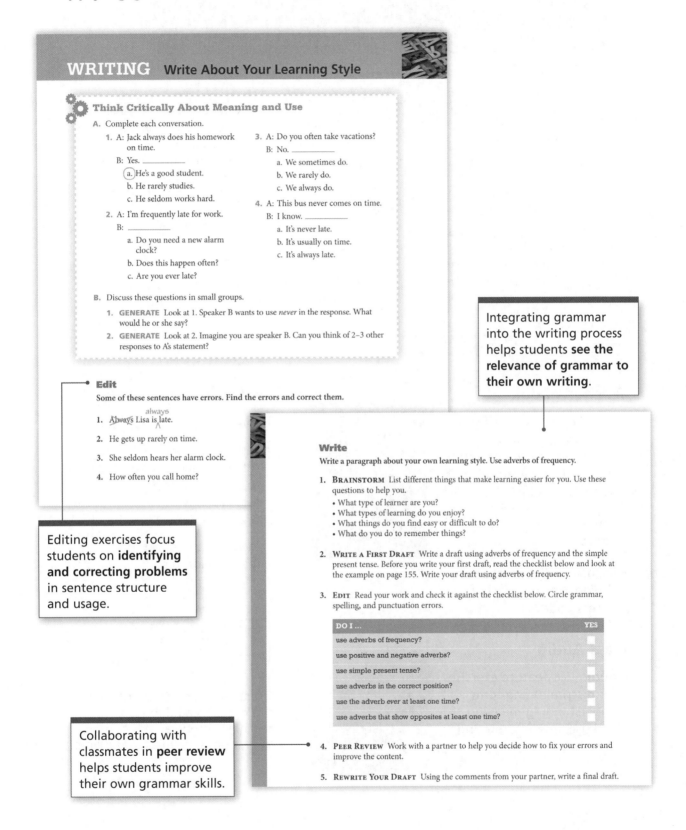

WRITING   Write About Your Learning Style

Think Critically About Meaning and Use

A. Complete each conversation.

1. A: Jack always does his homework on time.

   B: Yes. _____

   a. He's a good student.
   b. He rarely studies.
   c. He seldom works hard.

2. A: I'm frequently late for work.

   B: _____

   a. Do you need a new alarm clock?
   b. Does this happen often?
   c. Are you ever late?

3. A: Do you often take vacations?

   B: No. _____

   a. We sometimes do.
   b. We rarely do.
   c. We always do.

4. A: This bus never comes on time.

   B: I know. _____

   a. It's never late.
   b. It's usually on time.
   c. It's always late.

B. Discuss these questions in small groups.

1. **GENERATE** Look at 1. Speaker B wants to use *never* in the response. What would he or she say?

2. **GENERATE** Look at 2. Imagine you are speaker B. Can you think of 2–3 other responses to A's statement?

Edit

Some of these sentences have errors. Find the errors and correct them.

1. Always Lisa is late.

2. He gets up rarely on time.

3. She seldom hears her alarm clock.

4. How often you call home?

Write

Write a paragraph about your own learning style. Use adverbs of frequency.

1. **BRAINSTORM** List different things that make learning easier for you. Use these questions to help you.

   • What type of learner are you?
   • What types of learning do you enjoy?
   • What things do you find easy or difficult to do?
   • What do you do to remember things?

2. **WRITE A FIRST DRAFT** Write a draft using adverbs of frequency and the simple present tense. Before you write your first draft, read the checklist below and look at the example on page 155. Write your draft using adverbs of frequency.

3. **EDIT** Read your work and check it against the checklist below. Circle grammar, spelling, and punctuation errors.

DO I...	YES
use adverbs of frequency?	☐
use positive and negative adverbs?	☐
use simple present tense?	☐
use adverbs in the correct position?	☐
use the adverb *ever* at least one time?	☐
use adverbs that show opposites at least one time?	☐

4. **PEER REVIEW** Work with a partner to help you decide how to fix your errors and improve the content.

5. **REWRITE YOUR DRAFT** Using the comments from your partner, write a final draft.

Integrating grammar into the writing process helps students **see the relevance of grammar to their own writing**.

Editing exercises focus students on **identifying and correcting problems** in sentence structure and usage.

Collaborating with classmates in **peer review** helps students improve their own grammar skills.

Assessment

Choose the correct response to complete each conversation.

1. **A:** Do you often take vacations?
   B: _____

   a. No. We sometimes do.   **c.** No. We always do.

   b. No. We rarely do.   **d.** No. We often do.

2. **A:** How often do you wash your car?
   B: _____

   a. They usually do.   **c.** Yes, I do.

   b. Seldom.   **d.** No, I don't.

3. **A:** The train almost always comes late.
   B: _____

   a. I know. It's frequently on time.   **c.** I know. It's rarely on time.

   b. I know. It's usually on time.   **d.** I know. It's always on time.

> **Part Tests** allow ongoing assessment and evaluate the students' mastery of the grammar.

Teacher's Resources

Teacher's Book

- Creative techniques for presenting the grammar, along with troubleshooting tips, and suggestions for additional activities

- Answer key and audio scripts

- Includes a *Grammar Sense Online Practice* Teacher Access Code

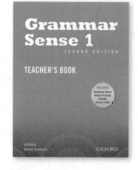

Class Audio

- Audio CDs feature exercises for discriminating form, understanding meaning and use, and interpreting non-standard forms

Test Generator CD-ROM

- Over 3,000 items available!

- Test-generating software allows you to customize tests for all levels of Grammar Sense

- Includes a bank of ready-made tests

Grammar Sense Teachers' Club site contains additional teaching resources at www.oup.com/elt/teacher/grammarsense

ONLINE PRACTICE

Grammar Sense Online Practice is an online program with all new content. It correlates with the *Grammar Sense* student books and provides additional practice.

FOR THE STUDENT

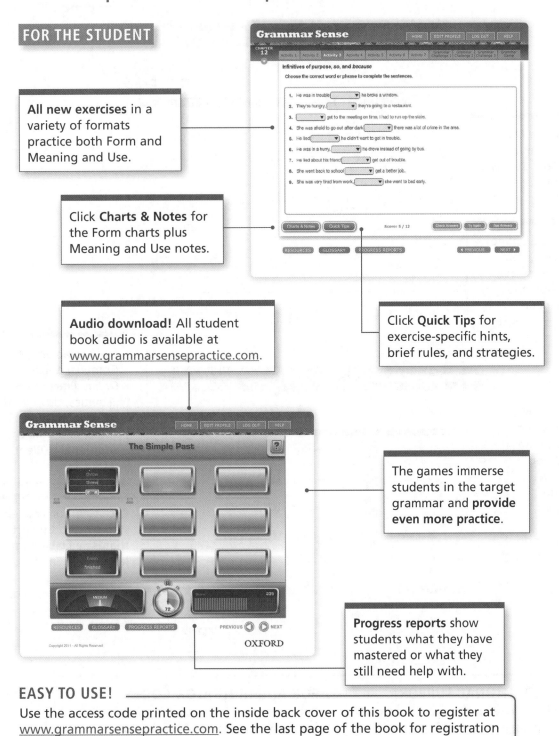

All new exercises in a variety of formats practice both Form and Meaning and Use.

Click **Charts & Notes** for the Form charts plus Meaning and Use notes.

Audio download! All student book audio is available at www.grammarsensepractice.com.

Click **Quick Tips** for exercise-specific hints, brief rules, and strategies.

The games immerse students in the target grammar and **provide even more practice**.

Progress reports show students what they have mastered or what they still need help with.

EASY TO USE!

Use the access code printed on the inside back cover of this book to register at www.grammarsensepractice.com. See the last page of the book for registration instructions.

Flexible enough for use in the classroom or easily assigned as homework.

Grammar Sense Online Practice automatically **grades** student exercises and tracks progress.

The easy-to-use online management system allows you to **review**, **print**, or **export** the reports you need.

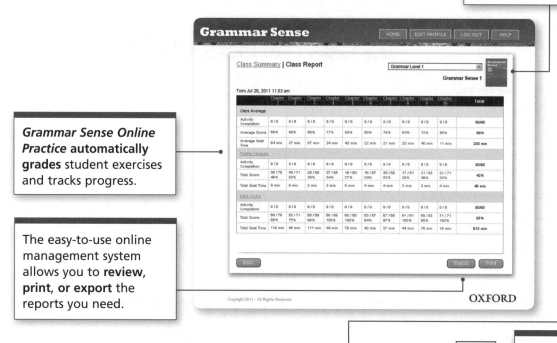

You can **access all** *Grammar Sense Online Practice* **activities**, download the student book audio, and utilize the additional student resources.

The **straightforward online management system** allows you to add or delete classes, manage your classes, plus view, print, or export all class and individual student reports.

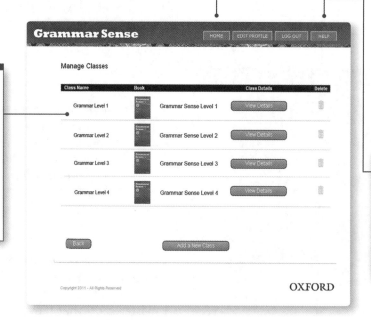

Click Help for simple, step-by-step support that is **available in six languages**: English, Spanish, Korean, Arabic, Chinese, and Japanese.

FOR ADDITIONAL SUPPORT
Email our customer support team at grammarsensesupport@oup.com and you will receive a response within 24 hours.

FOR ADMNISTRATOR CODES
Please contact your sales representative for an Administrator Access Code. A Teacher Access Code comes with every Teacher's Book.

Teacher's Book Introduction
Susan Iannuzzi

About the Teacher's Book

THE CHAPTERS

- **Overview:** Each chapter of the Teacher's Book begins with an overview of the grammar presented in the Student Book chapter. It enables the teacher to focus on the main points covered in the chapter, and highlights difficulties students may have with the structures.

- **Grammar in Discourse:** This section provides directions to help the teacher effectively teach the Before You Read, Read, and After You Read activities in the Student Book. It suggests creative ways to activate background knowledge, offers innovative reading strategies, and gives tips on checking comprehension.

- **Form:** This section offers two alternative ways to teach the inductive Think Critically About Form exercises: Method 1 for students who are unfamiliar with the structure and may need extra support, and Method 2 for students who are already familiar with the structure and may be able to work more independently. The section also contains step-by-step instructions for presenting the Form Charts, and directions for utilizing the Special Sections such as Informally Speaking.

- **Meaning and Use:** This section offers advice on teaching the inductive Think Critically About Meaning and Use exercises. It also provides step-by-step instructions for presenting the Meaning and Use Notes and directions for using the Special Sections such as Vocabulary Notes and Beyond the Sentence.

- **Trouble Spots:** These notes, placed at strategic points throughout the Teacher's Book, alert the teacher to problems that students may have with the grammar. They suggest how to address these problems effectively, and, where relevant, direct the teacher to parts of the Student Book that clarify or offer practice of the grammar point.

- **Cultural Notes:** These occasional notes give background about American culture that students typically do not know, and that may help their understanding of the topic in the Student Book. The teacher can relay this information to students as appropriate.

- **Writing:** This section provides step-by-step instructions for guiding students through each stage of the scaffolded writing task at the end of each chapter.

AT THE BACK OF THE BOOK

- **Student Book Audioscript:** A complete audioscript is available for every listening activity in the Student Book.

- **Student Book Answer Key:** The Teacher's Book contains the answers to all the Student Book exercises. (The answers are not available in the Student Book.)

Teaching Techniques for the Grammar Classroom

TEACHING STUDENTS AT THE BASIC LEVEL

Students at this level may be expected to have different levels of exposure to grammar. Some students will have a solid understanding of form, but only basic ideas of the meaning and use of that form. Still other students may not have had much focus on form, but they can communicate well. Teachers should focus on correct form to reinforce or establish a good foundation in their students' grammar usage. In addition, the meaning and use information in each chapter is carefully chosen for students at the basic level. The information is not exhaustive, so as not to be overwhelming to students at this level. As students progress in their grammar studies, additional meaning and use information will be addressed. *Grammar Sense 1* provides students at this level with necessary guidance and a wealth of exercises to practice and expand their grammar knowledge.

PRESENTING THE FORM SECTIONS

Think Critically About Form Exercises

One of the most challenging aspects of teaching grammar is finding clear and concise ways to present new forms to students. The Think Critically About Form exercise in each chapter is a series of inductive tasks in which students work on *identifying* the target structure and its most important structural features. In these exercises, students are asked to return to the reading text in the Grammar in Discourse section of the chapter, and follow the steps to recognize or systematically analyze key aspects of the form (such as the number of different parts in a structure, the addition of suffixes, word order, agreement, and so on). This serves as an introduction to the structural features illustrated and explained in the Form Charts, which students may then consult to check their answers.

Form Charts

In chapters with particularly challenging structures, you may need to help students work through and internalize the information in the Form Charts before they start on the form exercises. The following is a compilation of some of the most successful techniques for guiding students through this section. Choose appropriate techniques based on your teaching style, class size, class level, and students' previous experience with the grammar point. Most importantly, vary the techniques you use to accommodate the different learning styles of your students—some students may prefer to read and discuss every example in the chart before moving on to the exercises, while others may need to study the material less intensively.

Whole Class Techniques

1. After students have finished the Think Critically About Form exercise, ask them to close their books. Elicit examples of the target grammar from the reading text by asking questions that will produce the target grammar. When possible, personalize your questions. For example, to elicit possessive pronouns, hold up a book and ask, *Whose book is this?* with the aim of eliciting responses such as *It's his. It's mine.* When students answer, write their responses on the board. If a student gives an incorrect response (e.g., *It is her.*), you should still write it on the board. Incorrect answers are as valuable as correct ones, because they can be used to focus students' attention on the structure. Likewise, if a student answers correctly but uses a different structure than the one you wish to focus on (e.g., *It's her book.*), write this answer on the board and ask if anyone knows an alternative response (e.g., *It's hers.*). Write students' responses on the board, and then have them open their books to the Form Charts and find sentences that use the same structures as those on the board.

2. To focus more closely on the various parts of a structure, copy the chart headings onto the board, or construct other types of contrastive charts (e.g., -*s*/-*es*/-*ies*, or singular/plural, etc.).

Elicit examples from the reading text to illustrate each point, or ask students to create their own examples. Have individual students come to the board and fill in the charts. Then ask the rest of the class to decide if their examples are correct or not, and to explain why.

3. After students have finished the Think Critically About Form exercise, ask them to silently review the Form Charts for a few minutes. Assess their understanding of the charts by asking questions about the form. For example, for *Yes/No* questions in the present tense, you might ask *Where is the subject? What word does the question begin with? How many* Yes/No *question forms are there?* In this way, you will be able to judge whether students have fully understood the form of the target grammar.

Pair or Group Work Techniques

1. Divide students into pairs or small groups. Assign each group a Form Chart and ask them to read and study the information. Then ask each group in turn to present the form in their chart to the rest of the class. Students can use their own example sentences to aid their presentation, in addition to those provided in the book.

2. Divide students into pairs or small groups. Write two correct sentences and one incorrect sentence on the board. (Make sure the error is one of *form*, not meaning and use.) Tell students that one sentence is incorrect. Ask them to work together to identify the incorrect sentence by looking at the Form Charts. Some students may know the answer without using the charts, but ask them to point to the information or example in the chart that shows why it is incorrect. This insures that they know how to interpret the charts.

PRESENTING THE MEANING AND USE SECTIONS

Think Critically About Meaning and Use Exercises

Once students have grasped the form of a given structure, the next challenge is to find creative and engaging ways to help them understand the meaning and use. The Think Critically About Meaning and Use exercises do just this by offering carefully constructed examples, often in the form of minimal pairs, and asking students to use contextual cues to draw inferences about key aspects of meaning and use. These inductive tasks serve as an introduction to the features of meaning and use that are further elucidated in the Notes that follow.

Meaning and Use Notes

Students need to read and absorb the Meaning and Use Notes before starting the exercises. What follows are some techniques for helping students work through the Meaning and Use Notes. Regardless of the technique you choose, it is important that you have a clear understanding of the scope of the Meaning and Use Notes before you present them. In some instances, a particular structure may have multiple meanings and uses, but the chapter will not address all of them. In Levels 1 and 2, certain meanings and uses of structures are omitted to avoid overwhelming the students with too much information, while in Level 3, basic meanings and uses may be de-emphasized in order to focus on more complex issues.

Whole Class Techniques

1. Give students an opportunity to read and ask questions about the Meaning and Use Notes. Check their understanding by writing several original sentences on the board and asking them to match the meaning and use in each sentence to the Meaning and Use Notes. With more advanced students you can include a few incorrect sentences among the examples and have students identify correct and incorrect meanings and uses. Before you do this, be sure you have a firm grasp of the meaning and use you are focusing on so you can clearly explain why the examples you provided are correct or incorrect.

2. If there are several Meaning and Use Notes, or if you think students will find the content challenging, have them read and demonstrate their understanding of one Note at a time. Once they have read the Note, elicit sentences that demonstrate the meaning and use of the

Note they just read. For example, to elicit sentences with *used to* when talking about a situation that was true in the past but is not true now (Student Book 2, page 65, Note 1A), have students talk about something they did when they were younger but don't do today. This should elicit sentences such as *I used to eat a lot of candy. I used to play baseball every summer.*

Pair or Group Work Techniques

1. Divide students into pairs or small groups. Assign each pair or group a Note and ask students to study it. Then ask each pair or group to present their Note to the rest of the class. Students can create their own example sentences to aid their presentation, in addition to those provided in the book. Again, be sure you fully understand the meaning and use in question so you can tell students whether their examples are correct or incorrect and, most importantly, *why* they are correct or incorrect.

2. Divide students into pairs or small groups. Have each pair or group read one Note and create two example sentences to illustrate the information presented in the Note. Ask each pair or group to come to the front of the class to explain the Note and write their example sentences on the board. Ask the class if the sentences are correct examples of the information in the Note. If not, call on individual students to suggest alternate correct sentences.

General Teaching Techniques

Grammar Sense contains a wealth of exercises covering all four skills areas: reading, writing, listening, and speaking. Depending on your students, curriculum, and time frame, these exercises can be taught in many ways. Successful grammar teaching requires skillful classroom management and teaching techniques, especially in the areas of elicitation (drawing information from students), grouping procedures (groups, pairs, or individuals), time management (lengthening or shortening exercises), and error correction (peer or teacher correction, correction of spoken or written errors).

ELICITATION

Elicitation is one of the most useful teaching techniques in the grammar classroom. In essence, elicitation draws information out of the students through the use of leading questions. This helps students to discover, on their own, information about grammar forms as well as meanings and uses. For example, to elicit the difference in meaning between a gerund and an infinitive when used after the verb *stop*, write the following sentences on the board: *Ed stopped to eat cake. Ed stopped eating cake.* Then, in order to elicit the difference in meaning between the two sentences, ask questions such as, *In which sentence did Ed eat cake? Which sentence suggests that Ed is on a diet?* These questions require students to analyze what they know about the grammar and make inferences about meaning.

Knowing when to elicit information can be difficult. Too much elicitation can slow the class and too little elicitation puts students in a passive position. Avoid asking students to judge whether something sounds natural or acceptable to them because, as non-native speakers, they will not have the same intuitions about English as native speakers.

GROUPING STUDENTS

Group work is a valuable part of language learning. It takes away the focus from the teacher as the provider of information and centers on the students, giving them the opportunity to work together and rely on each other for language acquisition. Shyer students who may be less likely to speak out in class have an opportunity to share answers or ideas. Your class level will inform how you approach group work. Be sure to circulate among groups to monitor the progress of an activity, particularly at lower levels, and to answer any questions students cannot resolve on their own. Although students at the higher levels are more independent and can often manage their own groups, be attentive to the activities at hand, ready to offer feedback and keep everyone on-task. In classes where the level of students is uneven, try varying the composition of the groups to make the learning process interesting for everybody. Sometimes you can pair up a higher-level student with a lower-level student to give him or her an opportunity to help another classmate. However, other times you may want to group all the higher-level students together and offer them additional, more challenging activities. It is useful, especially in discussion activities, to conclude with a culminating task in which one or more students report back something (results, a summary) to the rest of the class using the target structure. This helps to refocus the class on the structure and provide a conclusion to the activity.

TIME MANAGEMENT

Some exercises are divided into steps, making it possible to shorten an activity by assigning part of it for homework or by dividing the class into two groups and assigning half the items to each group. Similarly, exercises can be lengthened. Many of the exercises in *Grammar Sense* require students to ask for or offer real-life information. You can ask students to create additional sentences within these activities, or have them do an activity again with a different partner. If your class does an activity well, ask them to focus on other aspects of the form, for example, transforming their affirmative sentences into negative ones, and vice-versa.

CHECKING EXERCISES

How you check exercises with students will depend on the level you are teaching. Having students check their answers in pairs or groups can be an effective technique, because it makes students revisit their work and resolve with other students the mistakes they have made. With lower levels, this requires careful teacher supervision. It is also possible at all levels to check exercises as a class, elicit corrections from students, and offer necessary feedback. It is often useful, especially for correcting editing exercises, to use an overhead projector. Be careful not to single out students when correcting work. Aim instead to create a supportive atmosphere whereby the class learns through a group effort.

CORRECTING ERRORS

Students can often communicate effectively without perfect grammar. However, in order to succeed in higher education or the business world, they need to demonstrate a high level of grammatical accuracy, and to understand that even a small change in form can sometimes result in a significant change in meaning. As students become aware of this, they expect to be corrected. However, their expectations as to how and when correction should be offered will vary. Many teachers have difficulty finding the optimal amount of correction—enough to focus students on monitoring errors, but not so much as to demoralize or discourage them. It is important to target specific types of errors when correcting students, rather than aiming to correct everything they say or write. The focus of the current lesson and your knowledge of your students' strengths and weaknesses will dictate whether you focus on form, pronunciation, meaning, or appropriate use. Discuss error correction with your students and determine how *they* would like to be corrected. Aim to combine or vary your correction techniques depending on the focus of the lesson and the needs of your students.

Spoken Errors

There are a variety of ways to correct spoken errors. If a student makes an error repeatedly, stop him or her and encourage self-correction by repeating the error with a questioning (rising) tone, or by gesturing. Develop a set of gestures that you use consistently so students know exactly what you are pointing out. For example, problems with the past tense can be indicated by pointing backwards over your shoulder, future time can be indicated by pointing your hand ahead of you, and third person can be shown by holding up three fingers. (Be careful not to choose gestures that are considered offensive by some cultures.) If your students feel comfortable being corrected by their peers, encourage them to help each other when they hear mistakes. Another option is to keep track of spoken errors during an activity, and then at the end elicit corrections from the class by writing the incorrect sentences you heard on the board. This way, students are not singled out for their mistakes, but get the feedback they need.

Written Errors

It is important to encourage students to monitor their written errors and learn strategies to self-correct their writing. Establish a standard set of symbols to use when marking students' work. For example, *pl* for *plural, agr* for *agreement, s* for *subject, v* for *verb*. When you find an error, do not correct it, but instead mark it with a symbol. Students will have to work out the exact nature of their error and correct it themselves. This will reduce your correction time and encourage students to learn for themselves by reflecting on their errors. Peer correction is another useful technique by which students can provide feedback on a partner's work. In order for it to be effective, give students clear and limited objectives and do not expect them to identify all the errors in their classmate's work. Note that students may be resistant to peer correction at first, and nervous about adopting others' mistakes. But once they develop trust in one another, they will be surprised at how much they can learn from their classmates.

1

Simple Present Statements with *Be*

Overview

The simple present with *be* is used to talk about conditions or characteristics that are true in the present. These include origin (e.g., *Reiko is from Japan.*), age (e.g., *Ali is 20 years old.*), occupation (e.g., *He is a student.*), and location (e.g., *He is in class now.*). Although *be* is a basic structure in English, many languages do not have an equivalent verb, and it is sometimes difficult for students to incorporate it into their English usage.

Form: The key challenges are remembering

- *be* has more forms than other verbs (*am, is, are*).
- students may have trouble hearing and writing contracted forms (e.g., *I'm, you're, she's*, etc.).

A) GRAMMAR IN DISCOURSE

Meet the Staff

A1: Before You Read

- Read or ask a student to read the questions aloud. Give students five minutes to discuss the questions in pairs. Then call on several students to report their partner's information to the class.
- Write the word *Compugames* on the board. Explain that *Compugames* is a company. Elicit opinions about what *Compugames* does. If necessary, separate the word *Compugames* into *Compu* and *games*. Elicit opinions based on the parts of the words. (*Compu* is from computer, so *Compugames* may be a company related to computer games.)

A2: Read

- Write the word *glossary* on the board. Explain that the glossary gives the meanings of important words in the Grammar in Discourse passages and that these words may be new to students. Encourage them to use the glossary before turning to a bilingual dictionary.

- Divide students into small groups. Assign one of the two conversations to each group. Ask groups to identify each person mentioned in the conversation and write one or two sentences about that person (e.g., *Carol Cheng*: *Carol is a new employee. She is the new sales manager.*).
- Ask groups to report their information about each person to the class.

Cultural Notes

Explain that in the United States it is common for students to work while attending college or university. This is because a college or university education can be quite expensive, and many students help pay for their tuition and/or living expenses. Also point out that the words *college* and *university* are often used interchangeably and do not usually imply a different type or level of education.

A3: After You Read

- Have students do this exercise individually and compare their answers with a partner. Tell them to mark the places in the text where they found the answers.
- Elicit the answers, encouraging students to use complete sentences (e.g., *John Louis is an assistant.*). Write answers on the board for visual support.
- Go over any problematic items with the whole class.
- As a follow-up, ask *Which job do you want?*

B) FORM 1

Affirmative Statements with *Be*, Subject Pronouns, and Contractions with *Be*

THINK CRITICALLY ABOUT FORM

- Have students work individually to complete questions 1–3. Encourage them to refer to the

Form charts to check their answers and get familiar with the new structures. As they work, write the example sentences on the board.

- **1. IDENTIFY** Elicit the subjects and verbs of the example sentences.

- **2. CATEGORIZE** Point to each sentence and ask students to identify whether the subject is singular or plural. Write the subjects on the board under the headings *Singular Subjects (I, you, Carol)* and *Plural Subjects (Dana and Diego)*. Ask students to identify the pronouns *(I, you)*.

- **3. ORGANIZE** Elicit that we use *are* with the singular subject *you* as well as with plural subjects (e.g., *we, you, they*).

- **4. RECOGNIZE** Give students a few minutes to look back at the conversations. Call on students to come to the board and write the sentences they found.

FORM CHARTS

- Ask students to look at the charts on page 12. Demonstrate how the charts work by reading aloud the example sentences in the *Singular* chart. Then call on individual students to do the same for sentences in the *Plural* chart. To demonstrate the relationship between the two charts, ask one student to read out a singular sentence *(e.g., I am an employee.)* and a second to read out the corresponding plural sentence *(e.g., Dana and I are employees.)*.

- To check understanding of the charts, prompt students at random with a pronoun (e.g., *he*) or name (e.g., *Diego*) and ask them to read the corresponding sentence from one of the charts (*He is in college.* or *Diego is in college.*).

- Direct students' attention to the heading *Subject Pronouns and Contractions with Be* at the top of page 13. Write *contraction* on the board and circle *contract*. Say that *contract* means "to make something smaller or shorter" and a *contraction* is a short form of two words.

- Ask a student to read out the first example in the *Singular* chart. Write *I am* on the board, then erase the *a* and replace it with an apostrophe (*'*). Explain that in the contraction *I'm*, the apostrophe takes the place of the

missing letter *a*. Also point out that the space between the two words is closed up. Have students read out the other examples.

- Put students in pairs to find four more contractions in the conversations. Ask the pairs to share their findings.

- Call on students to read aloud the bulleted notes that follow the charts. Discuss any difficulties, and encourage students to refer to the charts and bulleted notes as they do the exercises on the following pages.

Informally Speaking: Contractions with Noun + *Be* (p. 16)

- Remind students that contracted forms are created when the first letter of the verb *am, is,* or *are* is omitted. Tell students that when speaking, it is natural to use contracted forms, but sometimes this makes it difficult to hear the verb.

- Choose two students to read the text in the speech bubbles. Then tell the class you will play the recording and that they should listen to how the underlined form in the cartoon is different from what they hear. If needed, play the recording more than once.

- Have students point out the differences: *company is* in the cartoon vs. *company's* on the recording; *employees are* in the cartoon vs. *employees're* on the recording. Explain that the forms on the recording are considered informal spoken English. Point out that the forms in the cartoon are standard English, which we usually use when writing.

- Model the sentences under *What You Might Hear*, and ask students to repeat. Encourage them to practice the contracted forms of the first two sentences using their own names and ages (e.g., *My name's Robin. Juan's 21 years old.*).

C FORM 2

Negative Statements and Contractions with *Be*

THINK CRITICALLY ABOUT FORM

- Have students complete the tasks individually and compare their answers with a partner.

Direct students to the Form charts to help them check their partner's answers and get familiar with the structures. As they work, write the example sentences on the board.

- **1. ANALYZE** Ask three students to come to the board to underline the verbs in the sentence pairs. Elicit the answer to the question in the book (*not* comes after the verb).

- **2. COMPARE AND CONTRAST** Elicit or explain that the first is a contraction of *is* + *not* and the second is a contraction of *are* + *not*. Explain that the contractions are different because the subjects require different forms of *be*.

- **3. COMPARE AND CONTRAST** Elicit or explain that the first is a contraction of *He* + *is* and the second is a contraction of *They* + *are*.

- Ask students to look at 1a, 2a, and 3a. Elicit or explain that negative statements with *be* have three possible forms: a full form (e.g., *he is not)* and two contracted forms (*he isn't* and *he's not*). All three forms have no difference in meaning. Ask students to predict the three negative forms for *she* and *it* (*she is not, she isn't, she's not* and *it is not, it isn't, it's not.*).

- Repeat the procedure for 1b, 2b, and 3b, focusing on the negative forms of *they*. Ask students to predict the three negative forms for *we* and *you*.

Troublespots

Some students may try to negate sentences by putting *no* before the verb instead of *not* after the verb (*He no is happy* instead of *He is not happy.*). In addition, students may occasionally try to combine the two negative contractions (*We'ren't*). Remind students that they can use only one contraction at a time.

FORM CHARTS

- Give students a few minutes to read the charts and bulleted note on page 17.

- Call on students to read the sentences in the charts aloud.

- Ask students to close their books. Write on the board *I am not a game designer.* Practice the form by prompting students with singular and plural subjects (e.g., *he, Dana, we, they*).

- Give them a few minutes to read the charts and bulleted notes on page 18.

- Call on pairs to read out the examples in the charts (e.g., Student A: *You are not.* Student B: *You aren't. You're not.*).

- As a follow-up, have students write three original negative sentences using uncontracted forms. Put students in pairs and have them exchange sentences. Ask students to rewrite their partner's sentences using both forms of the negative contraction. Ask several pairs to share their sentences with the class.

D MEANING AND USE

Descriptions with *Be*

THINK CRITICALLY ABOUT MEANING AND USE

- Read or have a student read sentences a–d to the class. Ask students to answer the questions individually.

- **EVALUATE** Call on students to share their answers (health: c; age: a; job: d; country: b). Elicit the word or phrase in each sentence that led students to the answers (e.g., *Mexico is a country.*).

MEANING AND USE NOTES

- Divide the class into four groups. Assign each group a Note.

- Explain that each group will teach the class their Note by explaining or reading the information and example sentences to the class. The group must also write new sentences to illustrate each point in the Note.

- To present their Note, each group can assign one student to read or paraphrase the explanation, another to read the examples in the book, and another to write the group's sentences on the board. Circulate and help as necessary. Then call each group to the board to present their Note.

Beyond the Sentence: Using Pronouns in Paragraphs (p. 24)

The purpose of *Beyond the Sentence* is to give students practice with the meaning and use of grammar as it functions naturally in paragraphs and conversations.

- Tell students to read the first part of the Note.
- Review subject pronouns by eliciting and writing them on the board for visual support.
- Have students read the paragraph with no pronouns. Ask them to identify the subject of each sentence. (*Carol* or *Compugames*) Elicit students' opinions about the paragraph. Ask *Is it interesting?* (No) *What is strange about the paragraph?* (There are no pronouns. Every sentence starts with *Carol* or *Compugames*.)
- Ask students to read the paragraph with pronouns. Have them identify the subject of each sentence. (*Carol* and *She*, *Compugames* and *It*) Elicit opinions. Ask *Is this paragraph more interesting and easier to read?* (Yes)

Troublespots

Students may overuse subject pronouns at first. This can sometimes lead to confusion, as in this example: *Carol Cheng is 30 years old. She is a new employee at Compugames. Compugames is in Seattle. She is not from Seattle. She is from Taiwan.* Encourage students to check that their pronoun references are clear within the context of the paragraphs they write.

WRITING

THINK CRITICALLY ABOUT MEANING AND USE

- Have students do A individually. Then, in small groups, have them compare answers and discuss any differences.
- Have them stay in groups and do B.
- As a class, review any difficult items from A. Then elicit answers to B:

  1. EVALUATE (Bangkok)

  2. DRAW A CONCLUSION (We use *it* for things, animals, and places. Bangkok is a place, so we need the pronoun *it*.)

WRITE

The purpose of this activity is to give students practice using forms of *be* and subject pronouns by writing a paragraph about someone.

1. Brainstorm

As a class, start a brainstorm on the board about a person. (Make it clear that students will write about a different person.) Write the brainstorming categories on the board, and elicit the kinds of details that students might write about. Have students work individually to make brainstorming notes about their person.

2. Write a First Draft

Before students begin writing, make sure they have read the checklist in the Edit section. Also have them look at the example on page 24. Remind students to use their brainstorming notes to write their description.

3. Edit

Direct students to read and complete the self-assessment checklist on page 26. Ask for a show of hands for how many students gave all or mostly *yes* answers. If desired, ask students to comment on some of the errors they found.

DO I ...	YES
describe this person?	☐
use the verb *be* in every sentence?	☐
use pronouns to replace some of the nouns?	☐
use contractions with *be*?	☐
use at least one negative statement?	☐

4. Peer Review

Pair students and direct them to read each other's work. Ask students to answer the questions in the checklist and discuss them. Give students suggestions of helpful feedback: e.g., *Are you sure this verb is correct? / Is the apostrophe OK here?*

5. Rewrite Your Draft

Students should consider their partners' comments from the peer review and rewrite as necessary. Encourage students to proofread their work again before turning it in.

2

Questions with *Be*

Overview

The simple present of the verb *be* is used to talk about states or characteristics in the present. *Yes/No* questions with *be* elicit whether something is true or not (e.g., *Are you a student?*). Information questions with *be* elicit new, specific, or factual information (e.g., *Who is your teacher? Where is she from? When is the test?*).

Form: The word order of questions in English presents a great challenge to learners. Students at this level may forget to invert the subject and verb and, instead, use rising intonation to signal a question.

A GRAMMAR IN DISCOURSE

Are You Best Friends?

A1: Before You Read

- To introduce the topic, ask *What are important qualities or characteristics in a friend?* Write students' answers on the board. Be prepared to give examples (e.g., *A friend is honest, fun, reliable, helpful, interesting.*).

- Read or ask a student to read the questions aloud.

- Put students in pairs and give them several minutes to discuss the questions. Encourage students to use the list of qualities on the board. Call on several pairs to share their answers.

- Write the word *quiz* on the board and elicit its meaning. If students are unsure, point to the quiz in the book. Explain that a quiz can be used to find out information about someone or something.

- Draw attention to the title of the quiz "Are You Best Friends?" and ask students to predict

what the questions will be about (e.g., *favorite music, movies, sports*). List their predictions on the board.

A2: Read

- Remind students about using the glossary by eliciting the meaning of one of the words, e.g., *cautious*.

- Ask students to look at the picture on page 28. Elicit the main differences between the two men. *(One is African American and the other is not, one is tall and the other is short, one is in athletic clothes and the other is in more formal clothes.)* Ask students to predict the relationship between the two men.

- Give students a few minutes to read the conversation and discover the relationship between the young men. (*They're best friends.*)

- Ask students to read the quiz and answer the questions.

- When students have finished, ask them to look at their original predictions. Elicit which topics they accurately predicted and circle them. Elicit other topics that were not predicted and add them to the list on the board.

- Ask for a show of hands: *How many of you are similar to your best friends? How many of you are different from your best friends?* Have several students share their answers to the quiz.

A3: After You Read

- Have students form small groups. Explain that they will compare their answers to the quiz to find out who is most similar to them.

- Ask several students to tell the class who is most like them and why. Take the opportunity to introduce the word *both* (e.g., *Yuki is most like me. We are both cautious. We are both private people. We are both spendthrifts.*).

Yes/No Questions and Short Answers with *Be*

THINK CRITICALLY ABOUT FORM

- Ask students to do questions 1–3 in pairs. Encourage them to refer to the Form charts and bulleted notes to check their answers and get familiar with the new structures. As they work, write example sentences a–f on the board.

- **1. ANALYZE** Have a student come to the board and write an *S* next to the statements (a, d, e, f), and a *Q* next to the questions (b, c).

- **2. IDENTIFY** Call another student to the board to circle the subjects and underline the verbs.

- **3. COMPARE AND CONTRAST** Call on individual students to analyze the order of subject and verb in each example. Elicit or provide a rule for the word order in statements and questions. (*In statements, the subject is first; in questions, the verb is first.*)

FORM CHARTS

- Read the first question and corresponding short answers aloud. Remind students that for all subjects except *I* there are two forms of the negative contraction. Both are used in short answers (e.g., *No, you aren't. No, you're not.*).

- Point out that *Yes/No* questions have a rising intonation. Write the first question on the board and draw a rising intonation arrow over the end of it.

- Call on students in threes to read out the remaining questions and short answers (one reads the question, one reads the *Yes* answer, and one reads both forms of the *No* answer).

- Have students close their books. Write on the board: *Are you here?* Have students ask and answer new questions by prompting pairs as follows: Rick – Lisa, *she – no* (Rick: *Is she here?* Lisa: *No, she isn't.*) Call on a third student to provide the alternate form (Soo-jin: *No, she's not*).

- Ask students to read the bulleted notes. Write on the board: *Yes, I am.* Under it write *Yes, I'm.* Ask *Is this correct?* (No)

- Brainstorm several adjectives, nouns, and prepositional phrases (e.g., *adventurous, an engineer, in a club*). Have students write three original *Yes/No* questions with these words.

- Put students in pairs to ask and answer their questions. Remind them to use contractions in negative short answers. Circulate and help as necessary.

- Ask several pairs to model a question and answer for the class. Refer them back to the charts and bulleted notes when necessary.

Information Questions with *Be*

THINK CRITICALLY ABOUT FORM

- Conduct this section as a whole-class activity. Before beginning, write the example sentences on the board.

- **1. ANALYZE** If students have difficulty distinguishing between *Yes/No* and information questions, encourage them to focus on the types of answers required by each question. (We answer *Yes/No* questions with a simple *yes* or *no*. Information questions cannot be answered with *yes* or *no*. We answer them with specific information.)

- Explain that information questions begin with *wh-* words. Ask students to identify as many *wh-* words as they can, and write them on the board. Point out that there is one word used in information questions that doesn't begin with *wh-*. Elicit or provide the question word *how* and add it to the list.

- **2. COMPARE AND CONTRAST** Call on a volunteer to circle the subject and underline the verb in each question. Elicit the word order: *wh-* word + *be* + subject.

FORM CHARTS

- Read a few of the questions and answers aloud. Point out that, unlike *Yes/No* questions, information questions do not have a rising intonation; they have a rising-falling intonation similar to statements.

- Put students in pairs, and have them ask and answer the questions in the charts. Then ask them to read the bulleted notes.
- Check students' recollection of contractions by prompting them with full forms (e.g., *I am, she is, we are, they are*) and eliciting the appropriate contraction (*I'm, she's, we're, they're*, etc.).
- Tell students to write down an original information question and its answer. Call several students to the board and have them write only the answer to the question.
- Ask the class to make up a question for each answer. Emphasize that the type of information often indicates which *wh-* word to use. For example, prepositional phrases about location or time (e.g., *on the table* or *at 5:00*) require *where* or *when*; adjectives (e.g., in sentences like *I'm fine.* or *She's tired.*) require *how*; and names or occupations (e.g., *My roommate is David.* or *I'm a teacher.*) require *who* or *what*.
- Elicit a question for each answer. Write it on the board above or to the left of the answers.
- As a follow-up, prompt students to make questions with any other *wh-* words that may not be represented in the examples on the board.

Informally Speaking: Contractions with *Wh-Word + Be* (p. 35)

- Remind students that contractions are created when one or more letters are omitted from the verb (e.g., *'re, 's*). Tell students that when we speak, it is natural to use contractions, but this sometimes makes it difficult to recognize the verb.
- Choose two students to read the text in the speech bubbles. Then tell the class you will play the recording and that they should listen to how the underlined form in the cartoon is different from what they hear. If needed, play the recording more than once so everyone can hear the difference.
- Have students point out the difference: *How are* in the cartoon vs. *How're* in the recording. Explain that the form on the recording is considered informal spoken English. The form in the cartoon is standard English, which we usually use when writing.

D MEANING AND USE

Questions with *Be*

THINK CRITICALLY ABOUT MEANING AND USE

- Ask students to identify how sentences 1a and 2a are similar. (They both ask about Fumiko and her country.)
- Put students in pairs to answer and discuss the first two questions. After a few minutes, elicit answers from the class:
  1. EVALUATE (1a asks if something is true or not.)
  2. EVALUATE (2a is an information question.)
- Elicit or point out that in 1a, the speaker has an idea about Fumiko's country of origin (in this case he is wrong), but in 2a, the speaker probably has no idea.
  3. INTERPRET Ask students to look only at the answer sentences. Elicit which answer gives more information (2b).

MEANING AND USE NOTES

- Divide the class into four groups. Assign each group a Note.
- Explain that each group will teach the class their Note by explaining or reading the information and example sentences to the class. The group must also write new sentences to illustrate each point in the Note.
- Groups can assign one student to read or paraphrase the explanation, one student to read the example sentences, and another to write the group's sentences on the board.
- Circulate and help as necessary. Then call each group to the board to present their Note.

Vocabulary Notes: Responses to *Yes/No* Questions (p. 40)

- Point out that, as in all languages, it is possible to use different levels of formality in English.
- Elicit the difference between *formal* and *informal*. (*Formal* is more polite, respectful, or official, whereas *informal* is more relaxed, casual, or less official.)

- Elicit the meaning of *certainty* (how sure something or someone is about something). Explain that *uncertainty* is the opposite.
- Ask students to read the Notes on their own.
- Check students' understanding by asking if a particular expression is more formal or less formal than another (e.g., *Is* Yeah *more formal than* Yes?). Also ask if one statement expresses more or less certainty than another (e.g., *Is* You got me. *more certain than* Maybe?).
- Divide the class into several large groups. Ask half the groups to brainstorm a list of settings in which formal language should be used. Ask the other half to brainstorm a list of settings in which informal language can be used.
- Have students share their lists. Write them on the board in two columns, one labeled *Formal* and the other *Informal*. Discuss any questions or disagreements as a class.

● WRITING

THINK CRITICALLY ABOUT MEANING AND USE

- Have students do A individually. Then, in small groups, have them compare answers and discuss any differences.
- Have them stay in groups and do B.
- As a class, review any difficult items from A. Then elicit answers to B:

    1.–2. SUMMARIZE (We answer *Yes/No* questions first with either a *yes* or a *no* and then with other information, although this is optional; We answer information questions with the information requested in the question. We do not use *yes* or *no*.)

WRITE

The purpose of this activity is to give students practice in using information questions and *Yes/No* questions with *be* by interviewing a classmate. Explain that students will work in pairs to interview each other.

1. Brainstorm

As a class, start a brainstorm on the board about the interview. Write the brainstorming categories on the board, and elicit questions that could be asked. After each question, have several students offer possible answers. Have students work individually to brainstorm questions for their interviews. Allow 10–15 minutes for student pairs to interview each other. Encourage them to record their partner's answers under each brainstorming question.

2. Write a First Draft

Before students begin writing, make sure they have read the checklist in the Edit section. Remind them to use the best points from their brainstorming notes to write their interviews.

3. Edit

Direct students to read and complete the self-assessment checklist on page 42. Ask for a show of hands for how many students gave all or mostly *yes* answers. If desired, ask students to comment on some of the errors they found.

DO I...	YES
include *Yes/No* questions with the verb to *be*?	☐
include questions using *Who*, *What*, *When*, *Where*, *Why*, *How*?	☐
include questions that ask for information?	☐
include questions that ask if something is true?	☐

4. Peer Review

Pair students and direct them to read each other's work. Ask students to answer the questions in the checklist and discuss them. Give students suggestions of helpful feedback: e.g., *Could you add more detail here? / Is this question form correct?*

5. Rewrite Your Draft

Students should consider their partners' comments from the peer review and rewrite as necessary. Encourage students to proofread their work again before turning it in.

3 Imperatives

Overview

Imperatives are used for commands, warnings, instructions, and directions. In many instances, the use of an imperative signals some authority on the part of the speaker, such as a boss over an employee (e.g., *Don't be late for the meeting.*). However, imperatives are also used in more neutral situations, such as giving instructions or directions (e.g., *Go straight for three blocks and turn right.*).

Form: The imperative form is relatively easy for students, but the subtleties of use are often more difficult to master. Learners need to be careful when using imperatives so they are not perceived as being impolite or even rude.

A GRAMMAR IN DISCOURSE

The Adventures of an Office Assistant

A1: Before You Read

- Elicit students' opinions about what makes a job "good." Help with any new or difficult vocabulary that may come up (e.g., *boss, supervisor*). Write students' ideas on the board (e.g., *good wages/money, short hours, interesting work/co-workers, good benefits, low stress*).

- Put students in pairs. Give them about five minutes to discuss the questions and to list the things that they think an office assistant does.

- Bring the class together and ask several students to share their answers. Make a list of office-assistant duties on the board and keep it for later reference.

A2: Read

- Remind students about using the glossary by eliciting the meaning of one of the words, e.g., *immediately.*

- Put students into pairs. Ask them to read the conversations and make a list of Rob's duties. When everyone has finished, ask a student to come to the board and circle the duties that the class correctly predicted.

A3: After You Read

- Ask students to do the task alone and mark the places in the text where they found the answers. Then have them compare answers with a partner. Circulate and note any problematic items.

- Review answers as a class and go over any problematic items. For those items that are not Rob's duties (e.g., *write contracts*), ask *Is this a possible office-assistant duty?* (No) Encourage students to support their opinions with reasons (e.g., *Probably not. Contracts are very important. The boss writes contracts.*).

- As a follow-up, ask *Do you think Rob likes his job? Why or why not?*

B FORM

Imperatives

THINK CRITICALLY ABOUT FORM

- Give students about five minutes to complete questions 1 and 2. Then put them in pairs to compare answers. Have them refer to the Form charts and bulleted notes to check their answers and get familiar with the new structures. As they work, make two columns on the board labeled *Affirmative Imperatives* and *Negative Imperatives*.

- **1. CATEGORIZE** Elicit the answers and write them on the board in the correct column (affirmative imperatives: b, d; negative imperatives: a, c).

- **2. SUMMARIZE** Ask a student to come to the board and underline the verbs in the example sentences. Ask students to look at the verbs. Explain or elicit that we form affirmative imperatives with the base form of a verb and negative imperatives with *do not* or *don't* + the base form of the verb.

- **3. IDENTIFY** Have students look back at the conversations on pages 44–45 and find two more examples of affirmative imperatives and one more example of a negative imperative.

- Call one student to the board to write the affirmative imperatives in the appropriate column (*bring, take, copy, look, go*). Ask another student to write the negative imperative (*don't worry*) in the appropriate column.

FORM CHARTS

- Read or have students read aloud the sentences in the charts. Then ask students to read the bulleted notes silently.

- Ask students if they see a subject for any of the sentences. (No) Tell students that although they can't see a subject in the sentences, there is one. To demonstrate, point directly at a student and say *You.* Then pause for several seconds and say *Stand up, please,* motioning for the student to stand up. Elicit or explain that the subject is *you* (the person you are directly speaking to).

- Put students in groups. Have each group choose four verbs from the *Affirmative Imperatives* list and write four original sentences: two with affirmative imperatives and two with negative imperatives. Circulate and help as necessary.

- Conclude the activity by asking a student from each group to write one of their sentences on the board.

C) MEANING AND USE

Imperatives

THINK CRITICALLY ABOUT MEANING AND USE

- Write the following on the board: *a command, a warning, instructions,* and *directions.* Elicit or give their meanings. (A command tells

someone what to do. A warning tells someone about a danger. Instructions tell someone how to do something. Directions tell someone how to go somewhere.)

- **EVALUATE** Divide students into small groups to answer the questions. Circulate and help as necessary.

- Ask students to read the Meaning and Use Notes to check their answers. Review answers as a class and discuss any problematic items. (Sentence d gives a command; sentence c gives a warning of danger; sentence b gives instructions; sentence a gives directions.)

MEANING AND USE NOTES

- Keep students in their groups. Ask them to read Notes 1 and 2 and then think of one original sentence for each use of the imperative. They should also think of a context for each of their sentences (e.g., *who is talking to whom? what is happening?,* etc.). Circulate and help as necessary.

- Check students' understanding by eliciting a sentence and context for each use from each of the groups.

- For Note 1C, point out that *please* is not used with a warning. Ask students why (there is no time to be polite).

- Discuss Note 3 as a class. Elicit students' opinions as to why *you* is included in the example. (The speaker is giving specific commands to different people, and it is important to be very clear because they are each doing a different task.) Brainstorm other situations in which *you* might be used in an imperative (a team participating in a competition, a parent instructing several children to do something).

Vocabulary Notes: Prepositions of Location (p. 52)

- Explain that prepositions of location tell us where something is. Read or ask a student to read the sentences to the class.

- To illustrate the meaning of the prepositions *on, behind, next to, across from,* and *at,* ask two volunteers to come to the front of the class. Invite a more advanced student to write sentences on the board for visual support.

- Arrange the students so they are standing side by side facing the class. Place yourself with the first row of students and say *(Ken) is on the right and (Stefan) is on the left.* Then say *So Ken is next to Stefan . . . and Stefan is next to Ken.*

- Rearrange the pair so they are facing each other. Say *Now Ken is across from Stefan . . . and Stefan is across from Ken.*

- Have Stefan stand behind Ken and say *Stefan is behind Ken.* Then switch their positions and say *Ken is behind Stefan.*

- To talk about the student writing sentences at the board, say *(Ahmed) is at the board.* Again, ask the student at the board to write this sentence. Then have the student take his or her seat.

- Explain that *on* shows location. Use objects in the room as examples (e.g., *The door is on the right. The windows are on the left.*). Write these sentences on the board for visual support.

- Have students look at the map on page 53. Read the names of the streets and places to the class. Ask questions to check understanding (e.g., *Is the library on the corner of Cherry Street and Bank Street? Yes, it is. Is the hospital next to the supermarket? No, it isn't.*).

WRITING

THINK CRITICALLY ABOUT MEANING AND USE

- Have students do A individually. Then, in small groups, have them compare answers and discuss any differences.
- Have them stay in groups and do B.
- As a class, review any difficult items from A. Then elicit answers to B:

  1.–2. EVALUATE (1, 2, and 4; 3)

WRITE

The purpose of this activity is to give students practice in using imperatives and prepositions of location by writing a note.

1. Brainstorm

As a class, start a brainstorm on the board. Write the brainstorming categories on the board, and elicit related imperatives. Elicit other related details: e.g., *Where is the mailbox key? / Where is the watering can?* Have students work individually to make their own brainstorming notes to write their note.

2. Write a First Draft

Before students begin writing, make sure they have read the checklist in the Edit section. Remind students to use the best points from their brainstorming notes to write their note.

3. Edit

Direct students to read and complete the self-assessment checklist on page 56. Ask for a show of hands for how many students gave all or mostly *yes* answers. If desired, ask students to comment on some of the specific errors they found.

DO I ...	YES
use affirmative imperatives?	☐
use negative imperatives?	☐
use the imperative verb in the correct form?	☐
make no mention of *you* in the imperative statement?	☐
use prepositions of location?	☐
use a gentle and polite tone?	☐

4. Peer Review

Pair students and direct them to read each other's work. Ask students to answer the questions in the checklist and discuss them. Give students suggestions of helpful feedback: e.g., *Can you add more detail here? / Can you add a negative imperative?*

5. Rewrite Your Draft

Students should consider their partners' comments from the peer review and rewrite as necessary. Encourage them to proofread their work carefully before turning it in.

4 Introduction to Nouns

Overview

Nouns are the names of people, animals, places, things, or abstract ideas. Students may not find the concept of a noun difficult, but they may find the English noun system confusing, especially the use of the articles *a/an* and *the*.

Form: The key challenges are remembering

- plural forms of nouns, especially irregular plural forms, which must be memorized.
- pronunciation of plural forms.
- capitalization rules (even if students are familiar with capitalization in their native language, the rules may be different).

A) GRAMMAR IN DISCOURSE

A Nice Place to Live

A1: Before You Read

- Make two columns on the board. Label one *Advantages* and the other *Disadvantages*. Elicit or explain the meaning of *advantage* (something positive or good) and *disadvantage* (something negative or not good). Say *Think about your neighborhood. What do you like about it? What don't you like about it?* Write responses in the appropriate column on the board.

- Put students in pairs and give them five minutes to discuss the questions. Ask them to rank the qualities of a neighborhood in order of importance, including size, shops and other facilities, location (distance from work or school), price of housing, safety, schools, etc. Elicit rankings from different pairs, encouraging them to support their answers.

- Then say *You want to rent a new apartment. What things are important to you?* Elicit answers

(e.g., *size, parking, price, sunny rooms*) and write them on the board.

A2: Read

- Remind students about using the glossary by eliciting the meaning of one of the words, e.g., *kitchenette*.

- Keep students in pairs. Ask them to read the advertisements and then use the characteristics on the board to choose the apartment or house that is best for them. Elicit students' opinions and encourage them to support their answers. For example, students who think it is important to live in a large apartment would not choose a studio in downtown Danvers.

A3: After You Read

- Ask students to do this exercise in pairs. Encourage them to use the information in the table to determine the needs of each renter. For example, elicit that renters with children will need more space. Circulate and help as necessary.

- Elicit the pairs' choices, prompting them to give reasons. Discuss any disagreements as a class.

- As a follow-up, give students a few minutes to list characteristics of their dream home. Elicit students' answers and write them on the board in note form (e.g., *six bedrooms, five bathrooms, a swimming pool, a home theater*).

B) FORM 1

Singular Count Nouns

THINK CRITICALLY ABOUT FORM

- Have students work individually to complete questions 1 and 2. Encourage them to refer to the Form chart and bulleted notes to check their answers and get familiar with the new structures. As they work, write the example sentences on the board.

- **1. IDENTIFY** Call a student to the board to underline the three proper nouns (*Paul, John, Toronto*).

- **2. RECOGNIZE** Call another student to the board to circle the other singular noun in each sentence (*engineer, teacher, city, apartment*).

- Elicit the difference between the underlined and circled nouns. (The underlined nouns begin with a capital letter; the circled nouns begin with a lower-case letter.)

- Explain that the underlined nouns are called proper nouns, and the others are called common nouns.

- **3. APPLY** Elicit the phrases with *a* or *an* from the four sentences and put a large box around each phrase (*an engineer, a teacher, a city, an apartment*).

- Put students in pairs and ask them to think about why *a* or *an* is used in each example. Then elicit the answers. (*A* is used before nouns that begin with a consonant sound. *An* is used before nouns that begin with a vowel sound.) Discuss any difficulties as a class.

- As a follow-up, have students look back at the advertisements on pages 60–61 to find more examples of singular count nouns with *a* or *an*. Circulate and help as necessary. Elicit answers (*a living room, a large kitchen, a garage, an elevator,* etc.).

FORM CHARTS

- Give students a few minutes to read the chart. Then call on students to read aloud the sentences in the chart. Ask a student to tell you the rule for when to use *a* or *an*.

- Give students a few more minutes to read the bulleted notes. As students read, make three columns on the board. Label them *People, Places,* and *Things.*

- Check students' understanding of proper nouns and common nouns by asking for examples of each from the chart. Elicit or point out that we do not use *a* or *an* before singular proper nouns.

- Put students in pairs. Ask them to write down a proper noun and a common noun for each category on the board (people, places, or things).

- Ask several students to come to the board and write their pair's nouns in the correct columns.

- Review the nouns on the board as a class, ensuring that they are spelled correctly and in the correct column.

- Choose several nouns from the list and ask if *a* or *an* is used with them. (Choose some that follow *a*, some that follow *an*, and some proper nouns, which do not take an article.)

- Ask the pairs to choose one noun from each category (including at least one proper noun) and write original sentences.

- Elicit a sentence from each pair. Discuss any difficulties or questions as a class.

C FORM 2

Plural Count Nouns

THINK CRITICALLY ABOUT FORM

- Have students work individually to complete questions 1 and 2. Encourage them to refer to the Form chart and bulleted notes to check their answers and get familiar with the new structures. As they work, write the example sentences on the board.

- **1. IDENTIFY** Call a student to the board to underline the plural nouns that end in *-s* or *-es* (*teachers, balconies, plants*). Point out that these are regular nouns.

- **2. RECOGNIZE** Call another student to the board to circle the two irregular plural nouns (*children, people*). Make sure students understand what an irregular plural noun is (a noun that does not form the plural with *-s* or *-es*).

- If desired, have students look back at the advertisements on pages 60–61 to find more examples of plural count nouns. Circulate and help as necessary. Elicit answers (*two apartments, 2 bedrooms, no pets, 3 bedrooms,* etc.).

FORM CHARTS

- Call on students to read sentences in the chart aloud. Check students' understanding by asking them which nouns are irregular (*children, women*).

- Then give students a few minutes to read the bulleted notes.

- Direct students' attention to the list of irregular nouns in the second bulleted note. Give students a few minutes to study them. If desired, put students in pairs and allow them to practice. Then ask them to close their books for a short quiz.

- Quiz students only on the nouns in the note at this time. Say the singular noun and have students write the plural noun as quickly as they can. To check answers, ask a student to write the plural forms on the board.

- If you wish to have students learn additional irregular plural forms, refer them to Appendix 1 in the Student Book.

- Divide students into small groups. Ask them to think of six nouns and write their plural forms. Encourage students to choose two nouns from each category (people, places, or things). Circulate and help as necessary.

- Elicit the plural forms from each group and write them on the board. Provide irregular forms, if necessary.

- Ask the groups to choose three of the plural nouns and write a sentence for each. Circulate and help with vocabulary and grammar as necessary.

- Ask a student from each group to read the group's sentences aloud. Discuss any questions or difficulties as a class.

Pronunciation Notes: Pronunciation of Regular Plural Nouns (p. 67)

- To introduce the concept of syllables, tell students *The parts of words are called* syllables. *A syllable has just one vowel sound.*

- Demonstrate by writing the following words on the board: *pen* (1), *pencil* (2), *eraser* (3). Elicit answers. To reinforce the concept, repeat each word slowly and tap out the syllables on the board.

- Repeat with *dish* (1), *dishes* (2), and *dishwasher* (3).

- Explain that singular and plural noun forms do not always have the same number of syllables. Write on the board in a column: *apartment, doctor, box*. Model the words while students tap out the syllables (*apartment*: 3; *doctor*: 2; *box*: 1).

- Elicit the plural forms (*apartments, doctors, boxes*) and write them to the left of the singular forms. Model the pairs. Say *One of the plural forms has an extra syllable. Which is it?* Model the pairs again, and elicit the answer (*boxes*).

- Explain that there are other differences as well. Demonstrate the different pronunciations of *-s/-es* by modeling each plural and exaggerating the final /s/ in apartments, /z/ in doctors and /ɪz/ in boxes. Ask students to comment on the differences. (Some may have difficulty hearing the differences; others may hear them, but be unable to reproduce them.)

- Direct students' attention to the Pronunciation Notes.

- Read each Note aloud. Model the examples and have students repeat. Ensure that all students understand that the /ɪz/ ending in the second Note adds an extra syllable to the plural form.

- Put students in pairs to practice the examples. Circulate and help as necessary.

D) MEANING AND USE

The Functions of Nouns

THINK CRITICALLY ABOUT MEANING AND USE

- **1.–4. CATEGORIZE** Put students in pairs and give them a few minutes to answer the questions. As they work, make four columns on the board. Label them as follows: *Nouns As Subjects, Nouns As Objects, Nouns After* Be, *Nouns After Prepositions*.

- Check students' understanding of the key terms in the column headings by eliciting the meaning of *subject* (often the first noun or pronoun in the sentence; what the sentence is about), *object* (a word that follows a verb other than *be*) and *preposition* (a short word such as *in, on, under, to,* or *from*).

- Call on several students to come to the board and write the nouns in the correct columns (Nouns As Subjects: *flowers, roses, the library*; Nouns As Objects: *the door*; Nouns After *Be*: *flowers*; Nouns After Prepositions: *the bank*).

- Discuss any questions or difficulties.

MEANING AND USE NOTES

- Divide the class into four groups. Assign each group a Note.

- Explain that each group will teach the class their Note by explaining or reading the information and example sentences to the class. The group must also write a new sentence to illustrate each point in the Note.

- To present their Note, each group can assign one student to read or paraphrase the explanation, another to read the examples in the book, and another to write the group's sentences on the board.

- Circulate and help as necessary. Then call each group to the board to present their Note.

WRITING

THINK CRITICALLY ABOUT MEANING AND USE

- Have students do A individually. Then, in small groups, have them compare answers and discuss any differences.

- Have them stay in groups and do B.

- As a class, review any difficult items from A. Then elicit answers to B:

  1. ANALYZE (It doesn't end in -*s* or -*es*.)

  2. APPLY (*a doctor* in A's question and *a teacher* in B's answer)

WRITE

The purpose of this activity is to give students practice in using singular and plural nouns by writing an advertisement.

1. Brainstorm

As a class, start a brainstorm on the board about the features of an apartment or house. Write the brainstorming categories on the board, and elicit the kinds of details that students might write about. Have students work individually to make brainstorming notes for their advertisement.

2. Write a First Draft

Before students begin writing, make sure they have read the checklist in the Edit section. Also have them look at the examples on pages 60–61. Remind them to use the best points from their brainstorming notes to write their advertisement.

3. Edit

Direct students to read and complete the self-assessment checklist on page 72. Ask for a show of hands for how many students gave all or mostly *yes* answers. If desired, ask students to comment on some of the errors they found.

DO I ...	YES
list the features using a mix of singular and plural count nouns?	☐
use at least one irregular plural count noun?	☐
use the correct indefinite article (*a* or *an*) before each noun?	☐
include all details about the apartment?	☐
include a way for people to get in touch with me?	☐

4. Peer Review

Pair students and direct them to read each other's work. Ask students to answer the questions in the checklist and discuss them. Give students suggestions of helpful feedback: e.g., *Are you sure you need -es on this plural? / I think you need* an *here.*

5. Rewrite Your Draft

Students should consider their partners' comments from the peer review and rewrite as necessary. Encourage students to proofread their work again before turning it in.

5 Introduction to Count and Noncount Nouns

Overview

This chapter introduces the concept of count and noncount nouns. Count nouns can be counted and have both a singular and plural form (e.g., *one egg, two eggs*). Noncount nouns cannot be counted and do not have a plural form (e.g., *air*). This concept can be difficult for students whose native language does not have countability, e.g., Chinese. Other languages may have the concept, but nouns that are considered countable may be noncountable in English and vice versa.

Form: The key challenges are remembering

- noncount nouns are treated as singular nouns for the purposes of subject-verb agreement.
- noncount nouns do not have plural forms.
- some nouns can be used as both count and noncount nouns.

A GRAMMAR IN DISCOURSE

Protect Our Environment

A1: Before You Read

- Write the word *environment* in the middle of the board. Draw a circle around it and ask students what comes to mind when they think about this word. Elicit responses and write them on the board, forming a spidergram with lines coming from the word *environment*. Be prepared to provide your own responses (e.g., *water, pollution, forests, energy, smoke*).
- Put students in pairs and give them five minutes to discuss the questions. Call on several students to share their answers.

A2: Read

- Remind students about using the glossary by eliciting the meaning of one of the words, e.g., *conserve*.

- Conduct the reading of the flyer as a jigsaw activity. Divide students into groups of three or four. Half the groups will be responsible for the information in the *Conserve Energy* section and the other half will be responsible for the information in the *Recycle* section.
- Each group should choose a reporter. Ask the groups to read and identify which tips they follow and which they do not. Encourage students to discuss their reasons for not following some of the suggested tips.
- Ask reporters to share their groups' findings.

Cultural Notes

This flyer contains a lot of information about recycling and conserving energy. These are important issues to the American public. In some cities in the United States, there are laws requiring people to recycle materials such as plastic, metal, glass, and newspaper. Energy conservation is also important, especially in California, where there have often been electricity shortages.

A3: After You Read

- Ask students to do this exercise individually and then compare their answers in pairs. Remind them to note the places in the text where they found the answers.
- Go over any difficult items with the whole class.
- As a follow up, ask students to name additional ways to protect the environment. Encourage them to make suggestions for protecting specific resources such as water or forests.

B FORM

Count and Noncount Nouns

THINK CRITICALLY ABOUT FORM

- Put students in pairs to answer the questions. Encourage them to refer to the Form charts and bulleted notes to check their answers and get familiar with the new structures. As they work, write the sentence pairs on the board, underlining the nouns as in the book.

- **1. COMPARE AND CONTRAST** Call a student to the board to circle the nouns which have both singular and plural forms (*bottle – bottles, computer – computers*).

- **2. ANALYZE** Call another student to the board to put a checkmark next to the nouns with only one form (*garbage, electricity*).

- Explain that some nouns in English can be both singular and plural (e.g., *bottle – bottles* and *computer – computers*), while others can only be singular (e.g., *garbage* and *electricity*). Elicit or explain that nouns with singular and plural forms are called *count nouns*; nouns which do not have a plural form are *noncount nouns*.

FORM CHARTS

- Give students a few minutes to read the charts and bulleted notes. Then call on students to read out the sentences in the charts. Elicit the form of *be* that we use with each type of noun. (We use *is* with singular count nouns and *are* with plural count nouns. Noncount nouns also use *is*.)

- Check students' understanding of the bulleted notes by eliciting the basic differences between count and noncount nouns. (Nouns that can be counted are count nouns; nouns that cannot be counted are noncount nouns.) Also elicit which nouns have two forms and which have only one form (count nouns have a singular and plural form, noncount nouns have only one form.)

- Divide students into small groups and turn back to the flyer on page 75. Ask them to underline the count nouns and circle the noncount nouns.

- Meanwhile, make three columns on the board labeled *Count Nouns – Singular*, *Count Nouns – Plural*, and *Noncount Nouns*.

- Ask a volunteer from three of the groups to come to the board. Assign a column to each student and have them write the nouns they found for that category. (Singular count nouns: *home, office, night.* Plural count nouns: *tips, lights, bulbs, appliances, clothes, curtains, days, machines, computers, printers, cans, newspapers, bottles, schools.* Noncount nouns: *environment,*

energy, water, heat, equipment, glass, plastic, paper, furniture).

- Discuss any difficulties as a class.

C MEANING AND USE

Count and Noncount Nouns

THINK CRITICALLY ABOUT MEANING AND USE

- Put students in pairs and give them a few minutes to complete the questions. As they work, write the sentence pairs on the board.

- **1. IDENTIFY** Ask a student to come to the board to underline the noncount nouns and circle the count nouns. (Noncount nouns: *long hair, chocolate.* Count nouns: *a gray hair, the chocolates.*)

- **2. EVALUATE** Elicit the answer to question 2. (Sentences 1a and 2b are about individual items: *a gray hair, the chocolates.* Sentences 1b and 2a are general statements. 2a is about a category: *chocolate.* 2b is about a kind of thing: *long hair.*)

- In anticipation of Note 3, point out or elicit that some nouns, such as the ones on the board, are both count and noncount.

MEANING AND USE NOTES

- To ensure that students grasp the meaning and use of count and noncount nouns, present these notes as a whole-class activity.

- Call on one or more students to read the explanations and examples in each Note. As you finish each section, ask students to provide examples of their own. Discuss any difficulties.

- As a follow-up, write these sentences on the board (answers in parentheses are for teacher's reference):

  1. *Jealousy is not an attractive quality.* (Note 2B)

  2. *I always drink juice with breakfast.* (Note 2A)

  3. *I need new furniture, especially a new sofa.* (Note 1B)

  4. *I rarely eat cake, but the cakes from this bakery are special.* (Note 3)

- Put students in pairs and ask them to identify which Note each sentence represents. Elicit answers from each pair.

● WRITING

THINK CRITICALLY ABOUT MEANING AND USE

- Have students do A individually. Then, in small groups, have them compare answers and discuss any differences.
- Have them stay in groups and do B.
- As a class, review any difficult items from A. Then elicit answers to B:

  1. GENERATE (Answers will vary. When A uses a plural count noun, B's pronoun and verb need to change as well. For example, A: Where are the <u>flowers</u>? B: <u>They are</u> on the table.)

  2. APPLY (B: Are earrings a good gift?)

WRITE

The purpose of this activity is to give students practice in using count and noncount nouns by creating a restaurant menu.

1. Brainstorm

- As a class, start a brainstorm on the board about the menu.
- Write the brainstorming categories on the board, and elicit a number of suggestions for each menu category.
- Have students work individually to brainstorm ideas for their menus.

2. Write a First Draft

Before students begin writing, make sure they have read the checklist in the Edit section. Remind them to use the best ideas from their brainstorming notes to create their menus.

3. Edit

Direct students to read and complete the self-assessment checklist on page 84. Ask for a show of hands for how many students gave all or mostly *yes* answers. If desired, ask students to comment on some of the errors they found.

DO I ...	YES
use noncount nouns?	☐
use count nouns?	☐
use singular count nouns?	☐
use plural count nouns?	☐
use the correct article in front of each noun?	☐
use descriptive words for each noun?	☐

4. Peer Review

Pair students and direct them to read each other's work. Ask students to answer the questions in the checklist and discuss them. Give students suggestions of helpful feedback: e.g., *Are you sure this plural is spelled correctly? / I think this plural should be singular. Isn't it a noncount noun?*

5. Rewrite Your Draft

Students should consider their partners' comments from the peer review and rewrite as necessary. Encourage students to proofread their work again before turning it in.

Descriptive Adjectives

Overview

Adjectives are used to describe nouns. They can indicate, among other things, a noun's quality, size, age, color, origin, or shape (e.g., *beautiful, large, new, blue, Japanese,* and *round*).

Form: Adjectives in English always have the same form. They do not change to reflect singular/plural, male/female, or subject/object. Remembering to place adjectives before the noun can be difficult for students, especially for those whose first language requires adjectives to follow nouns. Another challenge is the use of *a* or *an* before adjective + noun combinations.

A GRAMMAR IN DISCOURSE

Westbrook College News

A1: Before You Read

- To introduce the concept of classified ads, say *Imagine you want to sell your* Grammar Sense *book at the end of the term. How can you tell other students?* Elicit answers and list them on the board. If students do not mention on-line or on a website, add this to the list. Ask students how the Internet might be useful for buying or selling used textbooks and other things.

- Put students in pairs. Give them a few minutes to discuss the questions. Ask students to brainstorm a list of ads they might find in a college newspaper or newsletter (e.g., *apartments for rent, lost property*). Elicit answers and write them on the board.

A2: Read

- Remind students about using the glossary by eliciting the meaning of one of the words, e.g., *collar.*

- Keep students in pairs. Have them read the ads

and compare them with the list on the board. To check understanding, ask *Which ads did you predict correctly? What else can we add to the list?*

Cultural Notes

You may wish to point out that in some countries (e.g., the USA, Canada, and England), it's common for people to buy and sell used items. People who do this often have enough money to buy new things, but they choose to buy used items because they want to save money. People who sell used items often do so because they feel that if others can reuse these items, it will reduce trash and help the environment. In addition, many international students also buy and sell used items because they will not be in the country they are studying in for a long time.

A3: After You Read

- Have students do this exercise individually. Remind them to mark the place in the ads where they found the answers.

- Call on students to read each item aloud and say *Yes* if they checked it or *No* if they did not.

- As a follow-up, ask *For which kinds of items are classified ads most useful? Why?* Encourage students to support their opinions with their own experiences of listing or responding to classified ads.

B FORM

Descriptive Adjectives

THINK CRITICALLY ABOUT FORM

- Have students work individually to do questions 1 and 2. Encourage them to refer to the Form charts and bulleted notes to check their answers and get familiar with the new structures. As they work, write the example phrases and sentences from these questions on the board.

- **1. IDENTIFY** Call a student to the board to underline the noun and circle the adjective in each of the phrases. (Underline *cars, collar, student, apartment;* circle *large, red, serious, nice.*) Elicit or point out that adjectives come before nouns in English.

- **2. ANALYZE** Call another student to the board to do the same for the sentences. (Sentence a: underline *cat, collar;* circle *black, red.* Sentence b: underline *cats, collars;* circle *black, red.*) Elicit which nouns are singular (*cat, collar*) and which are plural (*cats, collars*). Ask *Does the form of the adjective change with singular and plural nouns?* (No)

- **3. APPLY** Put students in pairs, and ask them to find four more adjectives in the ads. Have them note the noun that each adjective modifies. Circulate and help as necessary.

- Check answers. (Music: *love [songs], popular [favorites], great [condition];* Household items: *double [bed], student [desk], kitchen [table], wool [rug];* Roommate: *nice [apartment], old [house], lovely, inexpensive, sunny, quiet, perfect [apartment], serious [student], large [pets];* Lost: *black [cat], long [tail], red [collar];* Found: *black [backpack], two [textbooks], basic [biology], advanced [calculus]*).

FORM CHARTS

- Call on two students to read the sentences in the charts. The students should alternate reading the singular sentences and the plural sentences. For each sentence, elicit the placement of the adjective (after a form of *be* or before a noun).

- Give students a few minutes to read the bulleted notes.

- To check understanding, ask questions such as: *What do adjectives describe? Do adjectives change forms in English? Where can you find an adjective in a sentence? When do you use* a *in front of an adjective? When do you use* an?

- If desired, reinforce the use of *a* and *an*. Write the following on the board in three columns:

___ man	___ university	___ umbrella
___ old man	___ old university	___ orange umbrella
___ tall man	___ great university	___ gray umbrella

Call on students to come to the board and fill in *a* or *an* in each column. (Column 1: *a, an, a;* Column 2: *an, an, a;* Column 3: *an, an, a*)

- Divide students into two groups, and write these adjectives on the board: *lovely, green, inexpensive, busy, quiet, large.* Ask one group to write a sentence for each adjective based on the *Adjectives After* Be chart; ask the other group to write a sentences based on the *Adjectives Before Nouns* chart.

- Call on students to come to the board and write their group's sentences. As a class, check placement of adjectives, subject-verb agreement, and the use of *a, an,* and *the.*

C MEANING AND USE

Descriptions with Adjectives

THINK CRITICALLY ABOUT MEANING AND USE

- Put students in pairs and give them a few minutes to answer the questions. As they work, write the categories from question 2 in a single column on the board.

- **1. IDENTIFY** Elicit the adjectives and write them on the board to the right of the categories (*red, Korean, young, interesting, small, round*).

- **2. ANALYZE** Check answers by having several students come to the board and write the adjectives from the list in the correct categories on the board (quality/opinion: *interesting;* shape: *round;* age: *young;* color: *red;* origin: *Korean;* size: *small*). Keep these categories on the board for later reference.

MEANING AND USE NOTES

- Call on two students to read aloud the explanation and example in Note 1A. Elicit one new sentence for each category.

- Divide students into two groups. Ask them to read Note 1B and think of one new adjective for each category. Give the groups about five minutes to compile their lists. Circulate and help as necessary.

- Elicit the adjectives from each group and write them on the board under the correct categories.

- Have each group write three new sentences using the adjectives from the other group's list. Give the groups about five minutes to write their sentences. Circulate and help as necessary.
- Elicit the sentences from each group. Write them on the board exactly as you hear them. Check the sentences as a class.
- Call on two students to read the explanation and examples in Note 2. Elicit new phrases with the following nouns used as adjectives: *gold* (e.g., *a gold ring*), *biology* (e.g., *a biology class/teacher*), *university* (e.g., *a university campus/student*), *computer* (e.g., *a computer course/programmer*).

WRITING

THINK CRITICALLY ABOUT MEANING AND USE

- Have students do A individually. Then, in small groups, have them compare answers and discuss any differences.
- Have them stay in groups and do B.
- As a class, review any difficult items from A. Then elicit answers to B:

  1. ANALYZE (1. small = size; 2. hard = quality/opinion; 4. small = size)

  2. DIFFERENTIATE (In 3, *school* is an adjective because it describes *bus*.)

WRITE

The purpose of this activity is to give students practice in using adjectives by writing an advertisement about their personal belongings.

1. Brainstorm

As a class, start a brainstorm on the board about typical items that students might want to sell. Write the brainstorming categories on the board, and elicit a number of items that students might want to sell in each category. Then elicit adjectives that students could use to describe these items. Have students work individually to make brainstorming notes for their own ad.

2. Write a First Draft

Before students begin writing, make sure they have read the checklist in the Edit section. Also have them look at the examples on pages 88 and 96. Remind students to use their best points from brainstorming notes to write their ad.

3. Edit

Direct students to read and complete the self-assessment checklist on page 98. Ask for a show of hands for how many students gave all or mostly *yes* answers. If desired, ask students to comment on some of the errors they found.

DO I ...	YES
talk about the color of each object?	☐
talk about size?	☐
talk about quality?	☐
talk about origin?	☐
talk about shape?	☐
talk about age?	☐
use at least one noun as an adjective?	☐
use at least one adjective after the verb *to be*?	☐

4. Peer Review

Pair students and direct them to read each other's work. Ask students to answer the questions in the checklist and discuss them. Give students suggestions of helpful feedback: e.g., *Adjectives don't have a plural form, remember? / Are you sure you need the article an here?*

5. Rewrite Your Draft

Students should consider their partners' comments from the peer review and rewrite as necessary. Encourage students to proofread their work again before turning it in.

7 Possessives and Demonstratives

Overview

Possessives (nouns, adjectives, and pronouns) show ownership (e.g., *Maria's computer is fast. Her computer is fast. Hers is fast.*). They also describe relationships (e.g., *Peter's father is a manager. His father is a manager. His is a manager.*), and they identify physical characteristics (e.g., *His eyes are blue.*). Demonstratives (*this, that, these, those*) identify people and objects and tell if they are near or far (e.g., *This car is fast, but that car is slow.*).

Form: The key challenges are remembering

- possessive adjectives are used with nouns; possessive pronouns are not (e.g., *My grades are excellent. Mine are excellent.*).
- apostrophe placement in possessive nouns is critical to meaning (e.g., *the boy's room* vs. *the boys' room*).
- a possessive adjective agrees with the noun it replaces (the possessor), and not with the noun it modifies (e.g., *Peter is in Los Angeles. His mother is in San Diego. *Her mother is in San Diego.* Incorrect).

A GRAMMAR IN DISCOURSE

Keeping in Touch

A1: Before You Read

- Write the phrase *keep in touch* on the board and elicit its meaning (*stay in contact* or *correspond*). Ask *How do you keep in touch with your family and friends?* Write students' answers on the board (*telephone, email,* etc.).
- Put students in pairs and give them about five minutes to discuss the questions. Ask several students to share their preferences with the class.

A2: Read

- Remind students about using the glossary by eliciting the meaning of one of the words, e.g., *SUV*.
- Divide the class into two groups, and conduct the reading as a jigsaw activity: Ask half the students to read the first email (Alan's), and the other half to read the second email (Koji's). Give students about ten minutes to summarize the email in a few sentences.
- Put students in pairs, one from each group. Ask students to share their information and then talk about how their lives are similar or different from the person whose email they read.
- Bring the class together and elicit summaries. (Alan is in college. He is doing well in all classes except Spanish. Koji has a new job and a new SUV. His weekends are boring and his roommates' friends are quiet.)
- Call on several students to compare their lives to Alan's or Koji's.

A3: After You Read

- Have students do the exercise individually. Instruct them to correct the false sentences.
- Ask students to check their answers in pairs. Elicit answers, including the corrected false sentences.
- As a follow-up, ask students what they think the relationship is between Alan and Koji. (They are probably friends from school.) If they are unsure, direct their attention to the first paragraph of Alan's email (*our graduation ceremony*).
- If time permits, ask students if they prefer being in school or working. Discuss the advantages and disadvantages of each situation.

Possessive Nouns, Possessive Adjectives, and *Whose*

THINK CRITICALLY ABOUT FORM

- Put students in pairs and give them a few minutes to answer questions 1 and 2. Encourage them to refer to the Form charts and bulleted notes to check their answers and get familiar with the new structures. As they work, write the example sentences on the board; underline the possessive nouns in 1a and 1b.

- **1. CATEGORIZE** Call a student to the board to write *singular* and *plural* above the appropriate possessive nouns in 1a and 1b (*roommate's* is singular; *roommates'* is plural). Ask *How do you know this?* (If students do not know the possessive rules, they should be able to determine this from the follow-up sentences; point out the singular *He's* in 1a and the plural *They're* in 1b.)

- Elicit the position of the apostrophe for singular possessive nouns and plural possessive nouns. Emphasize that the placement of the apostrophe carries important information.

- **2. IDENTIFY** Call another student to the board to underline the nouns and circle the possessive adjectives in sentences 2a and 2b (nouns: *brother* in both sentences; adjectives: *my* in 1a, *their* in 2b). Ask *How many brothers are we talking about in sentence 2a?* (One) *How many brothers are we talking about in 2b?* (One) *How do you know?* (The noun is singular and the verb *is* agrees with it.)

FORM CHARTS

- Give students several minutes to read the information on Possessive Nouns.

- To check understanding, ask questions like: *How do we form the possessive of a singular noun?* (noun + *'s*) *How do we form the possessive of a regular plural noun?* (plural + *'*) *What about the possessive of irregular plural nouns* (irregular plural + *'s*).

- Ask students to copy the following sentences in their notebooks and add the missing apostrophes (answers in parentheses are for teacher's reference):
  1. *The cats tail is long.* (cat's)
  2. *The cats tails are short.* (cats')
  3. *Marys cats tail is short.* (Mary's cat's)
  4. *The mouses tail is long.* (mouse's)
  5. *The mices tails are long.* (mice's)
  6. *John and Marys house is big.* (Mary's: but the house belongs to both of them.)

- Call students to the board and have them fill in the missing apostrophes. Discuss as necessary to clarify any problems.

- Give students several minutes to read the information on Possessive Adjectives and *Whose*. As they read, write the subject pronouns *I, you, he/she/it, we, you,* and *they* in a column on the board.

- Elicit and write the possessive adjective for each subject pronoun on the board (e.g., *my, your,* etc.).

- Have students read aloud the example sentences in the Possessive Adjectives chart.

- To check understanding, create a third column on the board and write the following sentence next to *my*: *I'm smart. My parents are proud.* Say *Now change the subject to* You. Elicit the answer (*You're smart. Your parents are proud.*), and continue until the chart is complete (skipping over *It*).

- Direct students' attention to the charts with *Whose*. Explain that we use the question word *Whose* to ask about possession. To check understanding, hold up your book and ask *Whose book is this?* Elicit the full form (*It's your book.*). Continue with two or three questions that can be answered with your students' names: e.g., *Whose hair is brown?* (e.g., John's./ John's is.) *Whose eyes are blue?* (e.g., *Maria's are./Maria's eyes are blue.*) Call on several students to ask their own questions.

- Discuss any difficulties or questions.

C FORM 2

Possessive Pronouns

THINK CRITICALLY ABOUT FORM

- Put students in pairs and give them a few minutes to answer questions 1 and 2. Encourage them to refer to the Form charts and bulleted notes to check their answers and get familiar with the new structures. As they work, write the example sentences on the board.

- **1. IDENTIFY** Call a student to the board to underline the possessive adjectives + nouns *(My book, their cat)*. Ask *How many books are there?* (One) *How many cats are there?* (One)

- **2. APPLY** Call another student to the board to circle the possessive pronouns *(Mine, Theirs)*. Elicit the phrases replaced by the possessive pronouns *(My book, their cat)*.

FORM CHARTS

- Direct students' attention to the first two columns. Ask students if they notice any similarities or patterns. (The adjective and the pronoun possessive forms are similar, and with the exception of *my/mine* and *its*, the pattern is to add an *-s* to the adjective to create the pronoun.) Emphasize that *Its* is not used as a possessive pronoun.

- Read the sentences in the Form chart aloud while students follow in their books. Point out the shift from possessive adjective + noun in the first sentence to possessive pronoun in the second.

- Give students a few minutes to read the bulleted notes. To check understanding, ask *How many forms do possessive pronouns have?* (One. The same form is used for singular and plural.)

- Divide students into small groups. Have them choose three possessive pronouns and write an original example with each. Each example should have two sentences: the first with a possessive adjective and the second with a possessive pronoun (e.g., *My favorite class is history. Hers is chemistry.*). Write the example on the board.

- Elicit a sentence from each group and write it on the board. Check the sentences as a class.

D MEANING AND USE 1

Possessives

THINK CRITICALLY ABOUT MEANING AND USE

- Put students in pairs and give them a few minutes to answer questions 1 and 2. As they work, write the sentences on the board.

- **1. IDENTIFY** Call a student to the board to underline the possessive forms (sentence a: *my, Keiko's*; sentence b: *their, mine*; sentence c: *Mary's, her, brother's*). Discuss any questions or disagreements as a class.

- **2. EVALUATE** Elicit the answers (ownership: b; a human relationship: a; a physical characteristic: c). If desired, elicit phrases which cue the answers (ownership: *their car*; a human relationship: *My sister, Keiko's sister*; a physical characteristic: *Mary's eyes*).

MEANING AND USE NOTES

- Divide students into three groups. Assign each group a Note.

- Explain that each group will teach the class their Note by explaining or reading the information and example sentences to the class. The group must also write a new sentence to illustrate each point in the Note.

- To present their Note, each group can assign one student to read or paraphrase the explanation, another to read the examples in the book, and another to write the group's sentences on the board.

- Circulate and help as necessary. Then call each group to the board to present their Note. Discuss any questions or difficulties as a class.

E FORM 3

Demonstrative Adjectives and Demonstrative Pronouns

THINK CRITICALLY ABOUT FORM

- Put students in pairs to answer questions 1 and 2. Encourage them to refer to the Form charts and bulleted notes to check their answers and get familiar with the new structures. As they work, write the example sentence pairs on the board with the words underlined as in the book.

- **1. CATEGORIZE** Ask a student to come to the board to write *singular* or *plural* over the underlined words in 1a and 1b. (singular = *This, That*; plural = *These, Those*) Ask *How do you know?* (The verb *is* tells us that *This* and *That* are singular. The verb *are* tells us that *These* and *Those* are plural.)

- If helpful, use classroom objects to demonstrate the meaning of *this/these* (for objects that are near) and *that/those* (for objects that are farther away).

- **2. CATEGORIZE** Call another student to the board to write *adjective* or *pronoun* over the underlined words in 2a and 2b. (The first sentence of each example has a demonstrative adjective, *This* and *These*; the second sentence of each has a demonstrative pronoun, *That* and *Those*.) Ask *How do you know?* (*This* and *These* come before nouns; *That* and *Those* act as subjects before verbs.)

- Discuss any questions or difficulties as a class.

FORM CHARTS

- Call on several students to read aloud the sentences in the Form charts.

- Give students a few minutes to read the bulleted notes on pages 111–112. As they read, write these conversations on the board:

  1. A: *Is that a new shirt?*   2. A: *Are these yours?*
     B: *No, it isn't.*   B: *No, they aren't.*

- Elicit or point out that we use *it* or *they* in response to *Yes/No* questions with demonstratives. We do not use *this, that, these,* or *those*.

- Divide the class in half. Have each student in the first half write three pairs of sentences in which the first sentence contains a singular demonstrative adjective and the other contains a singular demonstrative pronoun (e.g., *This book is new. That is old.*). Ask students in the other half to write three pairs of sentences in which one sentence has a plural demonstrative

adjective and the other a plural demonstrative pronoun (e.g., *These books are new. Those are old.*) Circulate and help as necessary.

- Put students into pairs, one student from each group, to check each other's work.

- Elicit several pairs of sentences from different students. Discuss any questions or difficulties.

F **MEANING AND USE 2**

Demonstratives

THINK CRITICALLY ABOUT MEANING AND USE

- Have two students read the conversation aloud. (Note: Pleiades, a well-known star group or constellation, is pronounced /ˈpliəd,iz /.)

- Put students in pairs to answer and discuss the questions. Then elicit answers from the class:
  1. IDENTIFY (Sally: *This; these*; Brad: *that*; Sally: *That; those*)
  2. EVALUATE (*This* and *these* are near the speaker. *That* and *those* are far from the speaker.)

- To reinforce the concept of near and far, ask a student to come to the front of the class. Stand near the student and say *This is [Betty]*. Point to another student farther away and say *That's [Keiko]*. Write the sentences on the board. Elicit that both sentences use a demonstrative pronoun. Then elicit the difference between *this* and *that*. (We use *this* when someone or something is near the speaker; we use *that* when someone or something is farther away.)

MEANING AND USE NOTES

- Call on two or three students to read aloud the Notes and examples.

- Ask students to write four sentences about objects in the classroom, one with each demonstrative (*this, that, these,* and *those*).

- Divide the class into small groups to compare and check their sentences.

- Elicit examples from each group. Discuss any questions or difficulties.

THINK CRITICALLY ABOUT MEANING AND USE

- Have students do A individually. Then, in small groups, have them compare answers and discuss any differences.

- Have them stay in groups and do B.

- As a class, review any difficult items from A. Then elicit answers to B:

    1. SUMMARIZE (*That* is used because it refers to an object far away from the speaker.)

    2. APPLY (In 3, *this* would be used if the glass in 3 were close to the speaker. In 4, *this* would be used if the apartment were close to the speaker, or if A and B were in the apartment.)

WRITE

The purpose of this activity is to give students practice in using possessives and demonstratives by writing a paragraph about a photograph of their family and/or friends. Remind students in the previous lesson to bring a photograph of their family or friends to class.

1. Brainstorm

As a class, start a brainstorm on the board about a photograph that you have chosen for the activity. Write the brainstorming categories on the board, and elicit details that students could write about. Have students work individually to brainstorm ideas for their descriptions.

2. Write a First Draft

Before students begin writing, make sure they have read the checklist in the Edit section. Also have them look at the example on page 110. Remind them to use the best points from their brainstorming notes to write their paragraphs.

3. Edit

Direct students to read and complete the self-assessment checklist on page 116. Ask for a show of hands for how many students gave all or mostly *yes* answers. If desired, ask students to comment on some of the errors they found.

DO I ...	YES
show ownership?	☐
show possession?	☐
show physical characteristics?	☐
use an apostrophe to show possession with at least one singular and one plural noun?	☐
use demonstratives to show possession?	☐
use demonstratives to show location (near and far)?	☐

4. Peer Review

Pair students and direct them to read each other's work. Ask students to answer the questions in the checklist and discuss them. Give students suggestions of helpful feedback: e.g., *Are you sure the apostrophe is correct here? The noun is an irregular plural so you need -'s (not -s'). / Is* there *correct here or did you mean to use* their?

5. Rewrite Your Draft

Students should consider their partners' comments from the peer review and rewrite as necessary. Encourage students to proofread their work again before turning it in.

8

The Present Continuous

Overview

The present continuous is used to talk about actions that are happening right now (e.g., *The telephone is ringing.*). It is also used to describe activities that are ongoing but may not be happening at the moment of speaking (e.g., *I'm studying French, Spanish, and history this year.*). Students may be familiar with the "right now" use of the present continuous, but it is important that they learn the ongoing use as well. Both are common in English.

Form: The key challenges are

- spelling the present participle (*-ing* form) for verbs whose final consonant is doubled (*swim — swimming*) or whose final vowel is dropped (*live — living*).

- remembering to insert the subject between *be* and the *-ing* verb in questions.

A) GRAMMAR IN DISCOURSE

People Watching

A1: Before You Read

- To introduce the concept of *journal*, ask students *How can people remember their thoughts and feelings?* Elicit or provide the word *journal* and write it on the board.

- Put students in pairs and give them about five minutes to discuss the questions.

- Bring the class together. Ask *Who keeps a journal? What kind of information do you write in your journal?* (e.g., *observations or feelings about events, ideas, plans for the future*).

A2: Read

- Remind students about using the glossary by eliciting the meaning of one of the words, e.g., *gloomy*.

- Put students in pairs. Ask them to skim the journal entry quickly and describe entry (e.g., *observation and feelings about events*) and the writer's conclusion about the couple with briefcases and expensive clothes. (*They are married–I'm sure.*) The writer isn't sure about something. What is it? (*She isn't sure if the couple are fighting.*)

- Ask students to read the entry again and underline the information that makes the woman think the second couple are fighting (e.g., *They aren't talking; they aren't smiling. Perhaps she is thinking about happier times.*). Elicit answers.

A3: After You Read

- Give students a few minutes to do the exercise individually. Ask them to scan the journal entry and mark the places where they found the answers.

- Have students compare answers with a partner and return to the journal entry to check any answers that do not agree.

- Call on individuals to read the true/false statement aloud and give their answers. Discuss any problems as a class.

- As a follow-up, ask *Why do you think the writer wrote about this in her journal? Is it an accurate observation? Why or why not?* Encourage students to support their opinions with information from the entry. Also ask *Do we need more information to be sure?*

B) FORM

The Present Continuous

THINK CRITICALLY ABOUT FORM

- Ask students to work individually to answer question 1. Encourage them to refer to the

Form charts and bulleted notes to check their answers and get familiar with the new structures. As they work, write the following on the board in two columns, circling and underlining the example forms as they appear in the book: (First column) *Two people are waiting at the bus stop. She is pointing to her watch.* (Second column) *It isn't raining. They aren't talking.*

- **1. IDENTIFY** Direct students' attention to the first column on the board. Ask *How many parts does the present continuous have?* (Two) *What do you think they are?* Draw two lines under *are* and *is*, then elicit or explain that the first part is a form of *be*. Circle the base forms of the verbs *(wait, point)*, and elicit or explain that the second part is the base form of the verb + *-ing*.

- **2. RECOGNIZE** Put students in pairs to compare the examples they found in the journal. Elicit answers (and subjects where necessary) and write them on the board under the original examples *(The city is waking up, I'm sitting, She's complaining, He's reading, The man and woman are sitting, The woman/The man is wearing, A couple is standing,* etc.). Discuss any difficult or problematic items.

- **3. RECOGNIZE** Direct students' attention to the negative examples in the second column on the board. Underline *isn't* and *aren't*. Ask *Are these affirmative or negative?*

- Have students call out more examples of the negative form from the journal entry *(isn't listening, aren't talking, aren't smiling)* and write them on the board. Elicit or point out that we form the negative form of the present continuous with a form of *be* + *not* + the base form of the verb + *-ing*.

Trouble Spots

Since many languages do not have two present verb tenses, students may use the simple present instead of the present continuous (e.g., **I study English now.* Incorrect). Students may also leave out the appropriate form of *be* (e.g., **I studying English now.* Incorrect) or they may forget to add the *-ing* ending to the main verb (e.g., **I am study English now.* Incorrect).

FORM CHARTS

- Give students a few minutes to read the charts and bulleted notes. As they read, write the subjects *I, You, He/She/It, We, You,* and *They* in a column on the board.

- Have students close their books. Then point to the pronoun *I* and elicit the form of *be* that follows *I* (*am*). Add *am sleeping* to the first line, then point to each part of the sentence and say *Subject* + be + *base form* + -ing. Point to *You* and ask a student to change the sentence (*You are sleeping.*) Repeat for the remaining subjects.

- Have the students open their books. Call on pairs to read out corresponding affirmative and negative statements from the charts. (Be sure to draw attention to the Contractions chart under Negative Statements, and remind students about the two possible forms of *be* + *not*. Review as necessary.)

- Repeat the procedure for *Yes/No* questions and short answers and information questions and answers, having pairs of students read questions and answers from the charts. Discuss any difficulties with the class.

- As a follow-up, divide students into an even number of groups and ask each group to write three statements in the present continuous. Encourage students to use a variety of verbs and include pronoun subjects as well as subjects with people's names. Circulate and help as necessary, making sure that all the groups have written correct sentences.

- Ask the groups to exchange sentences. Say *These are answers to some questions. Now write one* Yes/No *question and two information questions for each answer.* Model the activity by writing this sentence on the board: *Maria is eating in the cafeteria.* Elicit the *Yes/No* question and possible information questions (e.g., *Is Maria eating in the cafeteria? Who is eating in the cafeteria? Where is Maria eating? What is Maria doing?*). Give students about five minutes to write their questions. Circulate and help as necessary.

- Check by having groups ask and answer their questions. Discuss any difficulties as a class.

The Present Continuous

THINK CRITICALLY ABOUT MEANING AND USE

- Put students in pairs and give them a few minutes to answer the questions. Ask students to be prepared to support their answers.
- **1. EVALUATE** Elicit the answer (a). Ask *How do you know?* (Julie is talking to Paulo and telling him to take an umbrella, so it is probably raining right now.)
- **2. EVALUATE** Elicit the answer (b). Ask *How do you know?* (Carol is probably talking on the phone to Steve so she isn't writing her paper at this moment.)

MEANING AND USE NOTES

- Divide the class into four groups. Assign each group a Note.
- Explain that each group will teach the class their Note by explaining or reading the information and examples to the class. The group must also write a short dialogue to illustrate each point in the Note.
- To present their Note, each group can assign one student to read or paraphrase the explanation, two students to read the example dialogues in the book, and another to write the group's dialogue on the board.
- Circulate and help as necessary. Then call each group to the board to present their Note.

Beyond the Sentence: Combining Sentences with *And* (p. 130)

- Explain that combining sentences makes our writing more natural and interesting. Point out that we can use *and* to combine sentences.
- Ask students to read the first two paragraphs and examples. Check understanding by eliciting the difference between the two sets of examples. (The first set shows how to combine two sentences with two different subjects, *I* and *Alex*. The second shows how to combine two sentences with the same subject, *He*.)
- Read aloud paragraphs A and B in the second half of the box. Ask students which version is more natural and interesting (paragraph B).

Ask why. (There is less repetition. The sentences are longer and more natural.)

WRITING

THINK CRITICALLY ABOUT MEANING AND USE

- Have students do A individually. Then, in small groups, have them compare answers and discuss any differences.
- Have them stay in groups and do B.
- As a class, review any difficult items from A. Then elicit answers to B:
  1. EVALUATE (3 and 4)
  2. GENERATE (Answers will vary.)

WRITE

The purpose of this activity is to give students practice in using the present continuous by writing a paragraph about a public place.

1. Brainstorm

As a class, start a brainstorm on the board. Write the brainstorming questions on the board, and elicit answers. Then have students brainstorm their own ideas.

2. Write a First Draft

Before students begin, have them read the checklist in the Edit section.

3. Edit

Direct students to read and complete the self-assessment checklist on page 132. Ask for a show of hands for how many students gave all or mostly *yes* answers.

4. Peer Review

Pair students and direct them to read each other's work. Ask students to answer the questions in the checklist and discuss them. Give students suggestions of helpful feedback: e.g., *Are you sure this form is OK?*

5. Rewrite Your Draft

Students should consider their partners' comments and rewrite as necessary. Encourage students to proofread their work again before turning it in.

The Simple Present

Overview

The simple present is used to describe events that the speaker views as unchanging, including habits, routines, and states and conditions (e.g., *I love shopping. I shop every weekend, but I don't buy many things.*). The simple present is also used to describe general truths, definitions, and scientific facts (e.g., *Infants sleep most of the day. The word* rehearsal *means "a practice for a performance." Water boils at 100° centigrade.*).

Form: The key challenges are remembering

- the third-person singular form (*-s/-es*) is different from the other forms.
- the negative form requires *do* or *does* + *not*.
- *Yes/No* questions and information questions require *do* or *does*.
- questions with a *wh-* word as subject do not require *do* or *does*.

A GRAMMAR IN DISCOURSE

Career Path Asks: "What Do You Do?"

A1: Before You Read

- Ask students *What is your dream job? Is it possible for you to be a student and do this job now? Why or why not?* Give students a few minutes to think about this on their own. Elicit answers from two or three students, helping with vocabulary as necessary. On the board, write the jobs and the reasons why students can or cannot do them now.

- Put students in pairs and give them about five minutes to discuss the questions. Ask them to take notes about their partner's jobs and their opinions about the ease or difficulty of working while studying. Elicit jobs that students have.

A2: Read

- Remind students about the glossary by eliciting the meaning of one of the words, e.g., *rehearse*.

- Put students in pairs and ask them to read the introduction to the interview. Elicit why Kyla is an unusual student. (She is a professional ballet dancer.)

- Ask students to predict the topics that the interview might ask about (e.g., *family, friends, work hours, free time*). Elicit students' suggestions and list them on the board. Then have them read the interview and put a check next to any questions that address the topics from the list on the board.

- To check understanding, ask students which topics they predicted correctly and what other topics they can now add to the list on the board. Then elicit students' answers to the question *What makes Kyla an unusual student?*

A3: After You Read

- Have students answer the true/false questions individually and compare their answers with a partner. Remind them to mark the places in the interview where they found the answers.

- Circulate, noting any difficult or problematic items, and go over them with the whole class.

- As a follow-up, ask *Do you think it is a good idea for students to work while they attend high school?* You may want to conduct a debate, with half the class speaking in favor of working while studying and the other half supporting studying without working. Explain that in a debate, students may have to defend a position they do not necessarily believe or agree with. Make sure each group makes a list of reasons to support their position. Also, make sure to allow students enough time to prepare for the debate, and give each side equal time to present its position.

Simple Present Statements

THINK CRITICALLY ABOUT FORM

- Have students work individually to complete questions 1 and 2. Encourage them to refer to the Form charts and bulleted notes to check their answers and get familiar with the new structures. Circulate and help as necessary.

- **1. COMPARE AND CONTRAST** Write sentences 1a–1c on the board. Call on individual students to say the subjects aloud (*I, She, They*) as you circle them in the sentences. Elicit the verbs used in the sentences (*come, comes, come*) and underline them. Then elicit that the verb form for *She* is different; it ends in -*s*.

- **2. COMPARE AND CONTRAST** Write sentences 2a–2c on the board. Ask students to call out the subject in each sentence and circle it. (*I, He, They*) Elicit the three words that come after each subject (*do not walk, does not walk, do not walk*). Then elicit that the verb form in 2b (*does*) is different from the other two forms.

- **3. IDENTIFY** Put students in pairs to find three affirmative sentences and one negative sentence in the interview. Circulate and help as necessary.

- Elicit the answers from different pairs. (Some affirmative sentences: *I have ballet class from 10:30 to 12:00. Then we rehearse from 12:00 to 3:30 and 4:30 to 6:00. I go home and make dinner. Then I study or read and go to bed. I live alone.* Negative sentence: *I don't have much free time.*)

FORM CHARTS

- Give students a few minutes to read the charts and the bulleted notes. Check students' understanding by eliciting the affirmative and negative forms of verbs in the simple present (*live, lives, do not live, does not live*).

- To check understanding further, call a student to the board to write affirmative statements with *live* and *work*. Then call on students to change the sentences to negative statements. Emphasize that we do not add -*s* to the base form when we make negative statements with *does*.

- Write the verbs *teach* and *have* on the board. Elicit a sentence each with *he* or *she* and write them on the board. Direct students' attention to the third-person verb form. Elicit or point out that -*es* is added to *teach*. Refer students to Appendix 4 in the Student Book for spelling rules. Ask students what *irregular* means. (Something is different and does not follow the usual rules.) Point out that *have* is irregular: the third-person singular form is *has*.

- Write the following verbs on the board: *read, like, watch, have*. Ask half the class to write an affirmative sentence for each verb. Ask the other half to write a negative sentence for each verb. Encourage students to use a variety of subjects.

- Put students in pairs, with one partner contributing affirmative statements and the other contributing negative statements. Ask students to check the subject-verb agreement in their partner's sentences. Then ask students to change their partner's sentences to either affirmative or negative. Circulate and help as necessary.

- Elicit a sentence for each verb and write it on the board. Be sure to elicit a variety of subjects to focus students' attention on the third-person singular forms.

Pronunciation Notes: Pronunciation of Verbs Ending in -*s* and -*es* (p. 139)

- Explain that the simple present third-person singular ending is pronounced in three different ways. Write /s/, /z/, and /ɪz/ as column heads on the board. Say the words below aloud and write them in the correct column.

  knows (/z/)   *dances* (/ɪz/)   *cooks* (/s/)

- Present the rules for each category. Emphasize that the pronunciation of -*s*/-*es* depends on the final sound of the base form of the verb.

- Say the following words aloud and ask students which column their third-person forms belong in. Write the third-person forms on the board in the correct column.

wants (/s/)	*tastes* (/s/)	*washes* (/ɪz/)
uses (/ɪz/)	*laughs* (/s/)	*decides* (/z/)
cooks (/s/)	*plays* (/z/)	*calls* (/z/)

C FORM 2

Simple Present *Yes/No* Questions and Short Answers

THINK CRITICALLY ABOUT FORM

- Put students in pairs to answer questions 1–3 in their books. As students work, write the questions on the board.

- **1. ANALYZE** Ask a student to come to the board and circle the subject of each question (*you, she, they*). Ask *What word comes before each subject?* (*Do, Does, Do*).

- **2. COMPARE AND CONTRAST** Direct students' attention to question b. Elicit that it begins with *Does*, unlike the other questions which begin with *Do*. Elicit that the third-person singular forms are different in the simple present.

- **3. APPLY** Ask another student to come to the board and underline the main verb in each sentence. Elicit or point out that the main verb is the base form, which is the same in all persons.

- As a follow-up, have students look back at the first part of the interview on page 134 and find the *Yes/No* questions. Circulate and help as necessary. Elicit answers (*Do you get lonely? Does your family visit you?*).

FORM CHARTS

- Call on several pairs of students to read out the *Yes/No* questions and short answers in the charts.

- To check students' understanding, ask questions like: *How are* Yes/No *questions like negative statements?* (We form them with *do/does* and the base form of the verb.) *How are* Yes/No *questions different from negative statements?* (*Do/Does* comes before the subject.)

- Give students a few minutes to read the bulleted notes. Discuss and answer questions as necessary.

- Write on the board: *you, your best friend, your teachers, your city*. Ask students to write a *Yes/No* question for each subject. Circulate and help as necessary.

- Ask several pairs to ask and answer their questions for the class. Elicit any necessary corrections from students.

D FORM 3

Simple Present Information Questions

THINK CRITICALLY ABOUT FORM

- Have students work individually to complete questions 1 and 2. As students work, write the sample sentences on the board.

- **1. CATEGORIZE** Ask a student to identify the *Yes/No* questions (1a, 2a). Elicit that questions 1b and 2b are information questions. Ask *How do you know this?* (They begin with *Where* and *When*.)

- **2. ORGANIZE** Elicit that simple present *Yes/No* questions begin with *do* or *does* and information questions begin with *wh-* words such as *who, what, where, when, why*, and *how*.

- As a follow-up, have students look back at the first part of the interview on page 134 and ask them to find the information questions. Circulate and help as necessary. Elicit answers. (*How many hours a day do you dance? What do you do after rehearsal? Who do you live with? Where does your family live? Who teaches you? When do you study? How are you doing in school? What do you do in your free time?*)

FORM CHARTS

- Call on several pairs of students to read out the information questions and answers in the charts.

- Write on the board: *When do you exercise?* Check students' understanding of the form by prompting them to change the question with a variety of subjects (e.g., *he, I, she, they*) and *wh-* words (e.g., *Where, Why, When*).

- Write the following on the board: *When does he eat dinner? What smells good?* Put students in pairs and ask them to read the caution note to find out why the forms are different. Elicit the subjects (*he, What*) and the verbs (*does . . . eat, smells*), and ask students to give you a rule for forming questions with a *wh-*word as subject (*wh-*word + base form of verb + *-s/-es*).

- Ask students to write two original information questions, one with a subject pronoun and the other with *wh-* word as the subject.

- Call on several students to come to the board and write their questions. Elicit possible answers and discuss any problems.

The Simple Present

THINK CRITICALLY ABOUT MEANING AND USE

- Call on individual students to read sentences a–c aloud.
- Put students in pairs. Give them a few minutes to answer the questions. Ask them to be prepared to support their answers.
- **1.–4. EVALUATE** Elicit answers. For each answer, ask *How do we know?* (1. b, *every Sunday*; 2. c, *the word . . . means* signals a definition; 3. a, *3 million*; 4. *makes* in sentence b)

MEANING AND USE NOTES

- Divide the class into three groups. Assign each group a Note.
- Explain that each group will teach the class their Note by explaining or reading the information and example sentences to the class. The group must also write a new sentence or short conversation to illustrate each point in the Note.
- To present their Note, each group can assign one student to read or paraphrase the explanation, another to read the examples in the book, and another to write the group's sentences on the board.
- Circulate and help as necessary. Then call each group to the board to present their Note.

Beyond the Sentence: Linking Ideas in the Simple Present (p. 149)

This section is intended to give students practice with the meaning and use of grammar as it functions naturally in paragraphs and conversations.

- Explain that it is helpful to use sequence words when describing actions in a sequence. Using sequence words makes it easier for the reader or listener to follow the text or speech.

- Put students into pairs and have them circle the first word of each sentence in the first paragraph. Elicit that with the exception of the first, all the sentences begin with *I*.
- Ask students to circle the first word in each sentence of the second paragraph. Elicit that the sentences begin with a sequence word. Ask questions like: *Which paragraph is more interesting and why?* (The second paragraph because the sentences have more variety.) *Which paragraph is more organized and easier to follow?* (The second is more organized because the reader can follow the sequence more easily.)

THINK CRITICALLY ABOUT MEANING AND USE

- Have students do A individually. Then, in small groups, have them compare answers and discuss any differences.
- Have them stay in groups and do B.
- As a class, review any difficult items from A. Then elicit answers to B:

  1. EVALUATE (4 uses a stative verb: *owns*)

  2. COMPARE AND CONTRAST (Stative verbs express states and conditions; action verbs express actions.)

WRITE

The purpose of this activity is to give students practice in using simple present verb forms by writing a paragraph about an interesting job.

1. Brainstorm

As a class, start a brainstorm on the board about one or more interesting occupations (e.g., *brain surgeon, explorer, professional soccer or basketball player*). Make it clear that students will write about a different job. Write the brainstorming categories on the board and elicit the kinds of details that students might write about. (If you're working with several jobs, elicit a range of answers for each category.) Have students work individually to make brainstorming notes on their own jobs. If time allows, encourage them to research their jobs on the Internet.

1. Write a First Draft

Before students begin writing, make sure they have read the checklist in the Edit section. Also have them look at the example in E4 on page 150. Remind them to use the best points from their brainstorming notes to write their paragraphs.

2. Edit

Direct students to read and complete the self-assessment checklist on page 152. Ask for a show of hands for how many students gave all or mostly *yes* answers. If desired, ask students to comment on some of the errors they found.

DO I ...	YES
use statements with the simple present tense?	☐
use *yes/no* questions with the simple present tense?	☐
use stative verbs to show description, possession, and feelings?	☐
include factual information?	☐
include information about habits and routines?	☐

3. Peer Review

Pair students and direct them to read each other's work. Ask students to answer the questions in the checklist and discuss them. Give students suggestions of helpful feedback: e.g., *Are you sure this is the correct form here? / You haven't included a negative form. Do you want to add one?*

5. Rewrite Your Draft

Students should consider their partners' comments from the peer review and rewrite as necessary. Encourage students to proofread their work again before turning it in.

10 Adverbs of Frequency

Overview

Adverbs of frequency are often used with the simple present to tell how often something happens (e.g., *He is often late for class.*) or how often someone does something (e.g. *I sometimes work on weekends. I never go home early.*). Adverbs of frequency are not conceptually difficult for students, but using the correct form and placement can be challenging.

Form: The key challenges are remembering

- negative adverbs of frequency are not used in negative statements.
- adverbs can appear in more than one position in a sentence, but their movement is not unrestricted. The easiest way to explain their placement to beginning students is that they come after the verb *be* and before other verbs.

A GRAMMAR IN DISCOURSE

What Kind of Learner Are You?

A1: Before You Read

- Write these three occupations on the board: *psychologist, architect, chemist.* Elicit or explain their meanings. Ask *What skills does a person need in order to be successful in each job?* Elicit students' answers, and write them under each occupation.

- Divide students into small groups to discuss the questions in the book. Elicit students' opinions about their preferences. Ask students which of the three occupations on the board is best for them.

A2: Read

- Remind students about using the glossary by eliciting the meaning of one of the words, e.g., *manuals.*

- Organize a jigsaw reading. Divide the class into three groups. Assign a different paragraph to each group. Instruct students to read their paragraph and prepare a two-or three-sentence summary. Give students about ten minutes to do this. Circulate and help as necessary.

- Ask a representative from each group to come to the board and write the group's summary. Elicit students' opinions about which summary describes them best.

A3: After You Read

- Have students answer the true/false questions individually and compare their answers with a partner. Remind them to mark the places in the excerpt where they found the answers.

- Go over any difficult or problematic items with the whole class.

- As a follow-up, ask students to make a list of three or four suitable jobs for each person in the article. Discuss their ideas as a class.

B FORM

Adverbs of Frequency

THINK CRITICALLY ABOUT FORM

- Have students work in pairs to complete questions 1–3. Encourage them to refer to the Form charts and bulleted notes to check their answers and get familiar with the new structures. As students work, write example sentences a–d on the board.

- **1. IDENTIFY** Call on a student to come to the board and underline the adverbs of frequency. Check as a class, discussing any difficulties or questions (a. *usually*; b. *always*; c. *often*; d. *rarely*).

- **2. CATEGORIZE** Elicit the letters of those sentences with the verb *be* (a, c). Elicit that the adverb of frequency comes after the verb *be*.

- **3. CATEGORIZE** Elicit the verbs from sentences b and d (*follow, read*). Elicit that the adverb comes before other verbs.

- As a follow-up, have students look back at the article on page 155 to find more examples of sentences with adverbs of frequency. Circulate and help as necessary. Elicit answers (e.g., *Teachers like them because they always follow instructions. He is usually very good with ideas and concepts but sometimes has problems with details. Some learners rarely learn from books or pictures. Peter never reads computer manuals and seldom looks at diagrams. Do you always learn the same way?*).

FORM CHARTS

- Give students a few minutes to read the charts and the bulleted notes.

- Check understanding of placement by reading aloud an example from the first chart as the students follow along in their books. Call on one student to identify the adverb of frequency and another student to describe its placement in the sentence (after *be* or before the verb in affirmative sentences, before *be* + *not* or before *do/does* + *not* in negative sentences, after the subject in *Yes/No* questions and information questions). Continue doing this until you have read most of the sentences in the charts.

- Write two column headings on the board labeled *Positive Adverbs* and *Negative Adverbs*. Have students close their books. Check their understanding of positive and negative adverbs by choosing one of the adverbs from the positive adverbs list and saying it aloud (e.g., *usually*). Ask if this is a positive or a negative adverb (positive). Write it on the board under *Positive*. Say another adverb aloud. Ask a student to come to the board and write it in the correct column. Continue until all the adverbs of frequency are on the board.

- Divide students into small groups. Ask groups to choose two positive and two negative adverbs. Have them use their adverbs to write two

affirmative sentences, two negative sentences, and two questions. Encourage them to use a variety of verbs, including the verb *be*.

- Elicit sentences from different groups. Have students write their sentences on the board. Point out the position of the adverb with relation to the verb in each sentence. Check them as a class and discuss any problematic sentences.

Adverbs of Frequency

THINK CRITICALLY ABOUT MEANING AND USE

- Call on individual students to read the sentences aloud. Ask what all the sentences are about (students and their homework habits).

- **1. IDENTIFY** Put students in pairs to underline the adverbs of frequency. Check their answers (a. *usually*; b. *rarely*; c. *never*; d. *always*).

- **2. CATEGORIZE** Conduct a class discussion about who the best student is (Teresa) and who the worst student is (Mike). Ask for support from the sentences. Then, in pairs again, have them complete the chart.

- Call a student to the board to draw the chart and fill in the blanks (*from top to bottom*: d, a, b, c).

MEANING AND USE NOTES

- Give students a few minutes to read the explanations and examples in Note 1. Point out that the first five bullets are positive adverbs and the last three bullets are negative adverbs and, as such, we do not use them in negative statements. (Some students may ask you to assign exact percentages for the adverbs of frequency in the middle of the chart, but resist this, explaining that many native speakers disagree about such percentages.)

- To check understanding, give students a few minutes to write three sentences about themselves using three adverbs in Note 1A. Elicit sentences from several students and write them on the board. For sentences with *always*, *sometimes*, or *occasionally*, elicit a sentence with an alternative expression (e.g., *all the time, some of the time, once in a while*). Draw students' attention to the correct placement of these frequency expressions at the end of the sentence.

- Give students a few minutes to read Note 2. As students read, write the following sentences on the board:

  I rarely drive to work.
  I always sleep late on weekends.
  We almost never begin class late.

- Ask students to write sentences based on the examples on the board (e.g., *I usually take the train. I never wake up before 10:00. We almost always begin class on time.*). Elicit a sentence for each and write it on the board.

- Give students a few minutes to read Note 3. Then put students in pairs to ask and answer original questions with *ever*. Call a student to the front to model the activity with you. Ask (*Diego*), *do you ever eat breakfast?* Encourage the student to answer you honestly.

- If necessary, prompt students by writing the following on the board: *go skating, watch horror movies, cook for your friends.*

- Ask several pairs to ask and answer their questions at the front of the class.

Vocabulary Notes: *How Often . . . ?* and Frequency Expressions (p. 163)

These Notes present the question form *How often . . . ?* and adverbs of specific frequency that are used to answer this question.

- You may want to bring in a calendar for this activity. An old wall calendar that is large enough for all students to see would be best.

- Ask students to read the Notes. Elicit or explain that frequency expressions are necessary to answer questions with *How often . . . ?*

- Some students may already be familiar with the frequency expressions. To present their meanings, call a volunteer to the front of the room and point out on the calendar the meaning of several frequency expressions (e.g., *every day, once a week, twice a month*).

- Discuss any questions or difficulties as a class.

THINK CRITICALLY ABOUT MEANING AND USE

- Have students do A individually. Then, in small groups, have them compare answers and discuss any differences.

- Have them stay in groups and do B.

- As a class, review any difficult items from A. Then elicit answers to B:

  1.–2. GENERATE (Answers will vary. Some examples are: *Yes, and he never complains about it. / Yes, he never does it late*; Answers will vary. Some examples are: *Does your boss like this? / Why does this happen? / That's not good. What does your boss say?*)

WRITE

The purpose of this activity is to give students practice in using adverbs of frequency by writing a paragraph about their individual learning styles.

1. Brainstorm

As a class, start a brainstorm on the board about learning styles. Write the brainstorming questions on the board, and elicit the kinds of detail that students might write about. Encourage students to provide suggestions that cover the range of learning styles represented by the three students in the article on page 155. Have students work individually to make brainstorming notes on their own learning styles.

2. Write a First Draft

Before students begin writing, make sure they have read the checklist in the Edit section. Also have them look at the example on page 155. Remind them to use the best points from their brainstorming notes to write their paragraphs.

3. Edit

Direct students to read and complete the self-assessment checklist on page 166. Ask for a show of hands for how many students gave all or mostly *yes* answers. If desired, ask students to comment on some of the errors they found.

DO I ...	YES
use adverbs of frequency?	☐
use positive and negative adverbs?	☐
use simple present tense?	☐
use adverbs in the correct position?	☐
use the adverb *ever* at least one time?	☐
use adverbs that show opposites at least one time?	☐

4. Peer Review

Pair students and direct them to read each other's work. Ask students to answer the questions in the checklist and discuss them. Give students suggestions of helpful feedback: e.g., *We're supposed to use the simple present. Are you sure this is the correct form? / Is the position of* always *correct here? You've got it before* am, *but adverbs are supposed to go after forms of* be.

5. Rewrite Your Draft

Students should consider their partners' comments from the peer review and rewrite as necessary. Encourage students to proofread their work again before turning it in.

11

The Simple Past of *Be*

Overview

The simple past of *be* is used to talk about people, things, or situations that existed in the past (e.g., *I was excited about the project last week.*). These include conditions (e.g., *They were sick last week.*), physical characteristics (e.g., *I was a skinny child.*), and occupations (e.g., *My grandparents were teachers.*). The simple past of *be* can also be used to talk about location and origin (e.g., *We were at our friend's house last night. Her family was from Italy.*).

Form: The simple past of *be* is not usually difficult for students. Point out that *be* has two past forms (*was* and *were*). These forms combine with *not* to make the negative contractions *wasn't* and *weren't*.

A) GRAMMAR IN DISCOURSE

The Temples of Egypt

A1: Before You Read

- If possible, bring in some photographs of ancient Egyptian artifacts and buildings (e.g., *gold jewelry, paintings, statues, the pyramids, temples*). Ask students to guess where they are from. Ask them to reflect on how they knew this.

- Divide students into small groups to discuss the questions. Elicit students' knowledge of ancient Egyptian history and culture. Explain that the pharaohs were the ancient kings of Egypt and that the pyramids were their tombs.

A2: Read

- Remind students about using the glossary by eliciting the meaning of one of the words, e.g., *ritual*.

- Direct students' attention to the question *What was the difference between a temple and*

a pyramid? Write the following additional questions on the board: *How many parts of the temple does the article describe? Which parts of the temple were open to ordinary people? Which parts were open only to priests and the pharaoh?*

- Give students about ten minutes to read and answer the questions. Circulate and help as necessary.

- Elicit students' answers. (e.g., *A pyramid was a tomb for the pharaoh, but a temple was the home of a god. The article describes six parts of the temple. The courtyard was open to ordinary people. The second hall and sanctuary were only open to priests and the pharaoh.*)

A3: After You Read

- Have students do the matching activity individually and then compare their answers with a partner. Remind them to mark the places in the excerpt where they found the answers.

- Go over any difficult items with the whole class.

- As a follow-up, ask students why they think ancient Egyptian culture still interests people today.

B) FORM

The Simple Past of *Be*

THINK CRITICALLY ABOUT FORM

- Have students work individually to complete questions 1–3. Encourage them to refer to the Form charts and bulleted notes to check their answers and get familiar with the new structures. Circulate and help as necessary.

- **1. IDENTIFY** Write the underlined examples from the excerpt on the board: *The ancient Egyptians were great builders. For the ancient Egyptians a temple was the home of the gods.* Underline the verbs (*were* and *was*). Explain that the underlined forms are the two forms of the simple past of *be*. Ask *Are the forms affirmative or negative?*

- Call a student to the board to put two lines under each subject. Elicit which subject is singular (*temple*) and which is plural (*Egyptians*). Then ask *Which form of* be *do we use with singular nouns?* (was) *Which form do we use with plural nouns?* (were)

- **2. IDENTIFY** On the board, write shortened versions of the negative examples from the excerpt: *The temples and pyramids were not for ordinary people. An Egyptian temple was not a tomb.* Circle *were not* and *was not*. Ask *Are the sentences affirmative or negative?* Elicit or explain that *not* comes after the form of *be*.

- Ask *When do we use* was not *in these sentences?* (with singular nouns) *When do we use* were not? (with plural nouns)

- **3. RECOGNIZE** Put students in pairs to find more examples from the text. Circulate and help as necessary.

FORM CHARTS

- Give students a few minutes to read the charts and bulleted notes. As they read, write the subjects *I, you, he/she/it, we, you,* and *they* in a column on the board.

- Elicit the form that follows each subject and write it on the board (e.g., *I was, you were,* etc.). Ask *When do we use* was? (With *I* and with *he/she/it*). Point out that *were* is used for all other forms (singular *you* and plural *we, you,* and *they*).

- Call on pairs of students to read out corresponding affirmative and negative statements from the charts. Repeat the procedure for *Yes/No* questions and short answers and for Information questions and answers.

- Divide the board into three columns. In the first, write the following in a single column on the board: *Affirmative, Negative, Yes/No Questions, Short Answers,* and *Information Questions.* Label the second column *Was* and the third column *Were.*

- Call on a student to give you an original affirmative sentence with *was*. Ask another student for an original sentence with *were*. Write them on the board in their respective

columns. Call on another pair of students to change the sentences to negative statements. Repeat until the chart is complete.

- Put the students in pairs and ask them to write three *Yes/No* questions and three information questions with the simple past of *be*.

- Put pairs together to form groups of four. Ask students to ask and answer each other's questions. Circulate and help as necessary.

C MEANING AND USE

The Simple Past of *Be*

THINK CRITICALLY ABOUT MEANING AND USE

- Put students in pairs. Give them a few minutes to do the questions.

- **1. EVALUATE** Elicit the answers to question 1. (Sentences a, c, d, e, and f are about past situations. Sentence b is about a present situation.) Ask *How do you know?* (From the verb forms that are used: *was* and *were* are for past situations; *is* is for present situations.)

- **2. INTERPRET** Elicit answers to question 2. Have the pairs write sentences about themselves using the past time expressions *yesterday* and *last year.*

MEANING AND USE NOTES

- Present these notes as a whole-class activity. In preparation, write these sentences on the board (answers in parentheses are for teacher's reference):

  1. *My sister was fat as a child. Now she's thin.* (Physical Characteristics: body size is a characteristic.)

  2. *Ayrton Senna was from Brazil.* (Origin: Ayrton Senna, a famous Brazilian racecar driver who died in 1994, was from Brazil.)

  3. *I wasn't late for class yesterday. I am late today.* (States or Conditions: lateness is a state.)

  4. *My father was a dentist. Now he's retired.* (Occupation)

  5. *My books were on the desk.* (Location: the prepositional phrase with *on* shows location.)

- Call on five students to read the explanations and four groups of examples in Note 1.
- Put students in pairs. Ask them to match each sentence to one of the categories in Note 1.
- Elicit answers, asking students to support their opinions.
- Give students a few minutes to read Note 2. Then ask them to write three sentences about themselves using the following time expressions: *yesterday, last week,* and *five years ago.*
- Put students in pairs to check each other's sentences. Elicit several sentences for each expression.

Vocabulary Notes: *Was Born* and *Were Born* (p. 179)

- Explain that in English we use *was born* and *were born* to talk about someone's birth or their birthplace. Tell students that it is not acceptable to use *born* as a verb without *was* or *were* (e.g., **I born in New York.* Incorrect).
- Give students a few minutes to read the Vocabulary Notes. Discuss any difficulties.
- As a follow-up, write these prompts on the board and have pairs ask and answer each other's questions: *When – you – born? Where – your brother/sister – born? You – born – 1989? Your grandparents – born – before 1950?* Circulate and help as necessary. (Answers: When were you born? Where was your brother/sister born? Were you born in 1989? Were your grandparents born before 1950?)

WRITING

THINK CRITICALLY ABOUT MEANING AND USE

- Have students do A individually. Then, in small groups, have them compare answers and discuss any differences.
- Have them stay in groups and do B.
- As a class, review any difficult items from A. Then elicit answers to B:

  1. EXPLAIN (The question is in the simple past. Answers b and c are simple present, so they can't answer A's question.)

2. PREDICT (Answers will vary. Some examples are: *Maybe it wasn't Marta. / Maybe it was Marta in a wig! / Was it really Marta?*)

WRITE

The purpose of this activity is to give students practice in using forms of the simple past of the verb *be* by writing a paragraph about a famous person. Encourage students to do research in the library or on the Internet to find out more about the person they want to write about.

1. **Brainstorm**

   As a class, start a brainstorm on the board about a famous person that most students know about. (Make it clear that students will write about a different person.) Write the brainstorming questions on the board, and elicit the kinds of details that students might write about. Have students work individually to make brainstorming notes about their person.

2. **Write a First Draft**

   Before students begin writing, make sure they have read the checklist in the Edit section. Also have them look at the example on page 174.

3. **Edit**

   Direct students to complete the self-assessment checklist on page 182. Ask for a show of hands for how many students gave all or mostly *yes* answers.

4. **Peer Review**

   Pair students and direct them to read each other's work. Ask students to answer the questions in the checklist and discuss them. Give students suggestions of helpful feedback: e.g., *You haven't used a* Yes/No *question. What about adding one here?*

5. **Rewrite Your Draft**

   Students should consider their partners' comments from the peer review and rewrite as necessary. Encourage students to proofread their work again before turning it in.

12 The Simple Past

Overview

The simple past is used to talk about an action that started and was completed in the past. The action can be from the recent past (e.g., *I bought a pen this morning.*) or it can be from the distant past (e.g., *My great-grandfather bought this land a hundred years ago.*).

Form: The key challenges are remembering

- irregular past tense forms (e.g., *eat – ate*).
- negative forms require *did* + *not* + base form of verb.
- questions require *did* + base form of verb.
- subject *who* and *what* questions use the regular or irregular forms; they do not use *did*.

A GRAMMAR IN DISCOURSE

Fashions in History

A1: Before You Read

- Write the word *trend* on the board and elicit its meaning (the popular way of doing something or the way in which something is changing). Write the phrase *fashion trends* on the board and elicit its meaning (popular ways of dressing, changing styles of clothing). Then ask *Who starts fashion trends?* Write students' answers on the board (e.g., *movie actors, singers*).

- Divide students into small groups to discuss the questions. Elicit some of today's popular fashions. Write them on the board. Survey students' opinions by asking them to raise their hands if they like a particular fashion. Ask a few students to give reasons for their preferences and what they know about past fashions.

A2: Read

- Remind students about using the glossary by eliciting the meaning of one of the words, e.g., *elaborate*.

- To help students focus on the reading task, write the following questions on the board (answers in parentheses are for teacher's reference):

  1. *How did French women decorate their hair?* (They put paste on their hair and made elaborate styles. They also used feathers, lace, and ribbons. Sometimes they added vases of flowers or birdcages with live birds.)

  2. *Why did people wear gloves?* (They wore gloves to keep their hands soft.)

  3. *How did women make their skin pale? Why did they want pale skin?* (Women made their skin pale with powder. White skin was a sign of wealth and leisure.)

- Ask students to read the excerpt to find the answers. Remind them to mark the places in the text where they found the answers.

- Elicit the answers. Discuss any disagreements or problems.

A3: After You Read

- Have students work individually and compare their answers with a partner. Remind them to mark the places in the excerpt where they found the answers.

- Go over any difficult or problematic items with the whole class.

- As a follow-up, ask students if they think any of the fashion practices in the excerpt were silly or strange. Ask them what fashion trends today they think might be considered silly or strange a hundred years from now.

Simple Past Statements

THINK CRITICALLY ABOUT FORM

- Put students in pairs to do questions 1 and 2. Encourage them to refer to the Form charts and bulleted notes to check their answers and get familiar with the new structures.

- **1.–2. SUMMARIZE** Elicit answers (1. -*d*; 2. -*ed*). To illustrate, write the underlined verbs from the excerpt on the board (*covered, placed*) and circle the base forms (*cover, place*).

- Ask students to look at the excerpt again and find other examples of regular simple past forms (*added, owned, helped, protected, included*). Write them on the board and ask students to identify the base forms.

- **3. ANALYZE** Ask students to read the question. Give students a minute to look for a common ending. (There isn't one.) Ask them what *irregular* means. (different from what is normal or usual, not following the usual rules) Explain that irregular verbs are verbs that do not add -*d* or -*ed* to the base form to form the simple past. They have different forms that must be memorized. (Refer students to Appendix 8 in the Student Book for a list of irregular verbs and their simple past forms.)

- **4. APPLY** Write the circled example from the extract on the board: *did not have*. Elicit the number of parts in the verb (three).

- Ask students to find the second example of the negative simple past in the excerpt (*did not need*). Write it on the board under the first example. Ask students to compare the two examples. Direct their attention to the last word of each phrase. Elicit or point out that we form the negative form of the past tense with *did* + *not* + the base form of verb.

FORM CHARTS

- Give students a few minutes to read the charts and bulleted notes. Check understanding by asking students if the form of regular and irregular verbs changes with different subjects. (It doesn't.) Then ask them to read out several examples from each chart.

- To check understanding further, call a student to the board to write affirmative sentences with *live* and *help*. Then call on students to change the sentences to negative statements.

- Direct students' attention to the list of irregular verbs in the bulleted notes on page 187. Give students a few minutes to study the list. If desired, put the students in pairs and allow them to practice. Then ask them to close their books for a short quiz.

- Write the base forms of the following regular and irregular verbs on the board: *forget, place, make, meet, try, cook, dance, send, walk, give*.

- Ask students to write the simple past forms of the verbs as quickly as they can. Then have them exchange their answers with a partner and check each other's work.

- Elicit the simple past forms and write them on the board (*forgot, placed, made, met, tried, cooked, danced, sent, shop, gave*).

- Ask a student to come to the board and circle the five regular verbs (*placed, tried, cooked, danced, shopped*). If you haven't already done so, point out the spelling rule for verbs ending with a single consonant + *y* (*try* – *tried*) and one-syllable verbs ending with a consonant + consonant (*shop* – *shopped*). Refer students to Appendix 6 in the Student Book for other spelling rules.

Pronunciation Notes: Pronunciation of Verbs Ending in -*ed* (p. 190)

- Explain that the regular simple past ending is pronounced in three different ways. Divide the board into three columns labeled /t/, /d/, and /ɪd/. Say the words below aloud and write them in the correct column.

    talked   *planned*   *decided*

- Go over the rules for each category on page 190. Model each group of examples and ask students to repeat. Emphasize that when the base verb ends in a /d/ or /t/ sound, an extra syllable is added.

- Say the following words aloud and ask students which column they belong in. Write them on the board in the correct column:

    wanted   (/ɪd/)   *played*   (/d/)
    used   (/d/)   *washed*   (/t/)

cooked	(/t/)	*decided*	(/ɪd/)
tasted	(/ɪd/)	*called*	(/d/)
laughed	(/t/)	*watched*	(/t/)

- Elicit other regular simple past verbs, and have individuals come to the board and write the verbs in the correct category. Discuss any disagreements.

C FORM 2

Simple Past Questions

THINK CRITICALLY ABOUT FORM

- Put students in pairs to answer questions 1–3 in their books. As they work, write the questions on the board.

- **1. ANALYZE** Call a student to the board to put a check next to the simple past questions (1b, 2b). Ask *How do you know this?* (They both have *did*.)

- **2. DIFFERENTIATE** Call another student up to identify the *Yes/No* question in the simple past (1b). Ask the student to underline the words that come before and after the subject (*Did* and *eat*). Elicit that *eat* is the base form and not a simple past form.

- **3. DIFFERENTIATE** Ask another student to come up and identify the information question in the simple past (2b). Ask the student to underline the word that comes between the *wh-* word and the subject (*did*). Then have the student circle the verb that follows the subject (*start*). Elicit that *start* is the base form of the verb and not a simple past form.

FORM CHARTS

- Call on five pairs of students to read out the questions and answers in both sets of charts.

- Then give the students a few minutes to read the bulleted notes. As they read, write the following questions on the board (answers in parentheses are for teacher's reference):

  1. *Did he walk to class yesterday?* (Correct. — first bulleted note)

  2. *Did you goed to the airport last night?* (Incorrect — Did you go . . . ? — second bulleted note)

  3. *Did she received the card yesterday?* (Incorrect — Did she receive . . . ? — second bulleted note)

  4. *Who called last night?* (Correct. — first bulleted note)

  5. *Who did you see at the game?* (Correct. — second bulleted note)

  6. *What did happen to my books?* (Incorrect — What happened . . . ? — caution note)

  7. *How did you find my books?* (Correct. — first bulleted note)

  8. *Where did you met your friends yesterday?* (Incorrect — Where did you meet . . . ? — second bulleted note)

- Ask students to work individually and identify the correct and incorrect question forms. Then ask them to match each sentence to one of the bulleted notes. (If necessary do the first as an example.) When students finish, put them in pairs to check each other's work.

- Bring the class together and elicit whether each question is correct or incorrect. Place an X next to the incorrect questions. Call students to the board to correct them. Discuss any difficulties or questions as a class.

Informally Speaking: Spoken Forms of *Did* + Pronoun (p. 196)

- Choose a student to read the text in the speech bubble. Then tell the class you will play the recording and that they should listen to how the underlined form in the cartoon is different from what they hear. If needed, play the recording more than once.

- Have students point out the differences (*did you* in the cartoon vs. *didja* on the recording). Explain that the form in the cartoon is standard English, whereas the form on the recording is considered to be very informal spoken English. Stress that although they will hear native speakers use *didja*, the standard *did you* is preferable in both writing and speaking.

D) MEANING AND USE

The Simple Past

THINK CRITICALLY ABOUT MEANING AND USE

- Put students in pairs to answer the questions.
- **1.– 2. EVALUATE** Elicit which sentence shows that David has a job in Seattle now (a). Ask how we know this (*works* = simple present). Elicit that sentence b shows that David does not have a job in Seattle now.

MEANING AND USE NOTES

- Put the class into groups and assign each group a Note (Notes 1A and 1B can be handled by two groups, if desired).
- Explain that each group will teach the class their Note by explaining or reading the information and example sentences to the class. The group must also write a new sentence to illustrate each point in the Note.
- To present their Note, each group can assign one student to read or paraphrase the explanation, another to read the examples in the book, and another to write the group's sentences on the board.
- Circulate and help as necessary. Then call each group to the board to present their Note.

Beyond the Sentence: Connecting Ideas in the Simple Past (p. 199)

- Explain that it is important to use time expressions to help us connect ideas when we speak or write. To illustrate this, ask students to close their books and listen.
- Read out the paragraph in the book, omitting all of the bold time expressions. Then elicit opinions about how clear the paragraph is.
- Ask students to open their books and read the paragraph. Ask which version is clearer.

E) WRITING

THINK CRITICALLY ABOUT MEANING AND USE

- Have students do A individually. Then, in small groups, have them compare answers and discuss any differences.
- Have them stay in groups and do B.
- As a class, review any difficult items from A. Then elicit answers to B:

  1. EXPLAIN (Choice "a" isn't the answer because it isn't logical: 10-year-old boys don't usually drive people to school.)

  2. GENERATE (1. *I drove my 10-year-old brother to school. 2. I did my homework.*)

WRITE

The purpose of this activity is to give students practice in using the simple past by writing a paragraph about life in their country 100 years ago. Encourage students to research the topic in the library and on the Internet.

1. Brainstorm

Write the brainstorming questions on the board, and elicit relevant details. Have students work individually to make their own brainstorming notes.

2. Write a First Draft

Before students begin writing, make sure they have read the checklist in the Edit section on page 202. Remind students to use the best points from their brainstorming notes to write their paragraph.

3. Edit

Direct students to read and complete the self-assessment checklist on page 202. Ask for a show of hands for how many students gave all or mostly yes answers.

4. Peer Review

Pair students and direct them to read each other's work. Ask students to answer the questions in the checklist and discuss them. Give students suggestions of helpful feedback: e.g., *I think you've used the wrong form. / This might be a good place for a question.*

5. Rewrite Your Draft

Students should consider their partners' comments from the peer review and rewrite as necessary. Encourage students to proofread their work again before turning it in.

13 The Past Continuous

Overview

The past continuous is used to talk about an activity that was ongoing at a specific time in the past but is no longer happening (e.g., *In the 1970s, we were living in Canada.*). It is often used to describe two or more ongoing activities in progress at the same time in the past (e.g., *I was sleeping while my roommate was studying.*). These uses are presented in contrast to the simple past, which is used to express actions that happened at a specific time but did not continue. (Note: The use of the past continuous in complex sentences is taught in *Grammar Sense 2.*)

Form: The key challenges are

- spelling the present participle (*-ing* form) for verbs whose final consonant is doubled (*swim — swimming*) or whose final consonant is dropped (*live — living*).
- remembering to insert the subject between *be* and the *-ing* verb in questions.

A GRAMMAR IN DISCOURSE

Unusual Disasters in History

A1: Before You Read

- Write the word *disaster* on the board. Draw a circle around it and ask students what comes to mind. Write and circle their responses on the board in the form of a spidergram, with lines coming from the word *disaster*. Be prepared to provide your own responses to fill out the diagram (e.g., *hurricane, flood, storm, earthquake, fire, death, injury, rescue,* etc.).

- Divide students into small groups to discuss the questions. Brainstorm a class definition of the word *disaster* (e.g., *something very bad that affects a lot of people*).

- Elicit general categories of disasters (e.g., *natural disasters, financial disasters, space accidents*). Divide the board into three columns labeled *What?, Where?, and When?* Ask for three examples of different types of disasters and write them in the first column (e.g., *earthquake, stock market crash, Columbia Space Shuttle disaster*). Then elicit where and when such a disaster occurred. Write these in the second and third columns (e.g., *Japan – 2011; New York – 1929; USA – 2003*).

A2: Read

- Remind students about using the glossary by eliciting the meaning of one of the words, e.g., *legend.*

- Direct students' attention to the chart on the board. Ask them to look at the magazine article, and tell you how many and what disasters it talks about. (Two: the Great Chicago Fire and Boston's Sea of Molasses) Then have them quickly skim the article and tell you what information to put in the chart. Elicit the information and write it on the board. (fire – Chicago – October 8, 1871; explosion – Boston – January 15, 1919)

- Ask students to read the article carefully and determine the causes of these disasters. *(A cow kicked over a lantern and started the fire; the sun heated a tank of molasses and it exploded.)*

A3: After You Read

- Have students answer the true/false questions individually and compare their answers with a partner. Remind them to mark the places in the article where they found the answers.

- Go over any difficult or problematic items.

- As a follow-up, ask students if they know of any other disasters that were caused in unusual ways. Discuss as a class.

Past Continuous

THINK CRITICALLY ABOUT FORM

- Have students work individually to complete questions 1 and 2. Encourage them to refer to the Form charts and bulleted notes to check their answers and get familiar with the new structures. As they work, write the following on the board, underlining the verbs as shown: *Mrs. O'Leary was milking, firefighters were fighting.*

- **1. IDENTIFY** Have a student come to the board to circle the base forms *(milk, fight).* Elicit the two parts of the verb (simple past of *be* + base form of verb + *-ing*).

- Ask *Where else do we use a form of* be + *the base form of a verb* + -ing? (In the present continuous) Elicit or explain that the only difference is that the present continuous uses present forms of *be* (i.e., *am, is, are*), while the past continuous uses past forms of *be* (i.e., *was* and *were*).

- Point to the use of *was* and *were* in the examples. Ask *Why do we use* was *in the first example and* were *in the second example?* (Like the present continuous, the form of *be* agrees with the subject. The form *was* agrees with singular nouns; the form *were* agrees with plural nouns.) Point to the first example and ask students to predict the forms for *I, you, he/she/it,* etc. (*I was milking, He was milking,* etc.)

- **2. RECOGNIZE** Ask students to find two more affirmative examples of the past continuous in the article. Elicit examples and write them on the board *(was burning, was shining, were enjoying, was sitting, was spreading).* Have students justify the use of *was* and *were* by finding the subjects in the article *(the city/Chicago, The sun, people, a huge tank . . . , a giant wave . . .).*

- **3. LABEL** Write the circled example of the negative past continuous on the board *(was not moving).* Elicit the number of words (three) and what they are (simple past of *be* + base form of verb + *-ing.*) Ask students to predict the forms for *I* and other subject pronouns (*I was not moving, You were not moving,* etc.).

FORM CHARTS

- Give students a few minutes to read the charts and bulleted notes on both pages.

- Call on pairs of students to read out corresponding affirmative and negative statements from the charts. Repeat the procedure for *Yes/No* questions and short answers and for information questions and answers.

- To check understanding, write the following in a single column on the board: *Affirmative, Negative, Yes/No Question, Short Answer, Information Question.* Call three students to the board to write affirmative sentences with *work, drive,* and *swim.* Remind students of the spelling rules for *driving* and *swimming.* Refer students to Appendix 3 in the Student Book for spelling rules for verbs ending in *-ing.*

- Then call on one or more students to write the negative forms. Continue until the chart is complete.

C MEANING AND USE

The Past Continuous

THINK CRITICALLY ABOUT MEANING AND USE

- Put students in pairs and give them a few minutes to answer the questions.

- **1. EVALUATE** Elicit the answers (sentences a and b; past continuous).

- Then ask students to imagine the following scenario: A person woke up at 6:00 a.m., looked out the window, and saw rain. Ask *Did the rain start at exactly 6:00 or sometime in the past?* (sometime in the past) To illustrate, draw this timeline on the board:

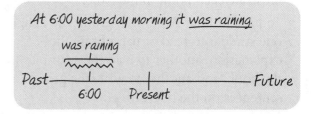

- Explain that the wavy line shows the activity was in progress: that is, it started before 6:00 and continued until 6:00 and probably after.

Explain that in English we use the past continuous for this.

- Put a similar timeline on the board to illustrate sentence b:

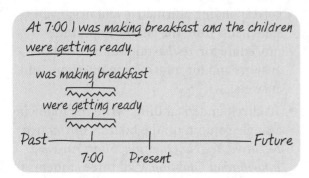

At 7:00 I <u>was making</u> breakfast and the children <u>were getting</u> ready.

was making breakfast

were getting ready

Past ———————————— Future

7:00   Present

- Ask *What do the wavy lines show?* (The activities were in progress; they started before 7:00 and continued until 7:00 and probably after.)
- **2. EVALUATE** Elicit the answers (sentence c; simple past.). Ask *Why do we use simple past verbs?* (To show that an action happened at a certain time but did not continue.)
- To illustrate, put a third line on the board:

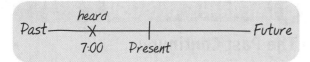

heard

Past ———X———————————— Future

7:00   Present

- Explain that the X shows that the action happened at a certain time but did not continue. Explain that in English we use the simple past for this.

MEANING AND USE NOTES

- Divide the class into three groups. Assign each group a Note.
- Explain that each group will teach the class their Note by explaining or reading the information and example sentences to the class. The group must also write a new sentence to illustrate each point in the Note.
- To present their Note, each group can assign one student to read or paraphrase the explanation, another to read the examples in the book, and another to write the group's sentences on the board.
- Circulate and help as necessary. Then call each group to the board to present their Note.
- As a follow-up, write these categories and

sentences on the board (answers in parentheses are for teacher's reference):

Activity in Progress at a Specific Past Time

Two Activities in Progress at the Same Time

Action that Happened but Did Not Continue

1. *She was sleeping at 11 p.m.* (activity in progress)
2. *Someone knocked at the door.* (action that happened but did not continue)
3. *I was eating dinner and my brother was working on his computer.* (two activities in progress at the same time)
4. *I was eating dinner while my brother was working on his computer.* (two activities in progress at the same time)

- Put students in pairs to determine which category each sentence represents.
- Elicit answers, asking students to support their opinions.

WRITING

THINK CRITICALLY ABOUT MEANING AND USE

- Have students do A individually. Then, in small groups, have them compare answers and discuss any differences.
- Have them stay in groups and do B.
- As a class, review any difficult items from A. Then elicit answers to B:

  1. EVALUATE (In 2, B uses the past continuous to describe an activity in progress at a specific time: *the sun was shining* [this morning]. In 4, B uses the past continuous to describe two activities in progress at the same time: [last night] *trying to study / playing loud music.*)

  2. EXPLAIN (Speaker A uses the simple past because "waking up" is not a continuous action. It happens at a specific time and does not continue.)

WRITE

The purpose of this activity is to give students practice in using the past continuous by writing an email about a natural disaster or major news event that happened recently.

1. Brainstorm

As a class, start a brainstorm on the board about a recent event. (Make it clear that students will write about a different event.) Write the brainstorming questions on the board, and elicit the kinds of details that students might write about. If desired, make suggestions to the class about topics they may want to write about: e.g., a disaster, a recent sporting event, something in the news, a traffic accident. Have students work individually to make brainstorming notes on their event.

2. Write a First Draft

Before students begin writing, make sure they have read the checklist in the Edit section. Remind students to use the best points from their brainstorming notes to write their email.

3. Edit

Direct students to read and complete the self-assessment checklist on page 216. Ask for a show of hands for how many students gave all or mostly *yes* answers. If desired, ask students to comment on some of the errors they found.

DO I ...	YES
use the past continuous for events in progress at the time of the event?	☐
use the simple past for events in the past but not in progress during the event?	☐
use affirmative and negative statements using the past continuous?	☐
use information questions using *Wh-* questions?	☐
use activities in progress at the time of the event?	☐
use at least one simultaneous activity?	☐
use a stative verb in the past continuous correctly?	☐

4. Peer Review

Pair students and direct them to read each other's work. Ask students to answer the questions in the checklist and discuss them. Give students suggestions of helpful feedback: e.g., *This seems like an action in progress to me. Maybe you should use the past continuous. / This seems like a finished action. Maybe you need the simple past here.*

5. Rewrite Your Draft

Students should consider their partners' comments from the peer review and rewrite as necessary. Encourage students to proofread their work again before turning it in.

14 Articles

Overview

The English article system is complex and challenging for nearly all students. Some languages do not use articles and others use them differently from English. At this level, the focus is on using the indefinite article (*a, an*) or no article to introduce a noun for the first time (e.g., *There's a new restaurant on Fifth Street. I have an idea. I bought new socks yesterday.*) and on using the definite article *the* to mention a noun for the second time (e.g., *The restaurant specializes in Asian food. Let's hear the idea. Show me the socks.*). The chapter also presents using the definite article when both speaker and listener share general knowledge about a noun in their environment (e.g., *The president is going to be on TV tonight.*).

Form: The key challenges are

- remembering to use the indefinite article before a singular count noun (e.g., *She is a teacher.*).
- understanding the idea of shared information between the speaker and listener.

A GRAMMAR IN DISCOURSE

How to Enjoy a New City

A1: Before You Read

- Bring in a map of your town, city, or area. Ask students what places or neighborhoods they know about. Elicit information about these places, for example, what people do there and what the areas are known for.

- Divide students into small groups to discuss the questions in their books.

- Write the phrase *Visiting new cities* on the board and then make two columns under it, one labeled *Pro* and the other *Con*. Elicit the meanings of *pro* and *con* (*for* and *against*).

- Ask for a show of hands of people who like to visit new cities. Elicit some of the reasons why they like visiting new cities. Write them in the *Pro* column. If students are reluctant to participate, provide your own reasons: e.g., *experience new culture, opportunities to see cultural events (plays, concerts), attend sporting events, and meet new people.* Elicit names of some of the students' favorite cities.

- Ask for a show of hands of people who do not like to visit new cities. Elicit reasons why and write them in the *Con* column. Again, be prepared to provide your own reasons, (e.g., *city life can be stressful, expensive, and dangerous*).

A2: Read

- Remind students about using the glossary by eliciting the meaning of one of the words, e.g., *ethnic*.

- Direct students' attention to the title of the magazine article ("How to Enjoy a New City"). Then ask students to look at the two columns on the board. Elicit which column most likely contains information that students will find in the reading (the *Pro* column).

- Ask students to read the magazine article and mark any information from the *Pro* column that they find.

- Call on students to identify the information found in both the article and the *Pro* column. Elicit other ideas that the article mentions which are not on the board.

- Elicit students' opinion as to which activities are interesting to them.

A3: After You Read

- Have students answer the true/false questions individually and compare their answers with a partner. Remind them to mark the places in the article where they found the answers.

- Go over any difficult or problematic items.
- As a follow-up, put students in groups and ask them to brainstorm ways to enjoy the city you live in. Call on each group to share its suggestions. Write them on the board to make a class list.

B) FORM

Indefinite and Definite Articles

THINK CRITICALLY ABOUT FORM

- Have students work in pairs to complete questions 1 and 2. Encourage them to refer to the Form charts and bulleted notes to check their answers and get familiar with the new structures. As they work, write the example sentences on the board.
- **1. IDENTIFY** If necessary, review the meaning of *count* and *noncount nouns*. Call a student to the board to underline the count nouns (a. map; b. museum; c. taxis, drivers; d. restaurants). Call another student to the board to circle the noncount nouns (b. art; d. food).
- **2. APPLY** Call a student to the board to draw two lines under *a* or *an* in sentences a–d. Call a student to the board to put a box around *the* in the sentences.
- Give students a few minutes to complete the chart in their books. As students work, draw the chart on the board.
- Elicit the answers and write them in the chart. (*a/an* and *the* are used before singular count nouns; *the* and no article are used before plural count nouns; *the* and no article are used before noncount nouns.)
- If time allows, ask students to look back at the magazine article and find more examples of indefinite/definite articles or no article + a noun (*a new city, cities, ethnic neighborhoods*, etc.).

FORM CHARTS

- Give students a few minutes to get familiar with the charts and bulleted notes.
- Call on students to read the phrases in the charts aloud.

- Write the following words on the board: *electricity, plan, equipment, computer, furniture, oil, car, homework, idea, decision*. Then make a two-column chart on the board. Label the column on the left *Count* and the column on the right *Noncount*.
- Call a student to the board to write the count nouns in the correct column (*plan, computer, car, idea, decision*). Call another student to the board to write the noncount nouns in the noncount column (*electricity, equipment, furniture, oil, homework*).
- Divide students into small groups and ask them to write one sentence for each noun using the appropriate indefinite article (*a, an,* or no article). Circulate and help as necessary.
- Have several students read one of their sentences to the class. Write them on the board and make corrections as a class.

C) MEANING AND USE

Indefinite and Definite Articles

THINK CRITICALLY ABOUT MEANING AND USE

- Put students in pairs to answer questions 1–3. Ask them to be prepared to explain how they arrived at their answers.
- **1. IDENTIFY** Elicit the answers (articles: a, The, an, The; nouns: movie, movie, soldier, soldier).
- **2. CATEGORIZE** Elicit the answers (a, c). Elicit the nouns that are introduced (*a great movie* and *an English soldier*). Ask which articles come before these nouns (*a, an*).
- **3. CATEGORIZE** Elicit the answers (b, d). Ask which article comes before each noun (*the*).

MEANING AND USE NOTES

- Divide the class into three groups. Assign each group a Note.
- Explain that each group will teach the class their Note by explaining or reading the information and example conversations and sentences to the class. The group must also write a new conversation or sentence to illustrate each point in the Note.

- To present their Note, each group can assign one student to read or paraphrase the explanation, two to read the conversations or different examples, and another to write the group's sentences on the board.

- Circulate and help as necessary. Then call each group to the board to present their Note.

- As a follow-up, put students into an even number of small groups. Ask them to write three sentences that introduce different nouns (e.g., *I read a great book last week. I saw a terrible play last night. I went to a restaurant on Sunday.*).

- Ask each group to exchange their sentences with another group. Then have them write a follow-up sentence or question for each noun that uses the noun again (e.g., *What's the name of the book? What's the name of the movie? How was the restaurant?*).

- Elicit pairs of sentences from each group. Write several of them on the board. Discuss any difficulties or questions as a class.

WRITING

THINK CRITICALLY ABOUT MEANING AND USE

- Have students do A individually. Then, in small groups, have them compare answers and discuss any differences.

- Have them stay in groups and do B.

- As a class, review any difficult items from A. Then elicit answers to B:

  1. EVALUATE (The word *the* completes B's sentence. We understand that one of the two gifts is a specific CD, so we need a definite article.)

  2. EXPLAIN (Because B is talking about a specific recipe: the recipe for A's eggs.)

WRITE

The purpose of this activity is to give students practice in using indefinite and definite articles by writing a blog update about a city they visited.

1. Brainstorm

As a class, start a brainstorm on the board about a city or town. (Make it clear that students will write about a different place.) Write the brainstorming categories on the board, and elicit the kinds of details that students might write about. Have students work individually to make brainstorming notes about their city.

2. Write a First Draft

Before students begin writing, make sure they have read the checklist in the Edit section. Remind students to use the best points from their brainstorming notes to write their blog entry.

3. Edit

Direct students to read and complete the self-assessment checklist on page 230. Ask for a show of hands for how many students gave all or mostly *yes* answers.

DO I ...	YES
use a mixture of indefinite and definite articles?	☐
use nouns that take no article?	☐
use a mixture of singular and plural count nouns?	☐
use noncount nouns?	☐
use at least one reference to a "shared information" noun?	☐
use at least one reference to a noun mentioned twice?	☐
use contrasting indefinite and definite articles?	☐

4. Peer Review

Pair students and direct them to read each other's work. Ask students to answer the questions in the checklist and discuss them. Give students suggestions of helpful feedback: e.g., *Are you sure you need* the *here? It's the first time you use the noun.*

5. Rewrite Your Draft

Students should consider their partners' comments from the peer review and rewrite as necessary. Encourage students to proofread their work again before turning it in.

15 Quantity Expressions

Overview

Quantity expressions indicate an amount of the nouns they modify. The focus in this chapter is on general quantity expressions (i.e., ones that do not specify exact amounts). Some general quantity expressions (e.g., *many, a lot of,* and *much*) refer to large amounts (e.g., *Many grammar rules are difficult. English grammar has a lot of rules. There isn' t much milk in the carton.*). Other quantity expressions (e.g., *a few* and *a little*) refer to small amounts (e.g., *A few grammar rules are easy. He has a little money.*). Finally, the quantity expression *no* expresses the concept of *none* (e.g., *No student can remember all the grammar rules.*).

Form: The key challenges are remembering

- which quantity expressions are used only with count nouns (*many, a few*) and which are used only with noncount nouns (*much, a little*).

- which quantity expressions are used in affirmative or negative statements.

A GRAMMAR IN DISCOURSE

Sustainable Communities

A1: Before You Read

- Write the word *sustain* on the board and elicit or explain its meaning (*to provide with the necessities of life*).

- Add the syllable *-able* to the end of *sustain*. Circle the syllable and ask students how it changes the word (*It changes the word from a verb to an adjective meaning "able to provide the necessities of life"*).

- Now write the word *community* under *sustainable*. Elicit the meaning (*a group of people living together in one place*). Then divide students into small groups and give them a few minutes to discuss the questions.

- Elicit answers, and write the goals they suggest on the board. Do not confirm or reject any ideas yet.

A2: Read

- Remind students about using the glossary by eliciting the meaning of one of the words, e.g., *resident.*

- Ask students to read the article and explain why people want to live in sustainable communities (*They don't like life in big cities*).

- Ask students to confirm which of the goals on the board are correct. Then ask them to make a list of other goals mentioned in the article (*respect the environment; don't put much emphasis on possessions; eat locally-grown fruits and vegetables; walk and bike a lot, rather than drive cars; work at home; no noise or pollution*).

A3: After You Read

- Have students do the exercise individually and compare their answers with a partner. Remind them to mark the places in the article where they found the answers.

- Go over any difficult or problematic items with the whole class.

- As a follow-up, put students in groups and ask them their opinion about living in a sustainable community. Write the following on the board: *What would you like/dislike about living in a sustainable community?* Ask groups to report back to the class, giving reasons for their ideas.

B FORM

Quantity Expressions

THINK CRITICALLY ABOUT FORM

- **1. IDENTIFY** Put students in pairs and give them a few minutes to do the question.

Encourage them to refer to the Form charts and bulleted notes to check their answers and get familiar with the new structures. As they work, write the underlined phrases from the article and the chart in question 2 on the board.

- Call a student to the board to circle the noun in each phrase (*communities, residents, communities, money, stuff, residents, traffic, work*)

- **2. CATEGORIZE** Keep students in pairs. Before they attempt to fill in the chart, ask them to look at the nouns on the board. Elicit which are count (*communities, residents*) and which are noncount (*money, stuff, traffic, work*). As students classify the noun in each phrase, label it with a *C* for count noun or *NC* for noncount noun.

- Have pairs complete the chart. Remind them to refer to the phrases on the board for help.

- Elicit the answers and write them in the chart (*a lot of*: both; *some*: both; *a few*: plural count nouns; *a little*: noncount nouns; *many*: plural count nouns; *much*: noncount nouns).

FORM CHARTS

- Give students a few minutes to read the charts and bulleted notes.

- Call on pairs to read aloud corresponding affirmative and negative statements. For plural count nouns, point out that we do not use *some* and *a few* in negative statements. Also explain that *no = not any*. For noncount nouns, explain that we do not usually use *much* in affirmative statements. *A lot of* is used instead.

- Repeat the procedure for *Yes/No* questions and short answers and information questions and answers.

- Check students' understanding by asking questions about the forms: *Can we use* no *in negative sentences?* (No, only in affirmative statements.) *Do we use* how much *in questions with count or noncount nouns?* (with noncount nouns)

- Put students in pairs. Ask them to look around the classroom, and write two affirmative sentences, two negative sentences, and two questions using a variety of quantity expressions: e.g., *The classroom has a lot of desks. We don't have any computers in the class. How many students are Korean?* Circulate and help as necessary.

- Have each pair exchange sentences with another pair and ask them to check each other's work. Remind them to look back at the charts and bulleted notes for reference.

- Bring the class together and elicit several examples of each type of sentence. Discuss any difficulties or questions as a class.

C MEANING AND USE

Quantity Expressions

THINK CRITICALLY ABOUT MEANING AND USE

- Put students in pairs to do the questions. As they work, write the sentences on the board.

- **1. IDENTIFY** Call a student to the board to underline the quantity expressions (a. *many, a lot of*; b. *a few, a little*; c. *no, no*; d. *a lot of, much*).

- **2. EVALUATE** Elicit answers. Write *large* or *small* above the quantity expressions on the board (a. *many, a lot of = large*; b. *a few, a little = small*; d. *a lot of, much = large*)

- **3. ANALYZE** Elicit answers. Write *none* above relevant examples (c. *no, no = none*).

MEANING AND USE NOTES

- Divide the class into four groups. Assign each group a Note.

- Explain that each group will teach the class their Note by explaining or reading the information and example sentences to the class. The group must also write a new sentence to illustrate each point in the Note.

- To present their Note, each group can assign one student to read or paraphrase the explanation, another to read the examples in the book, and another to write the group's sentences on the board.

- Circulate and help as necessary. Then call each group to the board to present their Note.

- As a follow-up, write on the board:
  1. *apartment/dorm room/house - furniture*
  2. *our school - interesting courses*
  3. *neighborhood - ethnic restaurants*
  4. *students at this school - homework*
- Put students in pairs and ask them to write a true sentence for each set of words. The sentences can be either affirmative or negative and must include a quantity expression.
- Elicit at least three sentences for each set of words. As a class, compare each group of sentences and decide whether each sentence expresses a large quantity, a small quantity, or no quantity.

WRITING

THINK CRITICALLY ABOUT MEANING AND USE

- Have students do A individually. Then, in small groups, have them compare answers and discuss any differences.
- Have them stay in groups and do B.
- As a class, review any difficult items from A. Then elicit answers to B:
  1. **CATEGORIZE** (1 and 3 refer to large quantities; 2 and 4 refer to small quantities.)
  2. **GENERATE** (Answers will vary.)

WRITE

The purpose of this activity is to give students practice in using quantity expressions by writing an email about their school.

1. Brainstorm

As a class, start a brainstorm on the board about the good qualities of a school in a different city. (If desired, prepare and distribute a fact sheet so students have specific details to work with.) Write the brainstorming questions on the board, and elicit the kinds of details that students might write about. Encourage them to use a range of quantity expressions. Have students work individually to make their own brainstorming notes.

2. Write a First Draft

Before students begin writing, read the checklist in the Edit section. Remind students to use the best points from their brainstorming notes to write their email.

3. Edit

Direct students to read and complete the self-assessment checklist on page 246. Ask for a show of hands for how many students gave all or mostly *yes* answers. If desired, ask students to comment on some of the errors they found.

DO I...	YES
use both affirmative and negative statements with quantity expressions?	☐
use quantity expressions with both plural count nouns and noncount nouns?	☐
ask and answer *yes/no* questions with quantity expressions?	☐
ask and answer information questions with quantity expressions?	☐
use expressions for general quantities?	☐
use expressions for large quantities?	☐
use expressions for small quantities?	☐

4. Peer Review

Pair students and direct them to read each other's work. Ask students to answer the questions in the checklist and discuss them. Give students suggestions of helpful feedback: e.g., *This is a noncount noun. Are you sure you can use* many *with it? / There aren't any questions. Can you add one?*

5. Rewrite Your Draft

Students should consider their partners' comments from the peer review and rewrite as necessary. Encourage students to proofread their work again before turning it in.

16

There Is and *There Are*

Overview

There is and *there are* are often used at or near the beginning of a sentence to introduce a noun for the first time; in the subsequent sentence, the noun or an equivalent pronoun is used at or near the beginning instead of *there* (e.g., *There are two good bookstores near campus. They both have good prices.*). *There is* and *there are* express existence and sometimes location (e.g., *There are many ways to send a letter. There is a post office on Main Street.*). *There is* and *there are* sentences are often used to state factual information (e.g., *There are ten provinces in Canada.*).

Form: The key challenges are remembering

- subject-verb agreement between the verb *be* and the noun that follows *there is/there are.*
- the difference between *there* and the possessive adjective *their.*
- the difference between *there is/there are* and the adverbial use of *there* for location (e.g., *The book is there by the window.*).
- the difference between *there are* and *they are/ they're*. Students may also have trouble recognizing and understanding the reduced form of *there are* (/'ðɛrər/) that often occurs in informal spoken English.

A GRAMMAR IN DISCOURSE

A Wonderful Gift

A1: Before You Read

- If possible, bring to class pictures or photographs of different works of art. Include a variety of art forms (e.g., *sculpture, painting, drawing*) and styles (*realistic, abstract*). Elicit the kind of art and, if possible, the name of the work. Write the information on the board.

Elicit the names of famous artists and write them on the board.

- Give students five minutes to discuss the questions in pairs. Ask them to take notes on their partner's preferences.
- Bring the class together and call on several students to share their partner's preferences. Add any new names or kinds of art to the lists.

A2: Read

- Remind students about using the glossary by eliciting the meaning of one of the words, e.g., *critical.*
- Organize a jigsaw reading. Explain that all students should read the newspaper article about the piece of art. Then ask half of the class to read the first letter, and the other half to read the second letter. Finally, ask students to summarize both the newspaper article and their assigned letter in a few sentences.
- Give students about ten minutes to read the material and write their summaries.
- Put students in pairs, one from each half of the class. Have the pairs compare their summaries of the newspaper article and then exchange information about the two letters.
- Call on several pairs to share their summaries with the class.

Cultural Notes

Point out that many newspapers around the world publish letters to the editor. Explain that in American newspapers, people are free to express their opinions and will often use language that is honest and sometimes not very polite.

A3: After You Read

- Have students answer the true/false questions individually and compare their answers with a partner. Remind them to mark the places in the article or letters where they found their answers.

- Go over any difficult or problematic items with the whole class.

- As a follow-up, ask students whether they agree or disagree with the opinions in the letters and why.

B) FORM

There Is and *There Are*

THINK CRITICALLY ABOUT FORM

- Put students in pairs to complete questions 1–3. Encourage them to refer to the Form charts and bulleted notes to check their answers and get familiar with the new structures. As they work, write on the board the sentences from the article in which the underlined examples occur.

- **1. IDENTIFY** Call a student to the board to circle the noun or noun phrase that follows each underlined example *(a new painting, houses and gardens, stores, a gray circle)*.

- **2. ANALYZE** Draw students' attention to the sentences on the board. Elicit that *there is* is followed by a singular noun and *there are* is followed by a plural noun. Make this clear by circling the plural ending *-s* on *houses and gardens* and *stores*.

- **3. RECOGNIZE** Ask students to look back at the article and letters. Have them find more examples of *there is/there are* and circle the nouns that follow them.

- Divide the board into two columns labeled *There is* and *There are*. Elicit answers and write them on the board. (Article: *There's no other painting like this, There isn't enough security*; First letter: *There are no houses and gardens, There aren't any stores, There are dark gray squares and light gray rectangles*; Second letter: *there are always many different opinions*) Discuss any difficulties as a class.

FORM CHARTS

- Give students a few minutes to read the charts and bulleted notes to get familiar with the structures.

- Call on several pairs of students to read out corresponding singular and plural affirmative statements from the charts.

- Elicit the contraction of *there is* (*there's*). Ask *Is there a contraction for* there are *in the charts?* (No) If desired, explain that in informal spoken English, it is common for native speakers to use a reduced form of *there are* which sounds like a contraction (/ˈðɛrər/). However, this form is never used in writing.

- Repeat the procedure for singular and plural negative statements. Point out the contraction of *aren't* and then draw their attention to the fifth bulleted point about *no* and *not any*.

- To check understanding, elicit something singular and something plural that your classroom does not have (e.g., *an air-conditioner, students from England.*). Ask students to generate sentences with *no* and *not any* and write them on the board (e.g., *There is no air-conditioner in the room. = There isn't an air-conditioner in the room. There are no students from England in the class. = There aren't any students from England in the class.*).

- Call on pairs to read aloud the *Yes/No* questions and short answers, and questions with *How much* and *How many*. Be sure to highlight the following: the inversion of *is/are* and *there*; the use of *any* with count nouns in *Yes/No* questions; the use of *How much* with noncount nouns and *How many* with count nouns.

- As a follow-up, write these sentences on the board (answers in parentheses are for teacher's reference):

  1. *There is a restaurant near the university.* (Correct)
  2. *There is not no swimming pool in this building.* (Incorrect)
  3. *How many students there are in this class?* (Incorrect)
  4. *Is there a class in this room at noon?* (Correct)
  5. *There aren't any cars in the garage.* (Correct)
  6. *How much is there money in your pocket?* (Incorrect)

- Put students in pairs and ask them to determine which sentences are correct and which are incorrect. Have them correct the incorrect sentences.

- Review the answers as a class. (Corrections for incorrect sentences: 2. *There is no swimming pool in this building.* or *There isn't a swimming pool in this building.* 3. *How many students are there in this class?* 6. *How much money is there in your pocket?*)

- Discuss any questions or difficulties as a class. Refer students back to the charts and bulleted notes as necessary.

C MEANING AND USE

There Is and *There Are*

THINK CRITICALLY ABOUT MEANING AND USE

- Put students in pairs to answer questions 1 and 2. Ask them to identify words or phrases in the sentences that help them determine their answers. As they work, write the example sentences on the board.

- **1. EVALUATE** Bring the class together and elicit the answer to question 1 (a). Ask *How do we know?* (The indefinite article *a* tells us that the noun *patient* is being used for the first time.) Point out that *there's* is often used in front of *a + noun* to introduce a singular count noun for the first time.

- **2. INTERPRET** Elicit the answer to question 2 (b). Ask *How do you know?* (The definite article *the* tells us that the doctor already knows about the noun. The word *again* tells us that this is not the patient's first call.)

MEANING AND USE NOTES

- Call on a pair of students to read aloud the explanation and examples in Note 1.

- Put the class in an even number of small groups, and have each group write two new examples: one that introduces a noun, and a second that mentions the noun again. (e.g., *There are 20 students in this class. They speak many different first languages.*) Ask half the

groups to begin their first sentence with *There is* or *There's* and the other half to begin their first sentence with *There are*.

- Keep the class in their groups. Call on two students to read aloud Note 2. Ask the groups to write three examples: one for location, one for existence, and one for fact.

- Call on the groups to read their sentences aloud. Write any problematic sentences on the board. Ask them to point out and correct any problems with meaning and usage.

- Ask students to reread the Caution Notes. Point out the differences in the uses of *there is/there are* and *there* vs. *their*. Discuss any questions or difficulties as a class.

- Proceed to the Caution Notes on page 256. Elicit new sentences to illustrate each point in the Note.

Beyond the Sentence: Combining Sentences with *But* (p. 259)

This section is intended to give students practice with the meaning and use of grammar as it functions naturally in paragraphs and conversations.

- Write the word *contrast* on the board and explain its meaning (to show a difference or a distinction between two things).

- Point out that it is common to combine sentences that contain contrasting information (e.g., *John is tall. His brother is short. = John is tall, but his brother is short.*)

- Read aloud the first paragraph of the section, then call on a student to read the first line of the example. Ask another student to read the combined sentence below. Elicit that the sentences are combined with *but*. Ask *What changes did the writer make to form the combined sentence?* (He or she changed the period in the first sentence to a comma, added the word *but*, and changed *plate* in the second sentence to *it*, to avoid using *plate* twice.)

- Point out that joining sentences makes writing smoother and more natural. Demonstrate this by reading paragraphs A and B aloud. Ask students which one flows better and is easier to follow (the second one).

THINK CRITICALLY ABOUT MEANING AND USE

- Have students do A individually. Then, in small groups, have them compare answers and discuss any differences.
- Have them stay in groups and do B.
- As a class, review any difficult items from A. Then elicit answers to B:

   1. PREDICT (B says "No, there aren't.")

   2. EVALUATE (The word *it* completes B's sentence. It refers back to "their car.")

WRITE

The purpose of this activity is to give students practice in using *there is/there are* by writing a paragraph about their neighborhood.

1. Brainstorm

As a class, start a brainstorm on the board about a typical neighborhood. (Make it clear that students will write about a different neighborhood.) Write key words from the brainstorming categories on the board (e.g., *good things, bad things, stores*), and elicit the kinds of details that students might write about. Prompt students to use *there is/there are*. Have students work individually to make brainstorming notes on their neighborhood.

2. Write a First Draft

Before students begin writing, make sure they have read the checklist in the Edit section. Also have them look at the example on page 259. Remind students to use the best points from their brainstorming notes to write their paragraph.

3. Edit

Direct students to read and complete the self-assessment checklist on page 262. Ask for a show of hands for how many students gave all or mostly *yes* answers. If desired, ask students to comment on some of the errors they found.

DO I ...	YES
make affirmative and negative statements with *there is* and *there are*?	☐
ask and answer *yes/no* questions with *there is* and *there are*?	☐
ask and answer questions about quantity with *how much* and *how many*?	☐
use *there is* and *there are* to introduce a noun?	☐
use *there is* and *there are* to express existence, location, and facts?	☐
use *their* and *there* at least once each in the entry?	☐
use *but* to combine sentences with contrasting information?	☐

4. Peer Review

Pair students and direct them to read each other's work. Ask students to answer the questions in the checklist and discuss them. Give students suggestions of helpful feedback: e.g., *You're talking about a plural noun. Are you sure you should start with* there is? / *These two sentences have contrasting information. Do you want to combine them with* but?

5. Rewrite Your Draft

Students should consider their partners' comments from the peer review and rewrite as necessary. Encourage students to proofread their work again before turning it in.

17 The Future with *Be Going To*

Overview

The future with *be going to* is used to express future plans (e.g., *I'm going to see a play on Friday.*) and to make predictions when there is evidence to support the prediction (e.g., *The boys are playing baseball in the street. Someone is going to get hurt.*). The future with *be going to* can also be used with *probably* to signal that a plan is less certain (e.g., *I'm not sure about my plans for the weekend. I'm probably going to see a play on Friday.*).

Form: The key challenges are remembering

- the verb following *to* in this structure is the base form and remains the same in all persons.
- contractions are not used in affirmative short answers.

A GRAMMAR IN DISCOURSE

Sports News Now

A1: Before You Read

- Bring in the contents page from several types of magazines (e.g., *sports, fashion, health and fitness, science, and entertainment*).
- Divide students into small groups and give one contents page to each group. Ask groups to determine the type of magazine their page is from.
- Elicit students' answers and write them on the board.
- Ask the groups to discuss the questions in their books. Have each group elect a secretary and reporter. Instruct the secretaries to take notes on their group's answers. When the groups are ready, ask reporters to report the information to the rest of the class.

A2: Read

- Remind students about using the glossary by eliciting the meaning of one of the words, e.g., *cautious.*
- Make three columns on the board labeled *Baseball, Soccer,* and *Basketball.* Divide the class into three groups, and assign a section of the contents page to each group.
- Write these questions on the board: *What team is in the article? Are there any specific players mentioned? Who are they? What is the section about? (Write one or two short phrases.)* Explain that groups should read their sections and answer the questions.
- When students are ready, ask for a volunteer from each group to write the information in the correct column on the board. (*Baseball:* New Jersey Diamonds; no players are mentioned; people's predictions about the Diamonds in their second championship. *Soccer:* Lancaster Lions; Victor Mundsen; Victor Mundsen's future plans. *Basketball:* Miami Twisters; Marta Sanchez and Holly Jones; Marta's retirement and Holly's role as the team's new star.) Discuss any questions or difficulties as a class.

A3: After You Read

- Have students do the true/false exercise individually. Remind them to mark the places in the article where they found the answers.
- Have students compare their answers in pairs. Circulate, note any problematic items, and go over them with the whole class.
- Call on students to report their answers.
- As a follow-up, ask students about their favorite sports and teams. Then ask if any of these teams are in the news these days and ask the students to tell you why.

The Future with *Be Going To*

THINK CRITICALLY ABOUT FORM

- Put students in pairs to complete questions 1 and 2. Encourage them to refer to the Form charts and bulleted notes to check their answers and get familiar with the new structures. As they work, find the sentences in which two underlined forms in the table of contents occur. Write them on the board, underlining the target forms.

- **1. ANALYZE** Call on students to identify whether the underlined form in each sentence has a singular or plural subject. (The form *are going to play* has a plural subject: the New Jersey Diamonds. The form *is going to be* has a singular subject: Holly Jones.).

- Elicit the verb form that follows *to* in both sentences. (Both verbs—*play* and *be*—are base forms.)

- Circle *are* and *is* in the example sentences. Ask *What verb do* are *and* is *come from?* (The verb *be*.) Ask students to predict a rule for forming the structure (subject + simple present of *be* + *going to* + base form of verb). Then ask them to predict the form for *I* and other subject pronouns (*I am going to, You are going to,* etc.). Have them predict the contracted forms as well (*I'm going to, You're going to,* etc.).

- **2. SUMMARIZE** Ask students to look at the sentences and predict the negative forms of the underlined phrases. Write all predictions on the board, even incorrect ones.

- Ask pairs to find two examples of negative forms of *be going to* in the table of contents (*aren't going to win, isn't going to play, I'm not going to lie*).

- Elicit the examples and ask students to compare the forms with the predictions on the board. Call up a student to circle the correctly predicted forms.

FORM CHARTS

- Give students a few minutes to read the charts and caution notes.

- Call on several pairs of students to read out corresponding affirmative and negative statements from the charts. Repeat the procedure for *Yes/No* questions and short answers and information questions and answers.

- Write the following in a single column on the board: *Affirmative, Negative, Yes/No Question, Short Answer,* and *Information Question.*

- Call on a student to give you an original affirmative statement with *be going to*. Write it on the board next to *Affirmative.* Call on another student to change the sentence to a negative statement. Repeat until the chart is complete.

- Write the following verbs on the board: *drive, win, fail, study.* Ask students to choose one or more of the verbs to write four sentences with *be going to*: one affirmative statement, one negative statement, one *Yes/No* question, and one information question.

- Put students in pairs to check each other's sentences.

- Call several students to the board to write one of their sentences. Discuss any difficulties or problems.

Informally Speaking: Reduced Forms of *Going To* (p. 271)

- Choose two students to read the text in the speech bubbles. Then tell the class you will play the recording and that they should listen to how the underlined form in the cartoon is different from what they hear. If needed, play the recording more than once so everyone can hear the difference.

- Have students point out the difference: *going to* in the cartoon vs. *gonna* on the recording. Say that the form on the recording is considered informal spoken English. The form in the cartoon is standard English, which students should use in both writing and speaking.

MEANING AND USE

The Future with *Be Going To*

THINK CRITICALLY ABOUT MEANING AND USE

- Ask students to answer the questions individually. As they work, write the two example sentences on the board.

- **1. ANALYZE** Determine how many students think example a is the future plan by asking for a show of hands. Do the same for example b. (Example a is the correct answer.)

- **2. ANALYZE** Repeat the procedure to elicit which example is a belief about the near future. (Example b is the correct answer.)

- Ask students how they know example a is the future plan. (The speaker has a plane ticket. This shows the speaker thought about the trip in advance and made advance preparations.)

- Ask students to explain why they think example b is a belief about the near future. (The speaker says "Be careful!" because he or she knows that untied shoes cause accidents. The shoe is clear evidence on which the speaker bases the prediction.)

MEANING AND USE NOTES

- Divide the class into three groups. Assign each group a Note.

- Explain that each group will teach the class their Note by explaining or reading the information and example sentences to the class. The group must also write a new sentence to illustrate each point in the Note.

- To present their Note, each group can assign one student to read or paraphrase the explanation, another to read the examples in the book, and another to write the group's sentences on the board.

- Circulate and help as necessary. Then call each group to the board to present their Note.

- As a follow-up, write these categories and sentences on the board:

    future plan
    less certain future plan

    prediction
    less certain prediction

    1. *They're probably going to win. The score is 2–1.*
    2. *He wants to go to medical school. He's going to take biology next semester.*
    3. *We're probably not going away this weekend. The weather report is bad.*
    4. *Look at this traffic! We're going to be late for work.*

- Put students in pairs and have them match the sentences to the categories. (Answers: 1. less certain prediction; 2. future plan; 3. less certain plan; 4. prediction)

Vocabulary Notes: Future Time Expressions (p. 275)

- Write the phrase *time expressions* on the board. Elicit some of the time expressions students already know (e.g., *yesterday, last week, now*).

- Point out that time expressions can refer to a specific time or a general time. Ask students to classify some of the time expressions they already know as either general or specific (e.g., *yesterday, last week*, and *now* refer to a specific time; *a while ago* and *nowadays* are more general).

- Have students read the information in the Notes. Discuss any difficulties or questions as a class.

WRITING

THINK CRITICALLY ABOUT MEANING AND USE

- Have students do A individually. Then, in small groups, have them compare answers and discuss any differences.

- Have them stay in groups and do B.

- As a class, review any difficult items from A. Then elicit answers to B:

    1. EVALUATE (In 1, it's used to talk about a future plan. In 2 and 4, it's used to ask about a future plan. In 3, it's used to make a prediction.)

2. COMPARE AND CONTRAST (It makes the meaning of B's answer more certain. When B says, "It's <u>probably</u> going to rain," it suggests that B is not 100% sure. There is still room for doubt.)

WRITE

The purpose of this activity is to give students practice in making predictions with *be going to* by writing an online magazine article about a famous person's future. If desired, encourage students to do research on the Internet to get recent information on the famous person they will write about.

1. Brainstorm

As a class, start a brainstorm on the board about a famous person. (Make it clear that student will write about a different person.) Write the brainstorming questions on the board, and elicit the kinds of details that students might write about. As necessary, make suggestions to the class about people they may want to write about: e.g., actors, politicians, athletes, musicians. Have students work individually to make brainstorming notes for their article.

2. Write a First Draft

Before students begin writing, make sure they have read the checklist in the Edit section. Also have them look at the examples on pages 266–267. Remind students to use the best points from their brainstorming notes to write their article.

3. Edit

Direct students to read and complete the self-assessment checklist on page 278. Ask for a show of hands for how many students gave all or mostly *yes* answers. If desired, ask students to comment on some of the errors they found.

DO I ...	YES
use the future with *be going to*?	☐
make affirmative and negative statements with *be going to*?	☐
ask and answer *Yes/No* questions?	☐
ask and answer information questions with *Wh-* question words?	☐
express future plans?	☐
make predictions?	☐
express less certain plans and predictions?	☐
use future time expressions?	☐

4. Peer Review

Pair students and direct them to read each other's work. Ask students to answer the questions in the checklist and discuss them. Give students suggestions of helpful feedback: e.g., *Maybe you should add* probably *here so this prediction sounds a little less certain. / Do you really need* be going to *here? It sounds like you're talking about the present.*

5. Rewrite Your Draft

Students should consider their partners' comments from the peer review and rewrite as necessary. Encourage students to proofread their work again before turning it in.

18 The Future with *Will*

Overview

Will has several uses. In first person, it is used to make promises (e.g., *I'm busy now. I'll call you back in a few minutes.*). *Will* is also used in first person when making a quick decision at the moment of speaking (e.g., *A: It's Jenna's birthday today. B: Is it? I'll send her some flowers.*). Finally, in all persons, *will* is used to make predictions about the future (e.g., *You will love Bermuda.*). (Note: Distinctions between the use of *will* and the use of *be going to* for predictions are addressed in *Grammar Sense 2.*)

Form: The key challenges are remembering
- *will* does not change with person or number.
- the verb following *will* is always in the base form.

A GRAMMAR IN DISCOURSE

Couch Potatoes Beware

A1: Before You Read

- Write the title "Couch Potatoes Beware" on the board. Ask if anyone has ever heard the expression *couch potato*. If so, elicit a definition and write it on the board. If no one has heard the expression, ask students to guess its meaning. Write responses on the board.

- Put students in pairs and give them five to ten minutes to discuss the questions.

- Bring the class together and ask students to raise their hands if they exercise regularly. Call on several students to describe their partner's exercise regimes.

A2: Read

- Elicit the meaning of *couch potato* from the glossary. Then ask students to skim the advertisement to find out why the title

is appropriate.

- Divide students into small groups to discuss their answers.

- Elicit several opinions and write them on the board.

- Then ask students to read the advertisement carefully and decide if they think it is effective or not.

- Call on several groups to share their answers.

A3: After You Read

- Have students do the true/false exercise individually and ask them to compare their answers with a partner. Remind them to mark the places in the advertisement where they found the answers.

- Circulate and help as necessary, noting any difficult or problematic items. Then review the answers with the whole class.

- As a follow-up, ask students if they think the exercise equipment in the ad really works. Encourage them to support their opinions with their own experiences of purchasing exercise equipment or other products from ads that promise easy solutions.

B FORM

The Future with *Will*

THINK CRITICALLY ABOUT FORM

- **APPLY** Ask students to read the sentences and complete the tasks. Encourage them to refer to the Form charts and bulleted notes to check their answers and get familiar with the new structures. As they work, write the example sentences on the board.

- Call a student to come to the board and underline the subject *(You, We).*

- Underline *will* in both sentences. Elicit or explain that the form of *will* is the same for different subjects.

- Circle the verbs after *will* and elicit or explain that another way to form the future is subject + *will* + the base form of a verb. Elicit or point out that the contracted form is subject + *'ll.*

- Ask students to predict the negative form (subject + *will* + *not* + base form). Elicit that the contracted form of *will* + *not* is *won't.*

- Have students look back at the ad and find examples of sentences with *'ll* and *won't.* Call on several students to read out the sentences. (*You'll be sorry in the summer. You won't be in shape.*, etc.)

FORM CHARTS

- Give students a few minutes to read the charts and bulleted notes.

- Call on several pairs of students to read out corresponding affirmative and negative statements and their contracted forms. Repeat the procedure for *Yes/No* questions and short answers and information questions and answers.

- Divide the class in half. Ask one half to write three affirmative statements with *will* or *'ll* and the other half to write three negative statements with *won't.*

- Put students in pairs, with one student from each half. Ask students to check their partner's sentences and then rewrite them as affirmative or negative statements. Call on several pairs to share some of their sentences with the class.

- Ask the pairs to write four questions using *will.* Encourage them to create both *Yes/No* and information questions. Call several students to the board to write two of their questions. Ask students to refer to the Form charts to identify and correct any errors they see. Discuss any difficulties or problems.

Informally Speaking: Reduced Forms of *Will* (p. 285)

- Choose a student to read the text in the speech bubble. Then tell the class you will play the recording and that they should listen to how the underlined form in the cartoon is different from what they hear. If needed, play the recording more than once.

- Have students point out the difference: *Jenny will* in the cartoon vs. *Jenny'll* in the recording. Explain that the form on the recording is considered informal spoken English. The form in the cartoon is standard English; students should use this form when writing and speaking, although they will hear native speakers using the informal form in conversation.

C MEANING AND USE

The Future with *Will*

THINK CRITICALLY ABOUT MEANING AND USE

- Call on pairs of students to read the conversations aloud.

- Put students in pairs to answer the questions.

- Draw the following chart on the board:

	PREDICTION	PROMISE	QUICK DECISION
Conversation A			
Conversation B			
Conversation C			

- Ask for a show of hands: *How many people think conversation a makes a prediction? A promise? A quick decision?* Tally the results and write them in the appropriate spaces on the chart. Do the same for b and c.

- Give answers; have students justify them:
  1. ANALYZE (prediction = a)
  2. ANALYZE (promise = b)
  3. DIFFERENTIATE (quick decision = c).

MEANING AND USE NOTES

- Divide the class into four groups. Assign each group a Note.

- Explain that each group will teach the class their Note by explaining or reading the information and examples to the class. The group must also write a new sentence or conversation to illustrate each point in the Note.

- To present their Note, each group can assign one student to read or paraphrase the explanation, another to read the examples in the book, and another to write the group's sentences on the board.
- Circulate and help as necessary. Then call each group to the board to present their Note. Discuss any difficulties or questions as a class.

Troublespot

Some students may ask about the distinction between the use of *will* and the use of *be going to* for predictions. If you choose to address this, explain that we usually use *be going to* when the speaker makes a prediction based on clear evidence that is present at the time he or she makes the prediction. You may wish to use the following examples:
1. I see clouds over there. It's going to rain.
2. Those boxes are very heavy. She's going to drop them.

WRITING

THINK CRITICALLY ABOUT MEANING AND USE

- Have students do A individually. Then, in small groups, have them compare answers and discuss any differences.
- Have them stay in groups and do B.
- As a class, review any difficult items from A. Then elicit answers to B:

  1. EVALUATE (In 2, speaker A uses *will* to make a prediction.)

  2. EVALUATE (In 3, speaker B uses *will* to make a quick decision.)

Write

The purpose of this activity is to give students practice in using *will* by writing a paragraph about election promises.

1. Brainstorm

As a class, start a brainstorm on the board about a candidate's election promises. Write shortened versions of the questions on the board (e.g., *Why ... president? / What ... promises?*), and elicit the kinds of details that students might write about. Have students work individually to make brainstorming notes about their own election promises.

2. Write a First Draft

Before students begin writing, make sure they have read the checklist in the Edit section. Remind them to use the best points from their brainstorming notes to write their paragraph.

3. Edit

Direct students to read and complete the self-assessment checklist on page 290. Ask for a show of hands for how many students gave all or mostly *yes* answers.

DO I ...	YES
make affirmative and negative statements with *will*?	☐
ask and answer *Yes/No* questions with *will*?	☐
ask and answer information questions with *wh-* question words plus *will*?	☐
use at least two contracted forms of *will*?	☐
use *will* for predictions?	☐
use *will* for promises?	☐

4. Peer Review

Pair students and direct them to read each other's work. Ask students to answer the questions in the checklist and discuss them. Give students suggestions of helpful feedback: e.g., *You haven't used any contractions. How about using* won't *in this negative statement? / This might be a good place for a Yes/No question. It will make your promise sound more dramatic.*

5. Rewrite Your Draft

Students should consider their partners' comments from the peer review and rewrite as necessary. Encourage students to proofread their work again before turning it in.

19 *May* and *Might* for Present and Future Possibility

Overview

Students often find modals challenging because the same modal can have very different meanings and uses. For example, *may* is used for permission as well as for present and future possibility. In this chapter, the focus is on *may* and *might* for present possibility (e.g., *Answer the door. It may/might be Sam.*) or future possibility (e.g., *We may/might go to see a play tonight, but I'm not sure.*). *May* and *might* are used in this context to indicate uncertainty. This is in direct contrast to *will* and *be going to*, which express certainty about the future (e.g., *He's going to go to San Francisco. He will have a good time there.*).

Form: Modals do not change with person or number and are always followed by the base form of the verb. Students may want to use an infinitive after a modal (e.g., **I can to go.* Incorrect). Students may also find questions and negative statements challenging since modals do not use the auxiliary *do*.

A GRAMMAR IN DISCOURSE

Optimist or Pessimist?

A1: Before You Read

- Write the words *optimist* and *pessimist* on the board. If students are unfamiliar with the words, elicit their meanings from the glossary.
- Put students in pairs and give them about five minutes to discuss the questions. Also ask them to reflect on their answers and decide whether they are optimists or pessimists.
- Ask several students to share their answers.

A2: Read

- Remind students about using the glossary by eliciting the meaning of a word, e.g., *risks*.

- Ask students to read and answer the quiz from the psychology magazine. Point out that they should answer every question. If neither of the statements sounds like them, they should choose the one that is closer to what they would say. Remind them to count up their answers according to the instructions at the end of the quiz.
- When students are finished, ask for a show of hands to find out how many optimists and how many pessimists are in the class.

A3: After You Read

- Have students do this exercise individually and then ask them to compare their answers with a partner. Remind them to mark the places in the quiz where they found the answers.
- Circulate and note any difficult or problematic items. Then review the answers with the whole class.
- As a follow-up, divide the class into small groups. Ask half the groups to think of a situation and write what an optimist would say in that situation. Ask the other half to think of a situation and write what a pessimist would say in that situation.
- Ask each group to share its answers. Encourage the class to think of what the opposite viewpoint would be in each situation.

B FORM

May and *Might*

THINK CRITICALLY ABOUT FORM

- Put students in pairs to answer questions 1 and 2. Encourage them to refer to the charts to check their answers and get familiar with the new structures. As they work, write the full sentences from the quiz on the board, underlining the verb forms as in the quiz. (*We may meet some interesting people. It may be good news. It might be bill. They may understand. I might be lucky.*)

- **1. APPLY** Check answers by calling a student to the board to circle the subject in each example (*We, It, It, They, I*).

- Elicit that *may* and *might* do not have different forms with different subjects and that the base form of the verb always follows *may* and *might*.

- **2. SUMMARIZE** Elicit the examples of negative forms with *may* and *might* that students have found (*might not talk, might not pass, may not listen*).

- Ask a student to come to the board to write a negative example of *may* and explain how it is formed (*may + not + main verb*).

- Call another student to the board to repeat the procedure with a negative example of *might*.

FORM CHARTS

- Give students a few minutes to read the sentences in the charts and the bulleted notes. Then call on several students to read several sentences from each chart aloud.

- Discuss any difficulties as a class.

- Write these sentences on the board (answers in parentheses are for teacher's reference):

    1. *I might go to the bank later today.* (Correct)

    2. *Bill may buys a new car.* (Incorrect — may buy)

    3. *We may move to a larger apartment next month.* (Correct)

    4. *Donna mayn't get to the airport on time.* (Incorrect — may not)

    5. *He might to see a film tonight.* (Incorrect — might see)

- Ask students to look at the sentences on the board and refer to the charts and bulleted notes to determine if the sentences are correct or incorrect.

- Put students in pairs to check their answers.

- Elicit whether each sentence is correct or incorrect. For the incorrect sentences, call students to the board to make corrections.

Present and Future Possibility

THINK CRITICALLY ABOUT MEANING AND USE

- Put students in pairs to answer the questions. Remind them to note the words that helped them arrive at their answers.

- **1. CATEGORIZE** Elicit the answers and ask students to explain how they knew the answers. (1a refers to a possibility in the future. Clues are the use of *might* and the time expression *tomorrow*. 2a refers to a possibility at the present. Clues are the use of *might* and the use of the simple present verb *are* in the first sentence.)

- **2. EVALUATE** Direct students' attention to 1b and 2b. Ask if these sentences indicate a possibility or a certainty (a certainty). Have a student explain how he or she knew this. (1b uses *will* without *probably*, which indicates a prediction that is certain. 2b uses the simple present, which is used when the speaker is certain or views something as true.)

- Confirm that students understand that 1a and 1b both refer to future time and that 2a and 2b both refer to present time.

MEANING AND USE NOTES

- Give students a few minutes to read the Notes.

- Read the explanation in Note 1A aloud. Then call on pairs of students to read the example conversations.

- Divide students into small groups. Ask half of the groups to write three sentences that use *may* or *might* for present possibility. Ask the other half to write three sentences that use *may* or *might* for future possibility.

- Have groups exchange their sentences so that groups that wrote present possibility sentences exchange with groups that wrote future possibility sentences. Ask students to check the meaning and use of the other group's sentences.

- Keep the students in their groups and read the explanation in Note 1B aloud. Then call on pairs of students to read the example conversations.

- Ask half the groups to write one conversation expressing present possibility and another expressing present certainty. Ask the other half to write one conversation with future possibility and another with future certainty.

- Elicit one conversation from each group and write it on the board. Do not correct any errors at this time; write the conversations exactly as the students report them.

- Ask the class to identify which conversations express possibility and which express certainty. Elicit how students know this.

- As a follow-up, ask which conversations refer to present time and which refer to future time. Elicit how students know this.

- Encourage students to correct any grammar errors in the sentences on the board. Call several students to the front to correct any errors. Have students refer back to the Notes if necessary.

Troublespot

Students who have studied modals before may be accustomed to assigning percentages of certainty to *may* and *might*. They may believe that *may* indicates a stronger certainty than *might*. However, these distinctions do not always hold true with all native speakers, so caution students against relying on these distinctions.

WRITING

THINK CRITICALLY ABOUT MEANING AND USE

- Have students do A individually. Then, in small groups, have them compare answers and discuss any differences.

- Have them stay in groups and do B.

- As a class, review any difficult items from A. Then elicit answers to B:

    1. EVALUATE (B's first sentence shows uncertainty, so *will* is incorrect.)

2. PREDICT (Answers will vary. Example: *She's finally decided. She'll stay with me.*)

WRITE

The purpose of this activity is to give students practice in using *may* and *might* by making predictions about their life in a new city.

1. **Brainstorm**

    As a class, start a brainstorm on the board about moving to a new city. Write the brainstorming questions on the board, and elicit the kinds of details that students might write about. Have students work individually to make brainstorming notes of their own.

2. **Write a First Draft**

    Before students begin writing, make sure they have read the checklist in the Edit section. Remind students to use the best points from their brainstorming notes to write their predictions.

3. **Edit**

    Direct students to read and complete the self-assessment checklist on page 304. Ask for a show of hands for how many students gave all or mostly *yes* answers. If desired, ask students to comment on some of the errors they found.

4. **Peer Review**

    Pair students and direct them to read each other's work. Ask students to answer the questions in the checklist and discuss them. Give students suggestions of helpful feedback: e.g., *You've used the phrase* I may to go *in this sentence. Do you see the error?*

5. **Rewrite Your Draft**

    Students should consider their partners' comments and rewrite as necessary. Encourage students to proofread their work again before turning it in.

20 *Can* and *Could* for Present and Past Ability

Overview

Students often find modals challenging because the same modal can have very different meanings and uses. For example, *can* is used to express both present and future ability as well as possibility and permission. In this chapter, the focus is on *can* and *could* to talk about ability. *Can* is used to talk about ability in the present (e.g., *I can type very quickly, but I can't type accurately.*). *Could* is used to talk about ability in the past (e.g., *I couldn't sleep last night.* or *By the age of four, my sister could use a computer.*).

Form: Modals do not change with person or number and are always followed by the base form of the verb. Students may want to use an infinitive after a modal (e.g., **I can to go.* Incorrect). Students may also find questions and negative statements challenging since modals do not use the auxiliary *do*.

A GRAMMAR IN DISCOURSE

The Youngest in His Class

A1: Before You Read

- Introduce the topic by asking *What does it mean to be smart? What are the characteristics of a smart person?* Write students' answers on the board. Be prepared to provide your own opinions (e.g., *Smart people learn things very quickly. Smart people have good memories. Smart people can read quickly and understand almost everything they read.*).

- Put students in pairs and give them about five minutes to discuss the questions. Point out that students do not have to use the child's name if they don't want to; they can simply refer to *a boy/a girl I know.*

- Call on several students to share their answers with the class. Be sure to elicit why they think the child is very smart. Ask *Does the child show any of the characteristics listed on the board?*

A2: Read

- Write the phrase *child prodigy* on the board and try to elicit its meaning. If students are unfamiliar with the term, direct students' attention to the glossary.

- Divide the class in half. Ask half the students to list the problems Jacob had as a young child. Ask the other half to list the problems he has now.

- Form pairs with one student from each half. Ask them to share their lists with each other.

- Make two columns on the board: *Problems as a Young Child* and *Problems Now*. Call students to the board to write one problem from their lists in the appropriate column. Continue until students have nothing else to add.

- Discuss the list as a class, making corrections as necessary.

A3: After You Read

- Have students answer the true/false questions individually and compare their answers with a partner. Remind them to mark the places in the article where they found the answers.

- Go over any difficult or problematic items with the whole class.

- As a follow-up, ask students if they would like to be the parent of a child prodigy. Discuss as a class.

Can and Could

THINK CRITICALLY ABOUT FORM

- Put students in pairs to complete questions 1 and 2. Encourage them to refer to the Form charts and bulleted notes to check their answers and get familiar with the structures. As they work, write the example sentences from the magazine article on the board, underlining the appropriate phrases.

- **1. APPLY** Call a student to the board to circle the subject of each sentence (*Jacob, He, the other children, Child prodigies, I*). Elicit that *can* and *could* do not have different forms for different subjects.

- Elicit that the verb form that follows *can* or *could* is always the same, the base form of the verb. Point out that both *can* and *could* are similar in form to *may/might/will* + verb.

- **2. SUMMARIZE** Call on several students to provide a negative form with *can* or *could* from the text (*couldn't read or write, couldn't tie, can't be, can't play*).

- Elicit a rule for the negative form of *can* and *could* (*can/could* + *not* + base form of verb).

FORM CHARTS

- Give students a few minutes to read the charts and bulleted notes. As they read, write these verbs on the board: *dance, swim, juggle, whistle, drive, ski*. In addition, label four strips of paper as follows, using one label per strip: *Affirmative Statement, Negative Statement, Yes/No Question, Information Question*. Fold the slips of paper so students cannot see what is written on them.

- Call on pairs of students to read out corresponding affirmative and negative statements from the charts. Repeat the procedure for *Yes/No* questions and short answers and for information questions and answers.

- Call four students to the front to choose one of the slips of paper you prepared in the first bulleted note above. Ask the students to choose two of the verbs on the board and write two

sentences on the board of the type indicated on their slip: one sentence with *can* and another with *could*. Check the sentences as a class, referring to the charts if there are questions.

- Draw students' attention to the pronunciation information in the last two bulleted notes at the top of page 310. Model the sentences in the notes and have students repeat. Then call on several students to read the sentences on the board aloud, correcting their pronunciation and stress as necessary.

- If time permits, repeat the process until all students have had a chance to write two sentences. Have students refer back to the charts and bulleted notes to check their work.

Present and Past Ability

THINK CRITICALLY ABOUT MEANING AND USE

- Put students in pairs to answer questions 1 and 2. Ask them to be prepared to explain how they determined their answers.

- **1. EVALUATE** Elicit that sentences a and c refer to present ability.

- **2. EVALUATE** Elicit that sentences b and d refer to past ability. Ask *How do you know?* (Both sentences have a phrase that indicates past time, e.g., *at the age of . . .*).

MEANING AND USE NOTES

- Read Note 1 aloud, calling on several students to read the examples.

- Ask students to write two sentences. The first sentence should be about something they could do at age ten that they cannot do now. The second sentence should be about something they can do now, which they could not do at age ten. Be prepared to give an example:

  I could stand on my head at age ten, but I can't stand on my head now.

  I couldn't drive at age ten, but I can drive now.

- Remind students that *but* is used to join sentences with contrasting information (see Chapter 16).

- Circulate and help with vocabulary as necessary.
- Call on several students to read one of their sentences aloud. Alternatively, you may want to collect the sentences and read them aloud at random, having students guess who wrote the sentence.

WRITING

THINK CRITICALLY ABOUT MEANING AND USE

- Have students do A individually. Then, in small groups, have them compare answers and discuss any differences.
- Have them stay in groups and do B.
- As a class, review any difficult items from A. Then elicit answers to B:

   1. EVALUATE (Both question and answer refer to past ability, so *could* is used.)

   2. DRAW A CONCLUSION (b)

WRITE

The purpose of this activity is to give students practice in using *can* and *could* by writing a paragraph about past and present abilities.

1. Brainstorm

As a class, start a brainstorm on the board to get students thinking about the paragraph they will write. Have students brainstorm ideas about a made-up person. (Make it clear they will later write about themselves.) Write the brainstorming questions on the board, and elicit the kinds of details that students might write about. Have students work individually to make brainstorming notes on their own past and present abilities.

2. Write a First Draft

Before students begin writing, make sure they have read the checklist in the Edit section. Remind students to use the best points from their brainstorming notes to write their paragraph.

3. Edit

Direct students to read and complete the self-assessment checklist on page 316. Ask for a show of hands for how many students gave all or mostly *yes* answers. If desired, ask students to comment on some of the errors they found.

DO I ...	YES
use *can* to show present ability?	☐
use *could* to show past ability?	☐
make affirmative and negative statements using *can* and *could*?	☐
ask and answer *Yes/No* questions using *can* and *could*?	☐
ask and answer information questions using *can* and *could*?	☐

4. Peer Review

Pair students and direct them to read each other's work. Ask students to answer the questions in the checklist and discuss them. Give students suggestions of helpful feedback: e.g., *You're talking about your past here, so you should use* could. / *You haven't included anything you couldn't do as a child. Is there anything you can add?*

5. Rewrite Your Draft

Students should consider their partners' comments from the peer review and rewrite as necessary. Encourage students to proofread their work again before turning it in.

21 Modals of Request and Permission

Overview

Students often find modals challenging because the same modal can have very different meanings and uses. In this chapter, the focus is on modals that are used to make requests and ask permission. *Can, could, will,* and *would* are used to make requests (e.g., *Can you get the door? Could you lend me some money? Will you go to the post office for me? Would you repeat that?*). The choice of modal depends on the level of formality, with *can* and *will* used in less formal situations, and *could* and *would* used in more formal situations. *Can, could,* and *may* are used to ask for permission (e.g., *Can we enter through this door? Could I borrow your pen? May I take this chair?*). *Can* is used in less formal situations, and *could* and *may* are used in more formal situations.

Form: Modals do not change with person or number and are always followed by the base form of the verb. Students may want to use an infinitive after a modal (e.g., **I can to go.* Incorrect). Students may also find questions and negative statements challenging since modals do not use the auxiliary *do.*

A GRAMMAR IN DISCOURSE

Standing Up For Yourself

A1: Before You Read

- Write the expression *standing up for yourself* on the board. Ask if any of the students has ever heard this expression. If so, elicit its meaning. If students are unsure of the meaning, direct their attention to the glossary to find the definition.

- Divide students into small groups and give them a few minutes to discuss the questions.

- Call on several students to share their answers with the class. If students are reluctant to discuss personal information, ask *Do most*

people you know express their true feelings, or do they hide them?

A2: Read

- Ask students to skim the interview very quickly and find the three types of people Dr. Grey talks about.

- Elicit the three types and write them on the board (*aggressive, assertive, unassertive*).

- Call on several students to say what type of person they think they are.

- Divide students into three groups. Assign one behavior type (*aggressive, assertive, unassertive*) to each group. Explain that each group will read the interview, define their group's behavior type, and find an example of that type of behavior.

- Ask groups to elect a reporter who will share the information with the class.

- Circulate and help as necessary.

- Call on reporters to share their group's information. If time permits, you may want to have each reporter write the group's information on a transparency. (Group 1: *Aggressive people are rude and think about their own needs only. For example, an aggressive person will not stay late to work. He or She will say his or her hours are from 9:00 to 5:00. Group 2: Assertive people express their feelings and needs honestly, but not in a rude way. An assertive person may not stay late for work, but will make another arrangement to help his or her boss. Group 3: Unassertive people will not express their feelings and will do what others want. An unassertive person will stay late for work, even if he or she already has plans.*)

- Discuss any questions or difficulties as a class.

A3: After You Read

- Have students do this exercise individually. Point out that the exercise presents six new situations; they should answer based on the information in the interview.

- Discuss the answers and any problematic items as a class.
- As a follow-up, ask *Do you think people can change? Do you think an aggressive person can become assertive? Do you think an unassertive person can become more assertive?* Encourage students to support their opinions with their own experiences.

B FORM

Modals of Request and Permission

THINK CRITICALLY ABOUT FORM

- Ask students to complete questions 1 and 2 on their own. Encourage them to refer to the Form charts to check their answers and get familiar with the new structures. As they work, write the underlined and circled questions from the interview in two columns on the board. Label the columns *Modals of Request* and *Modals of Permission*.
- **1. ANALYZE** Ask students to look at the first question on the board under *Modals of Request*. Call a student to the board to underline the subject (*you*). Elicit that the modal *can* comes before the subject. Explain that *can* is a modal of request: that is, we use it to ask someone to do something.
- Elicit the modals of request in the first column (*Could, Would, Will*). Confirm that students understand that the subject for all questions is *you* and that the modal comes before the subject.
- **2. ANALYZE** Direct students' attention to the first question in the *Modals of Permission* column. Call a student to the board to underline the subject (*I*). Elicit that the modal comes before the subject. Explain that in this question *could* is used as a modal of permission: that is, we use it to ask someone if we can do something.
- Elicit the modals in the other circled questions (*can, may*). Confirm that students understand that the subject for all questions is *I* and that the modal comes before the subject. (If desired, remind students that they have seen *can* and *could* in another context, as modals of present and past ability.)

FORM CHARTS

- Give students about five minutes to read the charts and the bulleted notes.
- Check students' understanding of the charts by asking a student to choose a question from one of the form charts and read it aloud. Ask the class to determine if the question uses a modal of request or a modal of permission. Ask *How do you know this?* (Modals of request are generally used in questions with *you*. Modals of permission are generally used in questions with *I* or *we*.).
- Ask students to write four questions and answers: two questions and answers expressing requests and two asking for permission. Have students refer to the charts and bulleted notes if necessary.
- Put students in pairs to check their questions.
- Call on several students to share one of their questions with the class.

C MEANING AND USE

Making Requests and Asking for Permission

THINK CRITICALLY ABOUT MEANING AND USE

- Put students in pairs. Give them a few minutes to do the questions.
- **1. CATEGORIZE** Elicit the answers. (Questions b, e, and f are requests.) Ask *How do you know?* (*You* is the subject for each question.)
- **2. CATEGORIZE** Elicit the answers. (Questions a, c, and d ask for permission.) Ask *How do you know?* (*I* is the subject for each question.)
- Discuss any difficulties or problematic items as a class.

MEANING AND USE NOTES

- Divide the class into four groups. Assign them Notes 1–4, one Note per group. (As Note 5 synthesizes the information in Notes 1–4, it will probably be more efficient to bring the groups together and discuss it as a class.)

- Explain that each group will teach the class their Note by explaining or reading the information and example sentences to the class. The group must also write a new sentence or conversation to illustrate each point in the Note.

- To present their Note, each group can assign one student to read or paraphrase the explanation, one or two students to read the examples and conversations in the book, and another to write the group's sentences or conversations on the board.

- Circulate and help as necessary. Then call each group to the board to present their Note.

- Read through Note 5 as a class. Discuss any difficulties or questions as a class.

WRITING

THINK CRITICALLY ABOUT MEANING AND USE

- Have students do A individually. Then, in small groups, have them compare answers and discuss any differences.

- Have them stay in groups and do B.

- As a class, review any difficult items from A. Then elicit answers to B:

  1. ANALYZE (*may* and *please*)

  2. EVALUATE (This conversation seems to take place between family members. That means they know each other well, so they don't need to be so polite with each other.)

WRITE

The purpose of this activity is to give students practice in using modals of request and permission by writing a conversation about an employee who is asking his boss for permission to do something.

1. Brainstorm

As a class, start a brainstorm on the board to get students thinking about their conversation. Write the brainstorming questions on the board, and elicit the kinds of details that students might write about. Have students work individually to make brainstorming notes on their conversation.

2. Write a First Draft

Before students begin writing, make sure they have read the checklist in the Edit section. Remind students to use the best points from their brainstorming notes to write their conversation.

3. Edit

Direct students to complete the self-assessment checklist on page 330. Ask for a show of hands for how many students gave all or mostly *yes* answers. If desired, ask students to comment on some of the errors they found.

DO I ...	YES
use modals of request and permission?	☐
make affirmative and negative statements?	☐
ask and answer *yes/no* questions using modals of request and permission?	☐
ask and answer information questions using modals of request and permission?	☐
include long and short answers?	☐
include questions asking for permission?	☐
use *please* and other expressions to be polite?	☐

4. Peer Review

Pair students and direct them to read each other's work. Ask students to answer the questions in the checklist and discuss them. Give students suggestions of helpful feedback: e.g., *You have* Do I ... ? *here. I think you meant* May I ... ? / *You haven't used any short answers. Can you add one here?*

5. Rewrite Your Draft

Students should consider their partners' comments from the peer review and rewrite as necessary. Encourage students to proofread their work again before turning it in.

22 Modals of Advice, Necessity, and Prohibition

Overview

Students often find modals challenging because the same modal can have very different meanings and uses. In this chapter, the focus is on modals that express advice, necessity, and prohibition. *Should* is used to give advice (e.g., *You should see a doctor for your injury.*) or to express an opinion (e.g., *People shouldn't drink coffee every day.*). *Must* is used in more formal situations to talk about something that is necessary (e.g., *You must assist customers with their bags.*). *Must* is also used to express rules, laws, and requirements, especially in writing (e.g., *All guests must check out before noon.*). *Have to* is used to talk about something that is necessary in less formal situations (e.g., *I have to pack for my trip this weekend.*). The negative form of *must* is used to express prohibition (e.g., *Passengers must not leave their baggage unattended.*). The negative form of *have to* is used to express a lack of necessity (e.g., *You don't have to walk me home.*).

Form: Modals do not change with person or number and are always followed by the base form of the verb. Students may want to use an infinitive after a modal (e.g., **I must to go.* Incorrect). Students may also find questions and negative statements hard since modals do not use the auxiliary *do*.

A GRAMMAR IN DISCOURSE

Rule Followers and Rule Breakers

A1: Before You Read

- Introduce the concept of a rule by eliciting some of the more familiar rules of your classroom or institution (e.g., *Students must not miss more than a certain number of classes. Homework must not be late. Students have to buy all the books for each class.*).
- Divide students into small groups and give

them a few minutes to discuss the questions. Encourage them to widen their discussion to other rules, e.g., *traffic laws or community laws.*

- Ask a student from each group to report the opinions of their group members.

A2: Read

- Remind students about using the glossary by eliciting the meaning of one of the words, e.g., *philosophy.*
- Ask students to read the introduction to the quiz on page 332 and tell you the writer's definitions of *rule follower* and *rule breaker.* Also ask them to tell you about the philosophies of rule followers and rule breakers. (Rule followers think people should always follow rules. Their philosophy is that rules are important and people have to follow them to make life orderly. Rule breakers break the rules. Their philosophy is that unreasonable rules don't have to be followed.)
- Ask students to take the quiz on page 333.
- Poll the students to find out how many rule followers (mostly *a* answers) and rule breakers (mostly *b* answers) there are in the class. Is there anyone who falls into the third category (mostly *c* answers)?

A3: After You Read

- Divide students into groups of four to compare and discuss their answers.
- If possible, have each student say who in their group is most like them and why. If time is limited, ask for volunteers to share their opinions.
- As a follow-up, ask students if they think most people are always rule followers or always rule breakers. Ask them to think of situations in which people should be rule followers. Also ask if they can think of any situations when it might be acceptable to be a rule breaker.

B FORM

Should, Must, and *Have To*

THINK CRITICALLY ABOUT FORM

- Put students in pairs to answer questions 1 and 2. Encourage them to refer to the Form charts to check their answers and get familiar with the new structures. As they work, divide the board into two columns labeled *Should/Must* and *Have To*, then write the example sentences in the appropriate columns. Underline or circle the verb forms as they appear in the book.

- **1. IDENTIFY** Ask students to identify the subjects in the five examples with *should/must* (*people, A person, You, Every car, Students*). Elicit that *should* and *must* have the same form for all subjects and that both modals are followed by the base form of the verb.

- **2. IDENTIFY** Ask students to identify the subjects in the two examples with *have to* (*We, The car, You*). Then ask *Does* have to *have the same form for all subjects?* (No, there are two forms in the examples.) Point out that *have to* (like *have* in the simple present) has two forms: *have to* + base form of the verb and *has to* + base form of the verb. Then ask students to predict the forms for *I* and other subject pronouns (e.g., *I have to stop, you have to stop, he/she/it has to stop*, etc.).

FORM CHARTS

- Give students a few minutes to read the charts and bulleted notes.

- Call on pairs of students to read corresponding negative and affirmative answers. Repeat the procedure for *Yes/No* questions and short answers and for information questions and answers. Discuss difficulties as a class.

- As a follow-up, make three columns on the board. Label the first column *Subject* and write the subject pronouns *I, You, He/She/It, We, You, and They*. Label the second and third columns *Modal* and *Base Form of Verb*.

- Explain that you will say a modal and a pronoun, and then you will call a student to the front to complete columns. Point out that students can use any main verb, except *leave* and *study*, which are already in the charts.

- Model the activity with a student. Say *The modal is* have to. *The pronoun is* She. Have the student write *has to* in the second column next to *She* and ask him or her to provide a verb in the third column (e.g., *read*). Ask students to check the answer against the appropriate chart. Continue using other modal/pronoun combinations, including negative forms, until the chart is complete.

- Then break the students into small groups and have them turn the examples on the board into *Yes/No* questions and information questions (e.g., *Does she have to study? When does she have to study?* or *Why does she have to study?*).

- Elicit answers and write them on the board. Discuss any difficulties or problems as a class.

C MEANING AND USE

Modals of Advice, Necessity, and Prohibition

THINK CRITICALLY ABOUT MEANING AND USE

- Before students attempt the questions, ensure that everyone understands the meaning of *advice* (something you think someone should do), *necessity* (something that is needed, necessary, or required), and *prohibition* (something that is not allowed).

- Put students in pairs to answer questions 1–3.

- Elicit answers. Discuss difficulties as a class.
  1. ANALYZE (a)
  2. ANALYZE (c)
  3. COMPARE AND CONTRAST (b, d; d is more formal.)

MEANING AND USE NOTES

- Divide the class into three groups. Assign each group a Note.

- Explain that each group will teach the class their Note by explaining or reading the information and example sentences to the class. The group must also write a new sentence to illustrate each point in the Note.

- To present their Note, each group can assign one student to read or paraphrase the explanation, another to read the examples in the book, and another to write the group's sentences on the board. Circulate and help as necessary. Then call each group to the board to present their Note.

- As a follow-up, write these sentences on the board (answers in parentheses are for teacher's reference):
    1. *People shouldn't eat chocolate every day.* (Note 1B)
    2. *I don't have to study English next term.* (Note 3: lack of necessity)
    3. *Workers in some professions have to wear a uniform.* (Note 2A)
    4. *Drivers must not exceed the speed limit.* (Note 3: prohibition)
    5. *You should see a doctor about your cold.* (Note 1A)

- Put students in pairs and ask them to decide which Note each sentence represents. Students should be specific as to which part of the Note applies to the sentence (e.g., *Sentence 1 is an example of an opinion, so it represents Note 1B.*).

- Bring the class together and review the answers. Discuss any difficulties or questions and, if necessary, refer students back to the Notes.

WRITING

THINK CRITICALLY ABOUT MEANING AND USE

- Have students do A individually. Then, in small groups, have them compare answers and discuss any differences.

- Have them stay in groups and do B.

- As a class, review any difficult items from A. Then elicit answers to B:

1. EVALUATE (Choice "a" is correct; we would use it if the sign says something like "Visitors cannot park here." We might use choice "b" if the first speaker says something like "We have to park here. Look at that sign." We can use choice "c" if there is a choice of places to park and the first speaker says something like "We don't have to park here. We can park in another place. Look at that sign.")

2. INTERPRET (b = necessity; a = prohibition; c = lack of necessity)

WRITE

The purpose of this activity is to give students practice in using modals of advice, necessity, and prohibition by describing laws in their country.

1. Brainstorm

As a class, start a brainstorm on the board about laws. Write short versions of the brainstorming questions on the board (e.g., *IDs, driver's licenses, car insurance, army, elections, schools,* and *taxes*) and elicit the kinds of details that students might write about. Have students work individually to make their own brainstorming notes.

2. Write a First Draft

Before students begin writing, make sure they have read the checklist in the Edit section. Remind students to use the best points from their brainstorming notes to write their description.

3. Edit

Direct students to read and complete the self-assessment checklist on page 342. Ask for a show of hands for how many students gave all or mostly *yes* answers. If desired, ask students to comment on some of the errors they found.

4. Peer Review

Pair students and direct them to read each other's work. Ask students to answer the questions in the checklist and discuss them. Give students suggestions of helpful feedback: e.g., *You've used the phrase* drivers must *to carry their IDs in this sentence. Do you see the error? / You haven't used any modals of advice. Maybe you could add one here.*

5. Rewrite Your Draft

Students should consider their partners' comments from the peer review and rewrite as necessary. Encourage students to proofread their work again before turning it in.

23 Object Pronouns; Direct and Indirect Objects

Overview

Object pronouns replace a noun in the object position of a sentence (e.g., *I enjoyed a <u>sandwich</u>. – I enjoyed <u>it</u>.* or *We called <u>John</u> last night. – We called <u>him</u> last night.*). Object pronouns can replace nouns that are direct or indirect objects. Direct objects usually follow verbs (e.g., *She read <u>my report</u>. – She read <u>it</u>.*). Indirect objects appear in sentences that have two objects, and they also occur after the prepositions *to* and *for* (e.g., *I sent a watch to my sister last year. We prepared dinner for our parents yesterday.*).

Form: The key challenge is remembering to use object pronouns instead of subject pronouns in the object position (e.g., *The teacher gave the award to Rachel and me last semester. *The teacher gave the award to Rachel and I.* Incorrect).

A GRAMMAR IN DISCOURSE

Holidays Around the World

A1: Before You Read

- Introduce the topic by eliciting the names of holidays that students are familiar with. Write them on the board. Ask students to describe each holiday in one or two sentences. Then elicit key words for each holiday and write them on the board (e.g., *Chinese New Year; a clean house, lucky words, red money envelopes; Ramadan: fasting, colored lanterns, visit people, feast after sundown*).

- Put students in pairs and give them about five minutes to discuss the questions. Some students may wish to discuss one of the holidays already mentioned. If so, encourage them to discuss how they personally celebrate the holiday.

- Call on several students to share their answers.

A2: Read

- Remind students about using the glossary by eliciting the meaning of one of the words, e.g., *incense.*

- Ask students to skim the article to identify how many holidays the excerpt describes (four) and what they are (Day of the Dead, Shichi-Go-San, Boxing Day, and Loy Krathong).

- Ask students to compare the names of the holidays in the book with the list on the board. Erase all the holidays on the board except for any matches.

- Write the following in a column on the board: *Where? Who? When? Why? How celebrated?*

- Divide students into small groups. Assign one holiday to each group. Explain that each group will read the introductory section and the part about their assigned holiday, and then report back to the class using the question words on the board as a guide. (Note: Point out to students that they will not find dates for Shichi-Go-San and Loy Krathong.) Have each group choose a secretary to write down the group's answers and a reporter to report back to the class.

- Ask the group reporters to share their information with the class. Discuss any questions or difficulties. Answers are:

Day of the Dead
Where: Mexico
Who: Families
When: November 1
Why: To remember ancestors
How celebrated: Everyone decorates their houses with skeletons. Many families visit the cemetery.

Shichi-Go-San
Where: Japan
Who: Children 3, 5, and 7 years old
When: not mentioned

Why: To honor children 3, 5, and 7 years old

How celebrated: Families pray for their children's good health, and the children are given a traditional drink. After that, the parents buy the children candy.

Boxing Day

Where: Britain and Canada

Who: Everyone

When: December 26

Why: To spend time with family and friends

How celebrated: People eat a special meal of roast lamb or other meat.

Loy Krathong

Where: Thailand

Who: Everyone

When: not mentioned

Why: To bring happiness

How celebrated: Thais make small boats, then they put candles and incense in the boats.

A3: After You Read

- Have students do this exercise individually. Remind them to mark in the excerpt the places where they found the information.

- Elicit the answers and support for each item. Discuss any problems as a class.

- As a follow-up, ask *Which of these four holidays would you like to celebrate? Why?* Encourage students to give reasons for their answers.

B) FORM 1

Object Pronouns

THINK CRITICALLY ABOUT FORM

- Put students in pairs to answer questions 1 and 2. Encourage them to refer to the Form chart and bulleted notes to check their answers and get familiar with the new structures. As they work, write the example sentences on the board.

- **1. IDENTIFY** Ask a student to come to the board and underline the object in each sentence (1a. Mrs. Allen; 1b. her; 2a. the manager; 2b. him).

- Elicit which objects follow a verb (Mrs. Allen, her) and which follow a preposition (the manager, him).

- **2. CATEGORIZE** Write the word *pronoun* on the board and elicit its meaning (a pronoun replaces a previously introduced noun).

- Elicit the nouns (Mrs. Allen, the manager) and the object pronouns (*her, him*).

FORM CHARTS

- Give students a few minutes to study the chart and bulleted notes.

- Check that students understand how the chart works by calling out a subject pronoun and eliciting the corresponding object pronoun. Elicit or point out that *you* and *it* have the same form in subject and object position.

- Ask students to cover the first two columns of the chart with their hand or a piece of paper. Point out that each example includes a subject pronoun and its corresponding object pronoun. Then call on a student to read the first pair of sentences in the example column. Ask the student to identify the subject pronoun in the first sentence and the object pronoun in the second. Ask *Why do we use* me *and not* I *in the second sentence?* (Because *me* is an object; it follows the verb *thanked.*) Repeat the procedure for the other examples.

- If time allows, divide students into small groups and ask them to write three pairs of sentences like the examples in the chart: the first sentence in each pair should use a subject pronoun, and the second should use the corresponding object pronoun.

- Have the groups exchange sentences and check each other's work. Encourage them to refer back to the chart. Then call on a student from each group to read one or two of the other group's sentences aloud. Ask the class to identify the subject and object pronouns.

- Discuss any difficulties or questions as a class.

C) FORM 2

Direct Objects and Indirect Objects

THINK CRITICALLY ABOUT FORM

- Put students in pairs to answer questions 1 and 2. Encourage them to refer to the Form charts and bulleted notes to check their answers and get familiar with the new structures. As they work, write the example sentences on the board.

- **1. IDENTIFY** Elicit the verb in the sentences (*sang*) and the direct object in each sentence (a. a folk song; b. it; c. a folk song).
- **2. RECOGNIZE** Elicit which sentence has a preposition (c) and what that preposition is (*to*).
- Call on a student to identify the indirect object (*children*).

FORM CHARTS

- Give students about five minutes to read the charts and bulleted notes.
- Draw students' attention to the first chart, and write this sentence on the board: *People make special food.* Elicit the verb (*make*) and the direct object (*special food*). Then elicit or point out the word order of the sentence (subject + verb + direct object). To the right of the sentence, write the pattern: *S + V + DO*.
- Draw students' attention to the second chart, and write this sentence on the board: *People make special food for their friends.* Have students compare the two sentences. Ask *What is similar?* (The subject, verb and direct object are the same.) *What is different?* (The second contains a prepositional phrase containing the preposition *for* and the indirect object *their friends*.) Elicit the word order (subject + verb + direct object + *for* + indirect object), and write the pattern on the board: *S + V + DO + To/For + IO*.
- Continue to the third chart and write this sentence on the board: *People make their friends special food.* Have students compare the second and third sentences. Ask *What is different?* (There is no preposition, and the indirect object comes before the direct object.) Elicit the word order, and write the pattern on the board: *S + V + IO + DO*.
- Direct students' attention to the bulleted notes under the heading "Verbs with Direct Objects and Indirect Objects." Read the bulleted notes aloud, and discuss any difficulties.
- **Direct Object + *To/For* + Indirect Object:** Make sure students understand that some verbs that follow this pattern take *to* after the direct

object and other verbs take *for*. Provide a few examples as students look at the list of verbs (e.g., He *brought the book <u>to</u> me. She described the film <u>to</u> the class. I baked a cake <u>for</u> him. He built a house <u>for</u> his family.*) Ask students to generate other examples.

- **Indirect Object + Direct Object:** Be sure students understand that the verbs listed can follow both patterns: (1) *S + V + DO + To/For + IO* and (2) *S + V + IO + DO*. Provide a few examples as students look at the list (e.g., *I baked a cake for Lee. – I baked Lee a cake. He brought flowers to Mary. – He brought Mary flowers.*). Ask students to generate other examples.
- If time allows, divide the class in half and have them look at the list of verbs again. Ask students in one half to choose three verbs and write sentences using the pattern *S + V + DO + To/For + IO.* Ask students in the other half to choose three verbs and write sentences using the pattern *S + V + IO + DO.* Remind students to refer to the charts for help.
- Put students in pairs made up of one student from each half. Refer students to the charts and bulleted notes, and ask them to check their partner's work. Then ask them to rewrite their partner's sentences using the other pattern (e.g., *We baked my mother a cake. – We baked a cake for my mother. I told jokes to my friends. – I told my friends jokes.*).
- Bring the class together and call on several students to share their pairs of sentences with the class. Discuss any difficulties or questions as a class, referring students back to the charts and bulleted notes as necessary.

D MEANING AND USE

Direct Objects and Indirect Objects

THINK CRITICALLY ABOUT MEANING AND USE

- Put students in pairs to do questions 1–3. As they work, write the example sentences on the board.
- **1. IDENTIFY** Call a student to the board to underline the direct objects (a. *a book*, b. *his*

retirement). Call another student to the board to circle the indirect objects (a. *his teacher*, b. *everyone*).

- Elicit the answers for 2 and 3, and discuss any dificulties or questions as a class.

  2. ANALYZE (*Greg bought a book. His teacher received the gift.*)

  3. ANALYZE (*The boss announced his retirement. He made the anouncement to everyone.*)

MEANING AND USE NOTES

- Give students five to ten minutes to read all three Notes silently. As students read, write these sentences on the board (answers in parentheses are for teacher's reference):

  1. *I mailed the letter yesterday.* (Correct)
  2. *We always bring to the picnic every year.* (Incorrect)
  3. *We cooked dinner for my cousin last week.* (Correct)
  4. *She gave a good explanation us.* (Incorrect)
  5. *We sold our old car to a college student.* (Correct)
  6. *He told a story to the children.* (Correct)
  7. *We said the police officer our names.* (Incorrect)

- Divide students into small groups. Ask them to determine which sentences are correct and which are incorrect.

- Call a student to come to the board and make an X next to the incorrect sentences (2, 4, 7). Elicit the Note that addresses why these sentences are incorrect (2. Note 1B points out that some verbs, including *bring*, always have a direct object. 4. Note 2 explains that the indirect object answers the question *To whom?* or *For whom?* and that it is usually a person, group, or institution. The indirect object *us* follows the direct object, so we need to put the preposition *to* in front of it. 7. Note 3B points out that the verb *say* must follow the pattern *direct object* + to/for + *indirect object*. It cannot be used with the pattern *indirect object* + *direct object*.).

- Discuss any questions or difficulties as a class.

- Ask the groups to correct the incorrect sentences and identify the direct and indirect objects in all the sentences. Encourage them to refer back to the Notes. Circulate and help as necessary.

- Elicit several possible corrections for sentences 2, 4, and 7 (e.g., 2. *We always bring soda/ chicken/salad to the picnic every year.* 4. *She gave us a good explanation.* or *She gave a good explanation to us.* 7. *We told the police officer our names.*).

- Call on several students to come to the board and underline all the direct objects and circle all the indirect objects (1. *letter* = DO; 2. DO = answers will vary, *picnic* = IO; 3. *dinner* = DO, *cousin* = IO; 4. *explanation* = DO, *us* = IO; 5. *car* = DO, *college student* = IO; 6. *story* = DO, *children* = IO; 7. *names* = DO, *police officer* = IO).

- Discuss any difficulties or questions as a class.

WRITING

THINK CRITICALLY ABOUT MEANING AND USE

- Have students do A individually. Then, in small groups, have them compare answers and discuss any differences.

- Have them stay in groups and do B.

- As a class, review any difficult items from A. Then elicit answers to B:

  1. GENERATE (*They owe a lot of money to the bank.*)

  2. IDENTIFY (A: *you* = indirect object; *German* = direct object; B: *me* = indirect object)

WRITE

The purpose of this activity is to give students to practice in using object pronouns and verbs that take direct and indirect objects by writing a paragraph. Explain that students will work in pairs in order to interview each other about how they celebrate their birthdays. They will then produce a paragraph describing how their partner celebrates.

1. Brainstorm

As a class, start a brainstorm on the board about birthday celebrations. Write short versions of the brainstorming questions on the board (e.g., *significant birthdays, songs, special activities, presents, special foods*), and elicit the kinds of details that students might write about. (If students come from different cultures, elicit as wide a range of answers as possible.) Put students in pairs, and allow 10–15 minutes for students to interview each other, using the brainstorming questions in the book. Encourage them to take notes as their partner answers their questions.

2. Write a First Draft

Before students begin writing, make sure they have read the checklist in the Edit section. Remind students to use the best points from their brainstorming notes to write their description.

3. Edit

Direct students to read and complete the self-assessment checklist on page 358. Ask for a show of hands for how many students gave all or mostly *yes* answers. If desired, ask students to comment on some of the errors they found.

DO I ...	YES
include sentences with object pronouns?	☐
include sentences with direct and indirect objects?	☐
include some sentences with direct object + *to/for* + indirect object?	☐
include some sentences with indirect object + direct object?	☐
use the correct verb with indirect and/or direct objects?	☐

4. Peer Review

Ask students to form new pairs, so they are working with a different person. Then direct them to read each other's work. Ask students to answer the questions in the checklist and discuss them. Give students suggestions of helpful feedback: e.g., *You've used a subject pronoun after the verb here. Can you fix it? / Did you check the order of the direct and indirect object here? I think you've reversed them.*

5. Rewrite Your Draft

Students should consider their partners' comments from the peer review and rewrite as necessary. Encourage students to proofread their work again before turning it in.

24 Infinitives and Gerunds After Verbs

Overview

Infinitives and gerunds function as nouns in sentences. In this chapter, the focus is on infinitives and gerunds after verbs. The infinitive consists of *to* + the base form of the verb (e.g., *to read, to swim, to have*). The gerund is formed by adding *-ing* to the base form of the verb (e.g., *reading, swimming, having*). Though the gerund looks like a verb form, it is used as a noun.

Form: The key challenge is spelling the gerund for verbs whose final consonant is doubled (*swim – swimming*) or whose final vowel is dropped (*have – having*). Students should already be comfortable with this as they have encountered spelling rules for forming the present participle (*-ing* form) in the simple present and past continuous in earlier chapters.

A GRAMMAR IN DISCOURSE

Advice to Business Travelers

A1: Before You Read

- Ask students *Is it important to be on time? Why or why not?* Elicit students' opinions. Ask students if their opinions change depending on the situation (e.g., *work, school, a movie*, etc.).
- Put students in pairs and give them about five minutes to answer the questions.
- Call on several pairs to share their opinions with the class.

A2: Read

- Remind students about using the glossary by eliciting the meaning of one of the words, e.g., *avoid.*

- Ask students to look at the headings in the article and identify the three kinds of information that international business travelers should find out about their destinations (e.g., *office hours, religious and national holidays, business customs*).
- Ask students to read the article more carefully and list two important pieces of advice for each of the three categories. In addition, ask them to note one other piece of general advice from the beginning of the article.
- Divide students into small groups to share their lists. Ask students to identify the two pieces of information they think are most important for business travelers. Students should be prepared to justify their opinions.
- Call on a member of each group to share the group's opinion with the class.
- Discuss any questions or difficulties.

A3: After You Read

- Have students do this exercise individually. Remind them to mark the places in the article where they found the information.
- Elicit students' answers and support for each item. Discuss any problems as a class.
- As a follow-up, ask students to consider what advice they would give to business travelers coming to visit their country (e.g., office hours, holidays, the importance of being on time, and other business customs).
- If time allows, ask *Do you think most people are forgiving or understanding when someone from another country makes a mistake? Why or why not?* Encourage students to support their opinions with their own experiences.

B FORM

Infinitives and Gerunds After Verbs

THINK CRITICALLY ABOUT FORM

- Put students in pairs to answer questions 1–4. Encourage them to refer to the Form charts to check their answers and get familiar with the new structures. As they work, write the example sentences from the article on the board, underlining and circling the appropriate forms as they appear in the article.

- **1.–2. IDENTIFY AND APPLY** Elicit the subject and verb in the first sentence (*travelers, need*). Point out that the infinitive (*to know*) is formed with *to* + the base form of the verb. Call several students to the board to write other examples of verb + infinitive from the text. Ask them to underline the infinitives (*need to know, like to talk, prefer to read*, etc.).

- **3.–4. IDENTIFY AND EXPLAIN** Elicit the subject and verb in the second sentence (*they, do . . . finish*). Point out that *working* looks like a verb, but it is actually a noun that functions as a direct object. Call students to the board to write other examples of verb + gerund. Ask them to circle the gerunds (*enjoy celebrating, don't like discussing, prefer beginning, avoid using*).

- Elicit that the gerund is formed by adding *-ing* to a verb.

FORM CHARTS

- Call on several students to read the sentences in the charts to the class. Then give students about five minutes to read the bulleted notes that follow the charts.

- Point out that it is important to remember which verbs are followed by infinitives, which are followed by gerunds, and which can be followed by either form.

- Make three columns on the board and label them: *Verb + Infinitive, Verb + Gerund*, and *Verb + Infinitive/Gerund*.

- Give students a few minutes to study the charts, and then have them close their books. Call a student to the board. Choose a verb from the

charts at random (e.g., *enjoy*) and ask *Which is correct: I enjoy to work, I enjoy working, or both?* Ask the student to write the correct phrase in the appropriate column. Repeat until all the verbs have been elicited.

- Give students a few minutes to study the three lists of verbs on page 363. Provide meanings for any verbs they are unsure of.

- Have students write sentences with two verbs from each list. For verbs that can take either the infinitive or gerund, have them write one sentence for each form.

- Put students in pairs to check each other's sentences by referring to the charts and bulleted notes.

- Ask several students to share one of their sentences with the class. Discuss any difficulties.

C MEANING AND USE

Infinitives and Gerunds

THINK CRITICALLY ABOUT MEANING AND USE

- Put students in pairs to do questions 1–2. As they work, write the example sentences on the board.

- **1. ANALYZE** Call on a student to identify the sentences that talk about an activity (b and c). Elicit the activity (*eating/to eat Mexican food*).

- **2. COMPARE AND CONTRAST** Elicit that b and c have the same meaning.

- Ask a student to describe how the meaning of sentence a might have a different meaning from sentences b and c. For example, in sentence a, the speaker could be talking about the smell or appearance of Mexican food.

MEANING AND USE NOTES

- Give students a few minutes to read both Notes.

- Divide students into small groups. Explain that each group will write six sentences, two sentences each for Notes 1A, 1B, and 2. Encourage students to use activities and states that are different from those in the book.

- Circulate and help as necessary.
- Call on a volunteer from each group to read the group's sentences aloud.
- Discuss any questions or difficulties as a class.

WRITING

THINK CRITICALLY ABOUT MEANING AND USE

- Have students do A individually. Then, in small groups, have them compare answers and discuss any differences.
- Have them stay in groups and do B.
- As a class, review any difficult items from A. Then elicit answers to B:

  1. EVALUATE (No, the meaning stays the same.)

  2. PREDICT (No, we can't replace the gerund with an infinitive because *dislike* only takes a gerund.)

Write

The purpose of this activity is to give students practice in using gerunds and infinitives by writing a paragraph giving advice to business travelers visiting their country.

1. Brainstorm

As a class, start a brainstorm on the board about things that business travelers need to know in general. (Make it clear that students will use other ideas about their own country.) Write the brainstorming questions on the board, and elicit the kinds of details that students might write about. Have students work individually to make brainstorming notes on business practices in their own country.

2. Write a First Draft

Before students begin writing, make sure they have read the checklist in the Edit section. Also have them look at the example on page 361. Remind students to use the best points from their brainstorming notes to write their paragraph.

3. Edit

Direct students to read and complete the self-assessment checklist on page 370. Ask for a show of hands for how many students gave all or mostly *yes* answers. If desired, ask students to comment on some of the errors they found.

DO I ...	YES
use infinitives after verbs?	☐
use gerunds after verbs?	☐
include infinitives and gerunds that refer to activities and states?	☐
include infinitives and gerunds that express likes and dislikes?	☐
include infinitives and gerunds that explain customs and habits?	☐

4. Peer Review

Pair students and direct them to read each other's work. Ask students to answer the questions in the checklist and discuss them. Give students suggestions of helpful feedback: e.g., *You've used an infinitive after* avoid *here. Are you sure that's correct? / Are you sure about the gerund form here? I think* expect *takes an infinitive.*

5. Rewrite Your Draft

Students should consider their partners' comments from the peer review and rewrite as necessary. Encourage students to proofread their work again before turning it in.

25 Comparatives

Overview

Comparative adjectives are used to talk about differences between people or things (e.g., *Carol is older than Nina. Elephants are larger than hippos.*). Comparative adverbs are used to talk about the difference between actions (e.g., *Mike runs more quickly than Steve.*). Comparatives are often used to express opinions (e.g., *Basketball is more exciting than baseball, but basketball is less exciting than soccer.*).

Form: The form of comparatives can present several problems. The key challenges are remembering

- the rules for forming comparatives: either adding *-er* to a one-syllable adjective or adverb, or using *more* + an adjective or adverb for longer adjectives and adverbs.
- the spelling rules for adding *-er* to the adjective or adverb: i.e., if the word ends in *-e*, add only an *-r*; if the word ends with a single vowel and a consonant, the final consonant is doubled before adding *-er*.
- irregular comparative forms for adjectives (e.g., *good – better, bad – worse*).
- irregular comparative forms for adverbs (e.g., *good – well, bad – badly*).

A GRAMMAR IN DISCOURSE

Smartphones

A1: Before You Read

- Introduce the topic by asking questions like *What's so great about cell phones? How do you think life was before cell phones? When was the last time you bought a new phone? What makes your new phone better than your old phone?* For each question, elicit answers from several students.

- Put students in pairs and give them about five minutes to discuss the questions.

- Elicit answers to the last question: *Besides making phone calls, what special things can your cell phone do?* Write the features they name on the board. Use the opportunity to preteach vocabulary like *application, feature, digital camera, signal* and *Wi-Fi*.

- Then do a class survey. Read off each feature and ask: *How many of your phones can do this?* Write the number next to each feature.

A2: Read

- Remind students about using the glossary by eliciting the meaning of one of the words, e.g., *application*.

- Have students scan the article and tell you how many types of cell phones the writer discusses and what they are. (The writer discusses two kinds: "feature phones" and "smartphones.")

- Have students read the article again and answer the following: *Which type do more people buy?*

- Elicit the answer. (More people buy traditional feature phones.) Then ask: *For which age group is this NOT true? What does this group tend to buy?* (It isn't true of 24–35 year olds. They tend to buy smartphones.)

A3: After You Read

- Have students do the exercise individually and compare their answers with a partner. Remind them to mark the places in the article where they found their answers.

- Go over any difficult or problematic items with the whole class.

- As a follow-up, ask students if they were surprised to learn that traditional feature phones outsell smartphones. Elicit opinions about why they think this happens and if they think smartphone sales will overtake traditional phone sales in the near future.)

B FORM

The Comparative with Adjectives and Adverbs

THINK CRITICALLY ABOUT FORM

- Put students in pairs to do questions 1 and 2. Encourage them to refer to the Form charts and bulleted notes to check their answers and get familiar with the new structures. As they work, copy the charts for both questions on the board.

- **1. APPLY** Elicit the comparative form for each word, and write it on the board. Ask *What ending do we use to form the comparative of these adjectives and adverbs? (-er) How many syllables do these words have?* (One)

- **2. APPLY** Elicit the comparative form of each word, and write it on the board. Ask *How do we form these comparatives? (more +* adjective or adverb)

- Ask students if they see any differences between the adjectives and adverbs in questions 1 and 2. Have them try to guess why some of the words take *-er* and others take *more*. Refer them to the charts to find their answers.

FORM CHARTS

- Give students a few minutes to read the charts and bulleted notes.

- Call on several pairs of students to read out the adjectives and their comparative forms in the first chart. Then have someone read aloud the corresponding bulleted notes.

- Think of other examples of one-syllable adjectives ending in a single vowel + consonant (e.g., *red, hot*) and elicit the comparative forms (e.g., *redder, hotter*).

- Repeat for the other charts and corresponding notes.

- Ask a student to tell you a very general rule for when to use the two different forms (Short adjectives take the *-er* ending. Long adjectives take *more*.).

- Check students' understanding by giving them a list of adjectives and adverbs and asking them to write the comparative forms: e.g., *young, fat, healthy, effective, accurate, comfortably, loud, loudly, strong, carefully, good* (adj.), *bad* (adv.). Encourage them to refer to the charts and bulleted notes.

- Call for volunteers to come to the board to write the comparative forms (*younger, fatter, healthier/more healthy, more effective, more accurate, more comfortably, louder, more loudly, stronger, more carefully, well, badly*). Discuss any difficulties or questions as a class.

- Direct students' attention to the chart and bulleted notes under the heading "The Comparative in Sentences." Call on students to read aloud the examples in the chart and highlight the use of *than* in each sentence.

- To check that students understand that the last part of a comparative sentence can have more than one form, write on the board: *Chris drives faster than Gloria.* Ask them to change the sentence so that it ends with a verb (*Chris drives faster than Gloria drives.*) and then with an auxiliary (*Chris drives faster than Gloria does.*). Repeat the procedure for the other sentences in the chart.

- As a follow-up, put students in pairs. Ask them to choose two adjectives and two adverbs and write four sentences with comparatives. Write two sample sentences on the board, one with an adjective and the other with an adverb (e.g., *My sister is taller than I am. My brother writes more effectively than I do.*). Encourage students to refer back to the charts and bulleted notes for support. Circulate and help with vocabulary and grammar as necessary.

- Call on each pair to share one of their sentences. Write the sentences on the board, and elicit corrections where necessary. Discuss any difficulties or questions as a class.

C MEANING AND USE

Making Comparisons

THINK CRITICALLY ABOUT MEANING AND USE

- Put students in pairs to answer the questions. Ask them to underline the words that led them to their answers. As they work, write the sentences on the board.
- Elicit the answers:
  1. EVALUATE (a)
  2. EVALUATE (c)
  3. EVALUATE (b)
- Call a student to the board to underline the people compared in sentence a (*Ruth, Susan*); the things compared in b (*my car, Lee's car*); and the action compared in b (*drives*).

MEANING AND USE NOTES

- Ask students to read each part of the Note.
- Divide students into small groups. Ask them to write three sentences: one sentence comparing people, one comparing things, and one comparing actions. At least one of the sentences should express an opinion. Have students refer to the Notes for help. Circulate and help with vocabulary as necessary.
- Ask a student from each group to read the group's sentences aloud. Discuss any questions or difficulties as a class.
- Ask the groups to choose one of their sentences and rewrite it with *less* so that the meaning is not changed. If none of the group's sentences are suitable, have them create an additional sentence using *less*. Elicit each group's new sentence.

WRITING

THINK CRITICALLY ABOUT MEANING AND USE

- Have students do A individually. Then, in small groups, have them compare answers and discuss any differences.

- Have them stay in groups and do B.
- As a class, review any difficult items from A. Then elicit answers to B:
  1. DRAW A CONCLUSION (a. less; b. better)
  2. PREDICT (c. That's great!)

WRITE

The purpose of this activity is to give students practice in making comparisons by writing a paragraph about two people they know.

1. Brainstorm

As a class, start a brainstorm on the board about two people. Write short versions of the brainstorming instructions on the board (e.g., *appearance, personality, actions*), and elicit the kinds of details that students might write about. Have students work individually to make their own brainstorming notes.

2. Write a First Draft

Before students begin writing, make sure they have read the checklist in the Edit section. Remind students to use the best points from their brainstorming notes to write their paragraph.

3. Edit

Direct students to read and complete the self-assessment checklist on page 384. Ask for a show of hands for how many students gave all or mostly *yes* answers. If desired, ask students to comment on some of the errors they found.

4. Peer Review

Pair students and direct them to read each other's work. Ask students to answer the questions in the checklist and discuss them. Give students suggestions of helpful feedback: e.g., *Are you sure about* from *here? We usually use a different word after the comparative. / The form* badder *doesn't exist. You need* worse *here.*

5. Rewrite Your Draft

Students should consider their partners' comments and rewrite as necessary. Encourage students to proofread their work again before turning it in.

26 | Superlatives

Overview

Superlative adjectives are used to express differences among three or more people or things (e.g., *Marco is the tallest person in our class. That gold bracelet is the most expensive item in the catalog.*). Superlative adverbs are used to express differences among three or more actions (e.g., *Anton can run the fastest of all his team.*). Superlative sentences are often used to express opinions (e.g., *History is the most interesting class, and it is the least difficult for me.*).

Form: The form of superlatives can present several problems. The key challenges are remembering

- irregular superlative forms for adjectives and adverbs (e.g., *good – the best, bad – the worst*).
- the rules for forming superlatives: either using *the* + adjective + *-est* for a one-syllable adjective or adverb, or using *the most* + adjective or adverb for longer adjectives and adverbs.
- the spelling rules for adding *-est* to the adjective or adverb: i.e., if the word ends in *-e*, add only *-st*; if the word ends with a single vowel and a consonant, the final consonant is doubled before adding *-est*.
- not to use *than* after superlatives.

A GRAMMAR IN DISCOURSE

The Greatest Invention Since Sliced Bread?

A1: Before You Read

- Introduce the topic of inventions by asking questions like *What's the difference between* invent *and* discover? (When you invent something, you create or design a thing that never existed before. When you discover something, you are the first to find or observe something that already existed.) *What are some of the characteristics that make an invention great?* (e.g., It improves the quality of people's lives. It may save lives, time, money, work, etc.)

- Divide students into groups. Give them about five minutes to do the first two questions, challenging them to see which group can come up with the most answers for each question.

- Ask the groups to count up their inventions and inventors, and see which group is the winner of each category. Invite a student from one group to come to the board and write the group's inventions and inventors. Then elicit ideas from the other groups and add them to the lists.

- As a class, elicit answers to the third question: *What are the most important inventions of all time?* Limit students to 10 ideas. Write these on the board in a separate list. Then, ask the groups to re-form and decide on the top three. Elicit answers, and have them justify their ideas.

A2: Read

- Remind students about using the glossary by eliciting the meaning of one of the words, e.g., *slice.*

- Take the opportunity to explain that the title plays on the idiom "[something] is the greatest thing since sliced bread." Native speakers typically use the phrase when they talk about a new invention or product that looks like it may greatly improve people's lives.

- Have students scan the article to find out who invented a machine for making sliced bread and in what year (Otto Rohwedder in 1928). Then write the following on the board and have students scan to find the answers:

1. *What invention in the article came before sliced bread?*

2. *What inventions in the article came after sliced bread?*

- Call on students for the answers (1. Before: the sandwich; 2. After: Monopoly, the Barbie doll, and the ATM)

A3: After You Read

- Have students fill out the chart individually and compare their answers with a partner. Remind them to mark the places in the article where they found the answers.
- Go over any difficult or problematic items with the whole class.
- As a follow-up, have students comment on the modern inventions in paragraph 3. Ask: *Did the writer's choice of inventions in this paragraph surprise you? Do you think we should add any of these to our list of the most important inventions of all time? What other categories can you suggest?* (e.g., *the most likely to save lives, the most destructive, the most energy-saving, the least Earth-friendly*).

B) FORM

The Superlative with Adjectives and Adverbs

THINK CRITICALLY ABOUT FORM

- Put students in pairs to do questions 1 and 2. Encourage them to refer to the Form charts and bulleted notes to check their answers and get familiar with the new structures. As they work, copy the charts for both questions on the board.
- **1. APPLY** Ask a student to read the words in the chart aloud. Then call a student to the board to write the underlined superlative forms from the article next to the correct adjective or adverb: *the smallest* (adj.), *the fastest* (adv.). Be sure students include the word *the* before the adjective or adverb.
- Elicit the word *the* and the ending of these superlatives (*-est*) and underline them in the forms on the board.
- **2. APPLY** Elicit the superlative form for each word. Be sure students include the word *the*

before the adjective or adverb. Ask *Can you give me a general rule for forming the superlative of these words?* (*the* + adjective or adverb + *-est*) *How many syllables do these word have?* (One)

- Elicit the superlative form of each word, and write it on the board. Ask *How do we form these superlatives?* (*the most* + the adjective or adverb). Underline *the most* in the forms on the board.
- Ask students if they see any differences between the adjectives and adverbs in questions 1 and 2. Have them try to guess why some take *-est* and others take *the most*. Refer them to the charts to find their answers.

FORM CHARTS

- Give students a few minutes to read the charts and the bulleted notes.
- Call on several pairs of students to read out the adjectives and their corresponding comparative and superlative forms in the first chart. Then have someone read aloud the corresponding bulleted notes.
- Think of other examples of one-syllable adjectives ending in a single vowel + consonant (e.g., *red, hot*) and elicit the superlative forms (e.g., *the reddest, the hottest*). Repeat for the other charts and corresponding notes.
- Elicit a general rule for when to use the two different forms of the superlative. (Short adjectives take the *-est* ending. Long adjectives take *the most*.) Also elicit that the rules for forming the superlative form are similar to the rules for forming the comparative form with regard to one-, two-, or three-syllable words. Discuss any difficulties or questions as a class.
- Check students' understanding of the rules by giving them a list of adjectives and adverbs and asking them to write the superlative forms: e.g., *young, fat, healthy, effective, accurate, comfortably, loud, loudly, strong, carefully, good* (adj.), *bad* (adv.). Encourage them to refer to the charts and bulleted notes.
- Call for volunteers to come to the board to write the superlative forms (*the youngest, the fattest, the healthiest/the most healthy, the most effective, the most accurate, the most comfortably, the loudest, the most loudly, the*

strongest, the most carefully, the best, the worst). Discuss any difficulties or questions as a class.

- Direct students' attention to the chart and bulleted notes under the heading "The Superlative in Sentences." Call on students to read aloud the examples in the chart. Then call on a student to read aloud the caution note on page 390.

- To check students' understanding of the caution note, write this sentence on the board and ask if it is correct: *They are the smartest students than all.* (No, you can't use *than* after a superlative form.) Elicit ways to correct the sentence with *in* and *of*.

- As a follow-up, divide the students into small groups. Ask them to choose two adjectives and two adverbs and then write four sentences with superlatives. Encourage students to refer back to the charts and bulleted notes for support.

- Circulate and help as necessary.

- Call a student from each group to the board to write one of the group's sentences. Elicit corrections where necessary.

- Discuss any difficulties or questions as a class. Refer students back to the charts and bulleted notes if necessary.

C MEANING AND USE

Superlatives

THINK CRITICALLY ABOUT MEANING AND USE

- Put students in pairs to answer the questions. As they work, write the example sentences on the board.

- When students are done, elicit the names of the people mentioned in the sentences (Dan, Rick, Bob).

- Ask them to underline the words that led to the answers. Remind students how many items are being compared: two actions and two people.

- **1. EVALUATE** Elicit the answer. (Sentence a compares actions. This sentence uses the verb *walk* as the basis for comparison.)

- **2. EVALUATE** Elicit the answer. (Sentence b compares Dan and Bob.)

- **3. INTERPRET** Elicit the answer. (The two sentences in example c refer to Bob as the fastest in the group of three and Rick as the slowest.)

MEANING AND USE NOTES

- Ask students to read each part of the Note.

- Divide students into small groups. Ask them to write four sentences with superlatives. Two of the sentences should be factual (e.g., *Mount Everest is the highest mountain in the world. Main Street is the busiest street in our town.*). Two of the sentences should express an opinion (e.g., *Chemistry is the most difficult subject. The tulip is the most beautiful flower.*). Circulate and help with vocabulary as necessary.

- Ask a student from each group to read the group's sentences aloud. Discuss any questions or difficulties as a class.

- Ask the groups to write a sentence using *least.* You may wish to allow them to express a fact or an opinion with this sentence.

- Elicit each group's new sentence.

- For Note 1C, write the following sentence on the board: *Mount Everest is the tallest mountain in the world.*

- Elicit the prepositional phrase (*in the world*) and erase it. Ask students if the sentence is still meaningful. (Yes, because this is common information, we don't need the prepositional phrase.)

- Point out that sometimes the prepositional phrase may be necessary to introduce the context, but it may not need to be repeated in the following sentences, as is the case in the example for Note 1C.

WRITING

THINK CRITICALLY ABOUT MEANING AND USE

- Have students do A individually. Then, in small groups, have them compare answers and discuss any differences.

- Have them stay in groups and do B.
- As a class, review any difficult items from A. Then elicit answers to B:

    1. EVALUATE (a)

    2. GENERATE (Answers will vary. Some examples: B: *Yes, in a few years it's going to be the most useful language for business. / C: I don't think so. It's the most difficult of all the languages at our school.*)

WRITE

The purpose of this activity is to give students practice in using superlatives by writing a paragraph comparing and contrasting three schools.

1. Brainstorm

As a class, start a brainstorm on the board about three typical schools (A, B, and C). Write short versions of the brainstorming questions on the board (e.g., *size, reputation, location, dorms, professors, students, campus*), and elicit the kinds of details that students might write about. (Make it clear that students will write about real schools that they know about.) Have students work individually to make brainstorming notes on their own three schools.

2. Write a First Draft

Before students begin writing, make sure they have read the checklist in the Edit section. Also have them look at the example on page 393. Remind students to use the best points from their brainstorming notes to write their paragraph.

3. Edit

Direct students to read and complete the self-assessment checklist on page 396. Ask for a show of hands for how many students gave all or mostly *yes* answers. If desired, ask students to comment on some of the errors they found.

DO I ...	YES
form the superlative with one-syllable adjectives and adverbs?	☐
form the superlative with two-syllable adjectives and adverbs?	☐
form the superlative with three-syllable adjectives and adverbs?	☐
include at least two irregular superlatives?	☐
compare three or more things, actions, or people?	☐
make statements of opinion about three or more things?	☐

4. Peer Review

Pair students and direct them to read each other's work. Ask students to answer the questions in the checklist and discuss them. Give students suggestions of helpful feedback: e.g., *The superlative always has the. You've left it out in a few places. / We don't use than in superlative sentences. I think you need of in this phrase. / Are you sure this form is OK? I'm pretty sure we don't form superlative adverbs with -est.*

5. Rewrite Your Draft

Students should consider their partners' comments from the peer review and rewrite as necessary. Encourage students to proofread their work again before turning it in.

Student Book Audioscript

CHAPTER 1

A2 (pp. 10–11)

Please refer to the conversations in the Student Book.

B1: Listening for Form (p. 13)

1. My name is Carol Cheng.
2. I'm from Taiwan.
3. I'm a new employee.
4. Compugames is a good company.
5. We're a new company.
6. The employees are very friendly.
7. I'm happy about my new job!
8. Your office is right here.

Informally Speaking (p. 16)

A: Your company'z great!
B: Yes, it is. Our employeez're happy.

B5: Understanding Informal Speech (p. 16)

1. David Kim'z a game designer.
2. The employeez're here.
3. The name'z Compugames.
4. Carol'z the sales manager.
5. The students're at school.
6. The president's from Seattle.

C1: Listening for Form (p. 18)

1. Carol is in the United States.
2. She isn't in California.
3. She's at Compugames in Seattle.
4. No . . . Seattle isn't in California.
5. The people at Compugames are friendly.
6. It's not a very big company.
7. Carol's happy there.
8. I'm happy for her.

D1: Listening for Meaning and Use (p. 22)

1. Kim and Linda are from China.
2. The school isn't big. It's small.
3. Fran isn't at school. She's at work.
4. Mr. Johnson is 50 years old.
5. They're doctors.
6. He isn't from Japan.

CHAPTER 2

A2 (pp. 28–29)

Please refer to the conversation and the magazine quiz in the Student Book.

B1: Listening for Form (p. 31)

1. A: Excuse me, are you Victor Tomes?
2. B: Yes, I am.
3. A: Is this your passport?
4. B: Yes. Thank you!
5. B: Are you a new student?
6. A: Yes, I'm Irina.
7. B: I'm a new student, too.
8. B: Are you from Russia?
9. A: Yes, I'm from St. Petersburg.

10. B: Oh, St. Petersburg is beautiful!

C1: Listening for Form (p. 34)

1. A: Is this Carson Street?
   B: Yes, it is.
2. A: Where is Apartment 7?
   B: Right here.
3. A: Are you the landlady?
   B: Yes, I am. I'm Ruth Nelson.
4. B: Who are you?
   A: I'm Hiro Yamada.
5. A: I'm here about the apartment. Is it available?
   B: Yes, it is.
6. A: Is the apartment on the ground floor?
   B: No, it's on the third floor.

Informally Speaking (p. 35)

A: How're the students?
B: They're great!

C3: Understanding Informal Speech (p. 35)

1. Where are the children?
2. What're their names?
3. When's the meal?
4. Who're your friends?
5. How's your class?
6. Where's your roommate?
7. What're your grades?
8. Where're your books?

D1: Listening for Meaning and Use (p. 37)

1. Are you a student here?
2. What's your major?
3. Is this your first year?
4. Are you from California?
5. Where are you from?
6. Are the students here friendly?
7. Who's your advisor?
8. Is she helpful?
9. What dorm are you in?
10. How's your room?

CHAPTER 3

A2 (pp. 44–45)

Please refer to the conversations in the Student Book.

B1: Listening for Form (p. 47)

1. Don't arrive late.
2. Listen carefully.
3. Give the contracts to Mr. Douglas.
4. Don't lose the mail.
5. Write down all appointments.
6. Be friendly.
7. Don't panic.
8. Don't take long lunch breaks.
9. Be careful with important papers.
10. Don't play games on the computer.

C1: Listening for Meaning and Use (p. 50)

1. Please write your name on the test.
2. Watch out! A car!

3. Don't sit there!
4. Turn left at the corner.
5. Add some salt and pepper to the mixture.
6. You be careful! That's hot!
7. Turn right at Baker Street.
8. Don't eat my sandwich.

CHAPTER 4

A2 (pp. 60–61)

Please refer to the advertisements in the Student Book.

B1: Listening for Form (p. 63)

1. hour
2. hospital
3. herb
4. hat
5. union
6. university
7. uncle
8. umpire

C1: Listening for Form (p. 66)

1. manager
2. children
3. books
4. man
5. teeth
6. woman
7. child
8. mice

C4: Pronouncing Regular Plural Nouns (p. 67)

A. 1. cars
   2. pencils
   3. wishes
   4. roommates
   5. nouns
   6. maps

D1: Listening for Meaning and Use (p. 69)

1. Eat the vegetables.
2. A skyscraper is a building.
3. Studios are apartments.
4. Read a newspaper.
5. Mr. Jones is the landlord.
6. Please clean the house.
7. Electricity and water are utilities.
8. A knife is a utensil.
9. Tony, open the door.
10. Chris is a swimmer.

CHAPTER 5

A2 (p. 74)

Please refer to the flyer in the Student Book.

B1: Listening for Form (p. 77)

1. Turn off the lights.
2. Don't use hot water.
3. Pollution is unhealthy.
4. Take buses.

5. Ride a bike.
6. Save electricity.

C1: Listening for Meaning and Use (p. 80)

1. Education is important.
2. Give me a coffee, please.
3. The table is glass.
4. Have a chocolate. They're good.
5. Put a glass on the table.
6. My hair is brown.
7. Play basketball with me tomorrow!
8. Time is up. Please hand in your paper now.

CHAPTER 6

A2 (pp. 88–89)

Please refer to the classified ads in the Student Book.

B1: Listening for Form (p. 91)

1. Look at this beautiful car.
2. Buy the blue suit.
3. The newspaper is old.
4. Close the door.
5. Are you happy?
6. Take the bus to school.
7. The train is late.
8. Maria and I are from Ghana.

C1: Listening for Meaning and Use (p. 94)

1. Tony's is a new restaurant.
2. The owner is a famous actor.
3. The chef is Italian, from Rome.
4. He is a wonderful cook.
5. The food at Tony's isn't cheap.
6. But the food is delicious.

CHAPTER 7

A2 (pp. 100–101)

Please refer to the email messages in the Student Book.

B1: Listening for Form (p. 104)

1. The students' essays are very good.
2. Whose class are you in?
3. Karen's parents are from Honduras.
4. Their parents are doctors.
5. Who's her teacher?
6. His plan is good.
7. Whose bag is on the floor?
8. Lynn's friends are in town.

C1: Listening for Form (p. 107)

1. Your roommate is really nice.
2. His guitar is expensive.
3. Our cousin is a famous singer.
4. Your cat is in my apartment.
5. Is the yellow jacket yours?
6. Is the book theirs?

D1: Listening for Meaning and Use (p. 109)

1. My brother Dan's cat is 16 years old.
2. Karen Foster's father is sick. He's in the hospital.

3. Bob and Josh are roommates. Bob's grades are **good**. His roommate's aren't.
4. Larry and Robin are parents. Lynn is their daughter.
5. My sister's in my house.
6. The Harris's car is new.
7. Paul's hair is brown. His brother Rick's hair is black.
8. Irina's apartment is on Main Street. Mine is on Elm Street.

E1: Listening for Form (p. 112)

A. 1. These socks are not mine.
2. Those books are interesting.
3. This tie is Alan's.
4. That is a beautiful painting.
5. This is my sister Wendy.
6. These are Jack's books, not mine.

F1: Listening for Meaning and Use (p. 114)

1. Let's get Jack clothes for his birthday. That jacket is nice.
2. It's expensive. How about those pants?
3. No. They're not good for a teenager. This shirt is a nice color.
4. Hmmm . . . I'm not sure. What about that sweater?
5. Good idea. Jack's always cold. Look, these sweaters are on sale.
6. Let's buy this blue one. Blue is his favorite color.

🎧 CHAPTER 8

A2 (p. 120)

Please refer to the journal entry in the Student Book.

B1: Listening for Form (p. 124)

1. A: Are you working?
   B: No, I'm not. I'm watching TV.
2. A: Are you watching the news?
   B: Yes, I am.
3. A: The weather is really bad here. Is it raining there?
   B: Yes, it is, but not much.
4. A: Is the baby sleeping?
   B: Yes, he is. He was tired.
5. A: Is Tom playing video games?
   B: No, he's not. He's at Tim's house.
6. A: Is Linda studying for her math test?
   B: Yes, she is. She's really worried about it.
7. A: How's the car? Is it running OK?
   B: No, it's not. In fact, it's at the garage.
8. A: Are the mechanics working on it?
   B: Yes, they are. But they're working slowly.

C1: Listening for Meaning and Use (p. 128)

1. A: Where are you going?
   B: To the store.
2. A: What courses are you taking?
   B: Italian and chemistry.
3. A: Who's singing?
   B: My sister. She's an opera singer.
4. A: Are you busy these days?
   B: Yes. I'm working long hours at my job, and I'm taking one night class.
5. A: Where are they playing?
   B: They're in the gym.

6. A: Where are you working?
   B: At the bank. I'm a teller.
7. A: How are your grades this semester?
   B: Not so great. I'm spending too much time at work.
8. A: Why are you crying?
   B: I'm watching a sad movie.

🎧 CHAPTER 9

A2 (pp. 134–135)

Please refer to the magazine interview in the Student Book.

B1: Listening for Form (p. 137)

1. Kyla doesn't live in Vermont.
2. She has a job.
3. She doesn't have much free time.
4. Kyla dances every day.
5. She studies every night.
6. Her parents worry about her.
7. Kyla misses her family, but she is happy.
8. She works very hard.

B4: Pronouncing the Third-Person -s and -es (p. 139)

1. speaks
   She speaks four languages.
2. smells
   The bread smells delicious.
3. washes
   My son washes the car every weekend.
4. leaves
   Andre always leaves his dirty dishes on the table.
5. notices
   Every time I arrive late, the teacher notices.
6. stops
   The bus stops very near my apartment.
7. pays
   Rob pays his rent on time every month.
8. teaches
   My best friend teaches ballet in her free time.

C1: Listening for Form (p. 141)

1. A: Do you need money?
   B: No, I don't.
2. A: Does the library open early?
   B: No, it doesn't.
3. A: Does your computer work well?
   B: Yes, it does.
4. A: Do your friends call you?
   B: Yes, they do.
5. A: Do you and your friends go to the movies?
   B: Yes, we do.
6. A: Do you have class today?
   B: No, I don't.
7. A: Do you and your brother need a ride to the mall?
   B: No, we don't.
8. A: Do you like your teachers?
   B: Yes, I do.

D1: Listening for Form (p. 144)

1. Where do you live?
2. Who lives with you?
3. How do you get to work?

4. Where do you eat lunch?
5. What do you do on Saturday morning?
6. Who does the shopping?
7. When does he go shopping?
8. What happens on Saturday night?

E1: Listening for Meaning and Use (p. 147)

1. A: Do you go to the gym?
   B: Yes, I do. I go on Mondays, Wednesdays, and Saturdays.
2. A: Where do polar bears live?
   B: In the Arctic.
3. A: Do you visit your family on holidays?
   B: Yes, I always see them on holidays.
4. A: What do architects do?
   B: They design buildings.
5. A: How does the pie taste?
   B: Delicious.
6. A: What do panda bears eat?
   B: They eat bamboo.
7. A: What do you do in your free time?
   B: I play tennis and go to the movies.
8. A: Do you like jazz?
   B: Yes, and I also like classical music.

CHAPTER 10

A2 (p. 154)

Please refer to the article from a science magazine in the Student Book.

B1: Listening for Form (p. 158)

Some adults occasionally get very angry when they drive. Experts call this "road rage." Road rage is dangerous because angry drivers usually drive carelessly and often cause accidents. These drivers never care about other drivers. They are generally rude and hostile. Angry drivers almost always drive very fast, and they frequently shout at other drivers.

C1: Listening for Meaning and Use (p. 161)

1. A: I need help with this bicycle! A piece is missing! I never look at diagrams to put things together.
   B: Oh, I always do. Let me help.
2. B: Do you usually follow instructions well?
   A: Yes, I always do.
3. A: I hardly ever make things in my free time. What about you?
   B: Me? I love to do things like that.
4. A: I usually don't make things or fix things, but I often cook. Do you ever cook?
   B: No, not me.
5. A: I like to collect recipes.
   B: I hardly ever do that.
6. B: I generally fix things around my house.
   A: That's great! Everyone's good at something.

CHAPTER 11

A2 (pp. 170–171)

Please refer to the excerpt from a history textbook in the Student Book.

B1: Listening for Form (p. 174)

1. My first home was in Chicago.
2. My family wasn't rich.
3. But we weren't poor either.
4. My parents were from Mexico.
5. They were teachers in Mexico.
6. But in Chicago my father was a taxi driver.
7. And my mother was a cook.
8. My brother, Diego, wasn't around often.

C1: Listening for Meaning and Use (p. 178)

1. David was in Germany for two years. His father was in the army there.
2. His father isn't in the army anymore. He's a salesman.
3. When David was young, he was often sick.
4. He was a good student, but he wasn't very athletic.
5. Now he's a long-distance runner.
6. He was the winner of a big race in Boston last weekend.

CHAPTER 12

A2 (p. 184)

Please refer to the excerpt from a history textbook in the Student Book.

B1: Listening for Form (p. 188)

1. Queen Victoria lived in the nineteenth century.
2. We call this time the Victorian Age.
3. At that time, women wore long dresses.
4. People thought a lot about modesty.
5. Victorian women played tennis in dresses.
6. People even covered piano legs in their homes.
7. The world is different now.

B5: Pronouncing Final -ed (p. 190)

A. 1. needed
      I needed a new coat this year.
   2. stopped
      I stopped at the supermarket on the way home.
   3. waited
      I waited for more than an hour.
   4. knocked
      I knocked on the door, but no one answered.
   5. gained
      I gained a lot of weight on vacation.
   6. borrowed
      I borrowed a cup of sugar from Emily.
   7. helped
      You helped me a great deal. Thank you.
   8. hated
      I hated the film on TV last night.

C1: Listening for Form (p. 193)

1. Why did English women wear high boots?
2. Who designed the boots?
3. Did women wear pants in the nineteenth century?
4. Does she have long hair?
5. When did Napoleon live?
6. Where do fashions usually start?

Informally Speaking (p. 196)

A: Jo-osh! What didja do to my new floor?

C4: Understanding Informal Speech (p. 196)

1. A: Diddie come home late last night?
   B: Yes. He got in at 9:00.
2. A: What time didja call him?
   B: About 10:00.
3. A: How diddie get home from the airport?
   B: He took a taxi.
4. A: Diddie have a good time in Hawaii?
   B: Yes, he loved it!
5. A: Didja invite him for dinner on Friday?
   B: Yes, I did.

D1: Listening for Meaning and Use (p. 198)

1. A few years ago, most men wore suits and ties to work.
2. Hats for men were very popular.
3. Most men owned several hats then.
4. Many people wear casual clothes to the office.
5. Most men don't wear hats.
6. In the nineteenth century, many women put white powder on their faces.
7. Jeans became popular in the 1950s.
8. Many young people own several pairs of jeans now.

 CHAPTER 13

A2 (pp. 204–205)

Please refer to the magazine article in the Student Book.

B1: Listening for Form (p. 208)

1. A fire in an office building on Main Street was burning out of control last night.
2. Two men were walking in front of the building.
3. They saw the fire on the first floor and called the fire department.
4. The firefighters arrived five minutes later.
5. The second floor of the building was burning.
6. Luckily, no one was working in the building at the time.

C1: Listening for Meaning and Use (p. 211)

1. I was living in San Francisco at the time of the last earthquake.
2. The earthquake hit at 5:05 P.M.
3. I was driving down the highway.
4. Suddenly, the road started to move.
5. Luckily, I wasn't traveling very fast.
6. I pulled over to the side of the road and stopped.
7. A lot of cars were moving very fast.
8. I saw several accidents.

 CHAPTER 14

A2 (p. 220)

Please refer to the magazine article in the Student Book.

B1: Listening for Form (p. 223)

Paris is an exciting city. It is a great city to visit. I spent time there last year. I liked the museums best. My favorite museum was the Musée d'Orsay. This museum is in an old train station. The station closed in 1939. The museum opened in 1986. It has famous paintings and sculptures. It was a wonderful place to spend an afternoon.

C1: Listening for Meaning and Use (p. 227)

1. A: Did you take a vacation this year?
2. B: Oh yes. We took two. In April we went on a trip to Yellowstone National Park.
3. B: And in the summer we went on a tour of France.
4. A: France, how wonderful! Did you enjoy the tour?
5. B: Oh yes. We loved France, and we had an excellent guide.
6. A: And did you enjoy the trip to Yellowstone Park?
7. B: Well, we had an accident on the way.
8. B: But the park was beautiful. The kids loved it.

 CHAPTER 15

A2 (p. 232)

Please refer to the online article in the Student Book.

B1: Listening for Form (p. 236)

1. Some people don't like this neighborhood, but I love it.
2. It's very quiet. We have almost no traffic.
3. Many families with small children live here.
4. We don't have any cafés or art galleries.
5. However, we have a lot of ethnic restaurants.
6. The city park is a few blocks away.

C1: Listening for Meaning and Use (p. 241)

1. We have many great food stores in Manhattan.
2. But Baldini's is my favorite. They sell a lot of wonderful Italian food.
3. The owner, Mr. Baldini, opened his shop many years ago in 1947.
4. He had no money then.
5. But now he has a lot of money. He's a millionaire!
6. A few people think that Baldini's is very expensive. But I don't agree.
7. I love pasta. And Baldini's sells many kinds of fresh pasta.
8. Everybody shops there, even a few celebrities.

 CHAPTER 16

A2 (pp. 248–249)

Please refer to the web news article and the online comments in the Student Book.

B1: Listening for Form (p. 251)

1. There's a large hall at the front of the apartment.
2. My bedroom is small. There aren't any closets.
3. But there are two windows with a view of the town.
4. The living room is nice, but there's no carpet on the floor.
5. There's a large kitchen at the back of the apartment.
6. There aren't a lot of cabinets in the kitchen.

C1: Listening for Meaning and Use (p. 256)

1. Is their house new?
2. Is there a supermarket near here?
3. Are there any paintings by Picasso in this museum?
4. That's Jack over there.
5. Is their child in school?
6. Look! There's my car!

CHAPTER 17

A2 (pp. 266–267)

Please refer to the table of contents of a magazine in the Student Book.

B1: Listening for Form (p. 270)

1. A: So . . . the world wants to know . . . Are you going to play for the Lions next year?
2. B: Oh . . . ah . . . well . . . Actually, I'm not going to be part of the team next season.
3. A: We're sorry to hear that . . . The fans are going to miss you.
4. A: So, tell us about your plans . . . What are you going to do next?
5. B: It was a difficult decision, but I'm going to play for a German team.
6. B: But, before that, I want to spend some time with my family. We're going to take a long vacation.

Informally Speaking (p. 271)

A: What are your plans for the weekend?
B: We're gonna go to the basketball game.

B3: Understanding Informal Speech (p. 271)

1. My sister is gonna get tickets for the game this weekend.
2. All my friends are gonna be here.
3. They're gonna watch me play.
4. Our team is not gonna play tonight.
5. The Astros are gonna win tonight.
6. The weather is gonna be nice for our game this weekend.
7. Our game is gonna be exciting.
8. My friends and I are gonna go to dinner after the game.

C1: Listening for Meaning and Use (p. 274)

1. Davis has the ball. He's running down the field. He's going to score!
2. I left the team last year, but I'm going to go back next season.
3. Okay, team, this year we're going to win the championship!
4. I think the coach is going to be angry with us. We didn't play well.
5. The coach called. The team isn't going to practice this afternoon.
6. They won the championship last year, but they aren't going to win again. Look at their record.
7. I'm going to run 25 miles a week so I can get ready for the race.
8. We're going to have a big celebration on campus when the season is over.

CHAPTER 18

A2 (p. 280)

Please refer to the advertisement in the Student Book.

B1: Listening for Form (p. 284)

1. A: I'm going to buy myself an exercise bike.
2. B: Why? You'll spend a lot of money on the bike.
3. B: But you won't use it.
4. A: I'll use an exercise bike.

5. A: I'm going to ride at least two miles a day.
6. B: Well, I don't believe you.

Informally Speaking (p. 285)

A: Don't worry. Jenny'll be great with the kids.

B4: Understanding Informal Speech (p. 285)

1. Use our lotion today and your skin'll feel softer.
2. Some of my friends'll believe anything.
3. Oh no! What'll your parents say?
4. The cold weather'll end tomorrow.
5. Who'll be the winner? You decide! Send your vote by email.
6. Use this product and your teeth'll be incredibly white!

C1: Listening for Meaning and Use (p. 287)

1. Don't be angry. I'll give you the money on Friday.
2. The Smiths won't arrive on time. They never do.
3. Hmm . . . I think I'll have a burger and French fries.
4. She'll let me take the test again. I'm fairly certain.
5. We'll probably see them at the park on Saturday.
6. I'll be very careful with your new car.
7. I have an idea. I'll get four tickets and we can all go together!
8. I'm sorry. I'll never be late again.

CHAPTER 19

A2 (pp. 294–295)

Please refer to the quiz from a psychology magazine in the Student Book.

B1: Listening for Form (p. 297)

1. A: Hurry up, Kim. We might miss our flight.
2. B: Don't worry! We have plenty of time.
3. A: Well, there may be a line at check in.
4. B: It only takes 30 minutes to get to the airport. Our flight doesn't leave for five hours.
5. A: I don't want to rush later on. I may not remember everything.
6. B: You have a lot of stuff. Did you weigh your suitcases? They might be too heavy!
7. A: No problem. They are fine. In fact, this one is light.
8. B: OK, so let's pack the car. The big suitcase might not fit so easily.

C1: Listening for Meaning and Use (p. 300)

1. A: My plane ticket . . . Oh no! It's not here. I lost it!
2. B: Look. It might be in your pocket.
3. A: You're right. Here it is.
4. A: It doesn't matter. This is going to be a terrible vacation. I know it.
5. B: That's not true. You might have a good time.
6. B: Hawaii is beautiful.
7. A: I'll hate it. I'm sure.
8. B: You may meet some interesting people.

CHAPTER 20

A2 (p. 306)

Please refer to the online magazine article in the Student Book.

B1: Listening for Form (p. 310)

A: My brother is really smart. He's only six and he can read the newspaper.

B: Well, my cousin Susan is smart, too. She's sixteen years old, and she just graduated from college. She can speak five languages. She could read at the age of three, and she could do high school math in elementary school.

A: Wow! Some people can't do elementary school math in high school!

B: Life isn't always easy for Susan. She can talk to professors, but she can't talk to other teenagers. She doesn't know what to say to them. She couldn't be in class with kids her own age, so she never had many friends.

A: Was she lonely?

B: Yes. She could read and talk to adults, but she couldn't be just a kid.

C1: Listening for Meaning and Use (p. 313)

1. John is a great skier. He skis every weekend.
2. Sshh . . . please be quiet. I'm trying to listen.
3. John Wayne died many years ago. He was a wonderful actor.
4. Marta and Paul are in Tokyo. They're lost, and all the signs are in Japanese.
5. Holly didn't have any sugar or eggs in the house this morning.
6. In college Mike went to bed after 2 A.M. He was always late for morning classes. Nowadays he goes to bed early. He's never late for work.
7. Let's play a song. I'll get my guitar. You play the piano.
8. I left my glasses at home. I had a problem in class this morning.

🎧 CHAPTER 21

A2 (pp. 318–319)

Please refer to the newspaper interview in the Student Book.

B1: Listening for Form (p. 322)

1. Excuse me, miss. Would you help me?
2. Doctor, can I go swimming?
3. Would you turn on the light, please?
4. May I see her now?
5. Can you explain this to me?
6. Where can I try this on?
7. Could you change the channel?
8. Will you help me tomorrow?

C1: Listening for Meaning and Use (p. 326)

1. Could I borrow your tape recorder?
2. Could you close the window, please?
3. May I please use the computer now?
4. Can we eat in the living room, please?
5. Would you buy a newspaper for me?
6. Could I speak to Lynn, please?

🎧 CHAPTER 22

A2 (pp. 332–333)

Please refer to the quiz from a magazine in the Student Book.

B1: Listening for Form (p. 336)

1. A: Are you going to take the job at the bank?
   B: I'm not sure. I don't have to decide until tomorrow.
2. A: I feel sick. Should I go home?
   B: I think so.
3. A: What time do we have to leave?
   B: At 6:00. The concert is at 7:00.
4. A: The sign says you must not take dishes from the cafeteria.
   B: Oh, OK. I'll ask for a carry-out bag.
5. A: Are we going to go soon?
   B: Yes. We have to be there by 10:00.
6. A: I'm thirsty. Let's have a cup of coffee.
   B: You shouldn't drink coffee when you're thirsty!

C1: Listening for Meaning and Use (p. 339)

1. Parents should always listen to their children.
2. Applicants for a learners' permit must be 15 years old.
3. People should drive carefully.
4. You don't have to knock. Just walk right in.
5. You really shouldn't leave assignments until the last minute.
6. You must not tell anyone about this. It's a secret!
7. I always have to help him with his homework.
8. The students at this college don't have to register for classes in person.

🎧 CHAPTER 23

A2 (pp. 346–347)

Please refer to the online article in the Student Book.

B1: Listening for Form (p. 349)

1. Mark and I had a picnic on the Fourth of July. We called our friends Jack and Lisa and invited them to the picnic.
2. Jack is a great cook. He helped us with the food. He made potato salad.
3. The potato salad was fantastic. Everyone liked it.
4. Lisa made an excellent chocolate cake. We all complimented her.
5. Mark ate all of the cake, so we teased him!
6. It was a great day. Holidays and friends always make me happy!

C1: Listening for Form (p. 352)

A. 1. In China, people celebrate Chinese New Year in January or February.
   2. They cook their guests delicious food.
   3. Some people also clean their houses before New Year's Eve.
   4. A lot of families hang lucky words on the sides of the door.
   5. Many old people play a Chinese game called "mahjiang."
   6. Adults give children red envelopes with money inside.

D1: Listening for Meaning and Use (p. 355)

1. I invited Sally to dinner.
2. I gave my phone number to her.
3. I cooked a special meal for her.
4. I even baked her a cake.

5. I expected Sally at 6:00.
6. I waited until 9:00. Then I left a telephone message for her.
7. I like Sally a lot . . .
8. But I won't make her dinner again!

 CHAPTER 24

A2 (p. 360)

Please refer to the magazine article in the Student Book.

B1: Listening for Form (p. 363)

1. I decided to go to Thailand on my last vacation.
2. I planned to see the markets in Bangkok.
3. But I also wanted to experience Thai culture.
4. I love trying new food.
5. I generally avoid eating spicy food, but Thai food is just right.
6. I expected to have a great time, and I did.
7. I tried speaking Thai, but no one understood me.
8. Everyone was very friendly. I really enjoyed traveling in Thailand.

C1: Listening for Meaning and Use (p. 367)

1. Susan hates to clean her house.
2. Josh doesn't like to get up early.
3. Holly doesn't enjoy movies.
4. Rob doesn't like working on Saturdays.
5. We don't like working late.
6. Derek hates to take tests.

 CHAPTER 25

A2 (p. 374)

Please refer to the online article in the Student Book.

B1: Listening for Form (p. 378)

1. Obviously, a laptop computer is a lot smaller than a desktop computer.
2. And a desktop computer has a bigger screen.
3. The desktop also has a larger keyboard.
4. Actually, a lot of people feel more comfortable with a desktop computer.
5. Most people type better on a desktop computer.
6. Of course, a laptop is more convenient.
7. It's lighter . . .
8. . . . so it's easier to carry.

C1: Listening for Meaning and Use (p. 381)

1. The temperature today is 90. The temperature yesterday was 80. Is today hotter than yesterday was?
2. Tyrone types 45 words a minute. Tamika types 62 words a minute. Who types more slowly?
3. Jack got an A on the test. Paul got a B. Who got a better grade?
4. Brad made five mistakes on his homework. Sasha made three mistakes. Who did the homework more accurately?
5. Two people can ride in a sports car. Five people can ride in an SUV. Which car is bigger?
6. Keiko's temperature is high. It's 101 degrees, but Koji's temperature is normal. Who probably feels worse?
7. Almost everyone failed Mr. Ryan's English test. Almost everyone passed Mr. Larkin's English test. Which test was more difficult?
8. You can use a computer to write letters and reports, do math, draw, and send messages. You can use a smartphone to send messages, do math, take pictures, look up information on the Internet, listen to music, and store important information. Smartphones can be carried in your pocket. Which machine is more convenient?

 CHAPTER 26

A2 (p. 386)

Please refer to the online newspaper article in the Student Book.

B1: Listening for Form (p. 390)

1. English is not the most common first language in the world to learn.
2. For example, Mandarin Chinese is a more common first language than English.
3. Today, however, English is the most popular second language in many non-English speaking countries.
4. This was not always true. A hundred years ago French was more popular than English.
5. It was the most common second language in the world.
6. Many people think that English is easier than other languages like Korean or Japanese.
7. This may be one reason why English is more popular than other languages.
8. But really, it is impossible to tell which language is the most difficult in the world.

C1: Listening for Meaning and Use (p. 393)

1. A: Where are you going to go to college next year?
   B: I don't know. I'm thinking about Lighthouse University, Westbrook College, and Cranberry University.
   A: You should go to Lighthouse University. It has the best reputation.
2. B: I know, but it's also the most expensive. My parents want me to go to Cranberry University because it's the cheapest.
3. B: And it's the closest to home.
4. B: And I can get in the most easily.
5. A: What about Westbrook College?
   B: Well, Cranberry has the most comfortable dorms.
6. A: That's important. But I think Lighthouse University has the most famous professors.
7. B: Yeah, but the students aren't very friendly. The students at Westbrook are the friendliest.
8. B: And its campus is the most beautiful.

Student Book Answer Key

GRAMMAR LANGUAGE

1. Nouns (p. 5)

A. 2. computers   4. desks   6. students
3. book   5. calendar

B. 2. house   4. pencils   6. girl
3. books   5. teachers

2. Verbs (p. 6)

B. 2. S   3. S   4. A   5. A   6. S

C. Underline: open, is, sit, am

3. Adjectives (p. 6)

2. B   3. B   4. A   5. A   6. B

4. Prepositions (p. 7)

B. Answers will vary.

C. 2. in (P), red (A)   5. under (P), green (A)
3. from (P), young (A)   6. expensive (A), on (P)
4. dirty (A), next to (P)

5. Subject Pronouns (p. 8)

B. 2. He   4. It   6. We
3. They   5. You

CHAPTER 1

A3: After You Read (p. 11)

2. c   3. d   4. a

Think Critically About Form (p. 12)

1. Circle: I, Dana and Diego, Carol, You
Underline: am, are, is, are
2. Singular subjects: I, Carol, You
Plural subject: Dana and Diego
Pronouns: I, You
3. are
4. Sentences with singular subject and verb:
My name is Carol Cheng.
This is Carol Cheng.
It's nice to meet you.
I'm a computer technician, and Diego is a game designer.

Sentences with plural subject and verb:
We're new employees, too.
And Dana and Diego are students, too.
They're in college in the morning.
In the afternoon, they're at work.

B1: Listening for Form (p. 13)

	AM OR 'M	IS OR 'S	ARE OR 'RE
2.	✓		
3.	✓		
4.		✓	
5.			✓
6.			✓
7.	✓		
8.		✓	

B2: Working on Affirmative Statements (p. 14)

2. am   5. am   8. are   11. are
3. is   6. is   9. is   12. are
4. are   7. is   10. is

B3: Working on Pronouns and Contractions (p. 14)

A. 2. It's   5. They're   8. You're
3. They're   6. I'm   9. It's
4. We're   7. She's   10. They're

B4: Completing Conversations (p. 15)

Conversation 1

Susan: Hi, John. I'm Susan Walker.

John: Oh, you're the new game designer. Welcome!

Susan: Thank you. It's nice to meet you.

John: It's nice to meet you, too.

Conversation 2

Beth: Steve, this is my roommate, Lisa.

Steve: Hi, Lisa.

Beth: Steve, you're from California. Lisa is from California, too.

Steve: Really? I'm from San Francisco.

Lisa: I'm from San Diego.

Lisa: Steve is handsome!

Ruth: Yes. And he's nice, too.

Conversation 3

Rosa: Jenny and I are computer technicians at ElectroDesign.

Juan: Oh! You're lucky!

Rosa: Yes, ElectroDesign is a great company.

Jenny: The employees are very happy.

Juan: My sons are computer technicians, too. They're employees at Reed.

B5: Understanding Informal Speech (p. 16)

2. employees are
3. name is
4. Carol is
5. students are
6. president is

Think Critically About Form (p. 17)

1. Underline: is, are
Not is after the verb.
2. Underline: isn't, aren't
Isn't is the contraction of *is+ not*. *Aren't* is the contraction of *are + not*.
3. Circle: He's, They're
He's is the contraction of *he+is*. *There is* the contraction of *are+ not*.

C1: Listening for Form (p. 18)

	AFFIRMATIVE	NEGATIVE
2.		✓
3.	✓	
4.		✓
5.	✓	
6.		✓
7.	✓	
8.	✓	

C2: Forming Negative Statements (p. 19)

2. Larry isn't from France.
3. Lisa and I aren 't students.
4. Our school isn't big.
5. I'm not Burmese.
6. You aren't/You're not in my class.

C3: Working on Pronouns and Negative Contractions (p. 19)

2. He's not a manager. OR He isn't a manager.
3. You're not teachers. OR You aren't teachers.
4. It's not big. OR It isn't big.
5. They're not in class. OR They aren't in class.
6. We're not Italian. OR We aren't Italian.

C4: Completing Conversations with Negative Forms of *Be* (p. 20)

Conversation 1
2. isn't/'s not

Conversation 2
1. aren't/'re not
2. aren't

Conversation 3
1. isn't
2. aren't

Conversation 4
1. 'm not
2. isn't

Conversation 5
1. isn't/'s not
2. isn't

Conversation 6
1. aren't
2. aren't/'re not

Think Critically About Meaning and Use (p. 21)

c. health   a. age   d. job   b. country

D1: Listening for Meaning and Use (p. 22)

	AGE OR CHARACTERISTIC	OCCUPATION	LOCATION OR ORIGIN
2.	✓		
3.			✓
4.	✓		
5.		✓	
6.			✓

D2: Defining and Describing Nouns (p. 22)

A. 2. flower
3. Rome and Venice
4. colors
5. dictionary
6. fruits
7. June
8. Pizza

B. Answers will vary.

D3: Describing Nouns (p. 23)

Answers will vary. Some examples are:
2. They're beautiful. They're not ugly. It's small. It isn't big.
3. They're beautiful. They're not ugly. It's big. It isn't small.
4. It's small. It isn't big. It's beautiful. It isn't ugly
5. It's ugly. It isn't beautiful. It's big. It isn't small.
6. He's young. He isn't old.

D4: Talking About Time, Dates, and Weather (p. 23)

Answers will vary. Some examples are:
2. It's 2:30.
3. It's 8:00 P.M.
4. It's Sunday.
5. It's in March.

D5: Introducing Yourself (p. 24)

Answers will vary.

D6: Using Pronouns in Paragraphs (p. 24)

Sally is 17 years old. She is not a normal teenager. In the afternoon she is an employee at Macro Games. She is not the only teenager there. Mark is an employee, too. He is only 16 years old. Both teenagers are students at West Valley High School. It is very near the offices of MacroAds.

Think Critically About Meaning and Use (p. 25)

A. 2. a   3. a   4. c

B. 1. Bangkok

2. We use *it* for things, animals, and places. Bangkok is a place, so we need *it* (not *he* or *she*).

Edit (p. 25)

2. India ^is in Asia.
3. correct
4. She^'s in the classroom.
5. They ^are happy.
6. I ~~am~~ 'm not a student.
7. Paolo ~~no~~ isn't Brazilian.
8. correct

CHAPTER 2

A3: After You Read (p. 29)

Answers will vary.

Think Critically About Form (p. 30)

1. Statements: a, d, e, f
   Questions: b, c
2. Circle: It, You, she, they, We, it
   Underline: is, Are, Is, are, are, isn't
3. In statements, the subject is first. In questions, the verb is first.

B1: Listening for Form (p. 31)

	QUESTION	STATEMENT
2.		✓
3.	✓	
4.		✓
5.	✓	
6.		✓
7.		✓
8.	✓	
9.		✓
10.		✓

B2: Forming *Yes/No* Questions (p. 32)

A. 2. Are you a smoker?
3. Is your family in the United States?
4. Is your English good?
5. Are you an active person?
6. Is your home big?

B. Answers will vary.

B3: Changing Statements into Questions (p. 32)

2. Is it interesting?
3. Are they friends?
4. Is she a Spanish teacher?
5. Are we late for the party?
6. Is she a spendthrift?

Think Critically About Form (p. 33)

1. Sentences 1b and 2b are *Yes/No* questions. Sentences 1a and 2a are information questions. The information questions begin with *How* and *Where*.
2. Circle: Marcia, Marcia, the classes, the classes
Underline: is, Is, are, Are
Yes, the order of the subject and the verb is the same.

C1: Listening for Form (p. 34)

	YES/NO QUESTIONS	INFORMATION QUESTIONS
2.		✓
3.	✓	
4.		✓
5.	✓	
6.	✓	

C2: Changing Statements into Questions (p. 34)

2. How is the apartment?
3. When is the appointment?
4. Where is the apartment?
5. Who is the manager? OR Who is Mrs. Hewitt?
6. Who are the other roommates? OR Who are Jada and Emily?

C3: Understanding Informal Speech (p. 35)

2. What are
3. When is
4. Who are
5. How is
6. Where is
7. What are
8. Where are

Think Critically About Meaning and Use (p. 36)

1. 1a   2. 2a   3. 2b

D1: Listening for Meaning and Use (p. 37)

2. b   4. a   6. a   8. a   10. b
3. a   5. b   7. b   9. b

D2: Asking If Something Is True (p. 38)

2. Is Julia athletic?   Yes, she is.
3. Are the windows open?   Yes, they are.
4. Is Julia happy?   Yes, she is.
5. Is Julia a bad student?   No, she isn't.
6. Is the shelf neat?   No, it isn't.
7. Is the ball on the bed?   No, it isn't.
8. Is the room messy?   Yes, it is.

D3: Asking for New Information (p. 38)

A. Answers will vary.

B. 2. What is your address?
3. Where are you from?
4. What are your hobbies?
5. Who is your best friend?
6. When is your birthday?

C. Answers will vary.

D4: Contrasting *Yes/No* and Information Questions (p. 39)

2. Are you from Mexico City?
3. Is it hot in Monterrey? OR Is Monterrey hot?
4. Is the neighborhood noisy?
5. Where are the stores?
6. How are the buses?

D5: Responding to *Yes/No* Questions (p. 40)

A. 2. I   3. I   4. F   5. F   6. F

B. Answers will vary. Some examples are:
2. I don't know.   5. Yes.
3. I don't think so.   6. Yeah.
4. Yep.

Think Critically About Meaning and Use (p. 41)

A. 2. a   3. b   4. b

B. 1. We answer Yes/No questions first with either a yes or a no and then with other information, although this is optional.
2. We answer information questions with the information requested in the question. We do not use *yes* or *no* in the answer.

Edit (p. 41)

2. Is ~~happy~~ the teacher happy?
3. Where is Dana ~~is~~?
4. Who are they?
5. correct
6. How are you ~~you~~?
7. Yes, I am.
8. She is 19 years old.

CHAPTER 3

A3: After You Read (p. 45)
Sentences to be checked:
2. ✓   4. ✓   6. ✓   7. ✓

Think Critically About Form (p. 46)
1. Affirmative imperatives: b, d. Negative imperatives: a, c
2. Affirmative imperatives: We use the base form of the verb. Negative imperatives: We use *don't/do not* + base form of the verb.
3. Affirmative imperatives:
   Please bring this contract to Mr. Douglas.
   Rob, take this to the mailroom immediately.
   Rob, call Snyder Supply Company for me, please.
   Rob, please copy this for me.
   Look under these papers and files.
   Go to the third floor.
   Turn right.

   Negative imperatives:
   Do not forget.
   Don't panic.
   Oh, and Rob, don't worry.

B1: Listening for Form (p. 47)

	AFFIRMATIVE	NEGATIVE
2.	✓	
3.	✓	
4.		✓
5.	✓	
6.	✓	
7.		✓
8.		✓
9.	✓	
10.		✓

B2: Working on Imperatives (p. 47)
A. 2. Talk   4. Listen   6. Open   8. Go
3. Take out   5. Read   7. Sit

B. 2. Don't talk to your partner.
3. Don't take out a pencil.
4. Don't listen to your partner's instructions.
5. Don't read Chapter 4.
6. Don't open the door.
7. Don't sit on the couch.
8. Don't go home.

B3: Forming Affirmative and Negative Imperatives (p. 48)
2. Be friendly to clients.
3. Don't call your friends.
4. Be polite.
5. Arrive on time.
6. Don't lose important files.
7. Don't be messy.
8. Help your co-workers.
9. Do your work.
10. Don't forget meetings.

Think Critically About Meaning and Use (p. 49)
d. a command to do something.
c. a warning of danger
b. instructions about how to do something
a. directions to a place

C1: Listening for Meaning and Use (p. 50)
2. warning   6. warning
3. command   7. directions
4. directions   8. command
5. instructions

C2: Giving Commands (p. 51)
A. 2. e   4. f   6. b   8. c
3. h   5. d   7. a

B. Answers will vary.

C3: Understanding Signs (p. 52)
2. Don't smoke   5. Don't take pictures.
3. Don't turn left.   6. Walk.
4. Don't swim.

C4: Working with Prepositions of Location (p. 53)
2. 1. on   5. 1. on
   2. next to   2. on/at
3. 1. on   3. on
   2. across from   4. on/at
4. 1. on   5. next to
   2. behind

C5: Identifying Imperatives (p. 54)
Answers will vary. Some examples are:
work, use, find, circle, talk about, ask, answer, write, compare, look, complete, listen, check, punctuate.

C6: Writing Instructions (p. 54)
A. 2. Boil   4. Lower   6. Serve
3. Add   5. Cook

B. Answers will vary.

Think Critically About Meaning and Use (p. 55)
A. 2. b   3. a   4. a

B. 1. 1, 2, and 4
2. 3

Edit (p. 55)
2. ~~Brings~~ *Bring* a jacket.   6. ~~No~~ *Don't* wear nice clothes.
3. ~~Not~~ *Don't* go to the party.   7. Don't ~~goes~~ *go* out.
4. correct   8. correct
5. ~~Be take~~ *Take* a map.

Part 1 TEST (pp. 57–58)

1. c	5. b	9. is	13. You	17. b
2. b	6. c	10. are	14. It	18. e
3. b	7. b	11. is	15. c	19. d
4. b	8. are	12. Is	16. f	20. a

CHAPTER 4

A3: After You Read (p. 61)

Derek Dobson = studio apartment
Sally and John Freeman = house
Paul and Jenny Rivera = apartment

Think Critically About Form (p. 62)

1. Underline: Paul, John, Toronto
2. Circle: engineer, teacher, city, apartment
3. We use *a* before a consonant sound and *an* before a vowel sound.

B1: Listening for Form (p. 63)

B2: Identifying Nouns (p. 63)

		CONSONANT SOUND	VOWEL SOUND
2.	hospital	✓	
3.	herb		✓
4.	hat	✓	
5.	union	✓	
6.	university	✓	
7.	uncle		✓
8.	umpire		✓

A. 2. C   3. P   4. P   5. C   6. C

B. Answers will vary.

B3: Working on Singular Nouns and *A/An* (p. 64)

Conversation 2
1. a
2. an
3. a

Conversation 3
1. a
2. a

Conversation 4
1. X
2. a
3. X

Conversation 5
1. an
2. An
3. a

Conversation 6
1. An
2. a

Conversation 7
1. a
2. X

Think Critically About Form (p. 65)

1. Underline: teachers, balconies, plants
2. Circle: children, people

C1: Listening for Form (p. 66)

	SINGULAR	PLURAL
2.		✓
3.		✓
4.	✓	
5.		✓
6.	✓	
7.	✓	
8.		✓

C2: Spelling Regular Plural Nouns (p. 66)

2. balconies
3. bedrooms
4. radios
5. boys
6. garages
7. potatoes
8. brushes

C3: Working with Irregular Plural Nouns (p. 66)

2. people
3. men
4. teeth
5. women
6. feet

C4: Pronouncing Regular Plural Nouns (p. 67)

A.

		/s/	/z/	/ɪz/
2.	pencils		✓	
3.	wishes			✓
4.	roommates	✓		
5.	nouns		✓	
6.	maps	✓		

B. 2. /s/   4. /z/   6. /ɪz/   8. /s/
3. /ɪz/   5. /s/   7. /ɪz/

Think Critically About Meaning and Use (p. 68)

1. Sentences a, b, and c have nouns used as subjects. Sentence d does not.
2. d
3. b
4. c

D1: Listening for Meaning and Use (p. 69)

		RECEIVES THE ACTION	DESCRIBES THE SUBJECT
2.	building		✓
3.	apartments		✓
4.	newspaper	✓	
5.	landlord		✓
6.	house	✓	
7.	utilities		✓
8.	utensil		✓
9.	door	✓	
10.	swimmer		✓

D2: Understanding the Functions of Nouns (p. 70)

1. the sink, bread, the laundry
2. the boys
3. island
4. at the park, at school, in Tonga, in the Pacific Ocean

Think Critically About Meaning and Use (p. 71)

A. 2. a   3. b   4. a

B. 1. It doesn't end in *-s* or *-es*.

2. Words that define or describe *father*: *a doctor* in A's question and *a teacher* in B's answer

Edit (p. 71)

2. correct

3. The Watson*s* are here.

4. The ~~childs~~ *children* are happy.

5. correct

6. Eat a*n* apple every day.

7. Kenya is *a* country in Africa.

8. correct

9. ~~A~~ Spain is a beautiful country.

10. correct

11. Marta and Stefan are student*s* in my class.

12. correct

CHAPTER 5

A3: After You Read (p. 74)

2. a   4. b   6. c   8. f
3. g   5. d   7. h

Think Critically About Form (p. 76)

Bottle and *computer* have both singular and plural forms. *Garbage* and *electricity* have only one form.

B1: Listening for Form (p. 77)

	COUNT NOUN	NONCOUNT NOUN
2.		✓
3.		✓
4.	✓	
5.	✓	
6.		✓

B2: Identifying Count and Noncount Nouns (p. 77)

2. pollution—N, problem—C, country—C
3. bicycle—C, pollution—N
4. curtains—C, room—C
5. person—C, office—C, equipment—N
6. newspapers—C, garbage—N

B3: Forming Sentences with Count and Noncount Nouns (p. 78)

2. Energy is not cheap.
3. The computers are not on.
4. The refrigerator door is open.
5. Our air conditioner is not energy efficient.
6. New furniture is expensive.

B4: Working on Count and Noncount Nouns (p. 78)

2. is   3. are   4. Are   5. is   6. Is

Think Critically About Meaning and Use (p. 79)

1. Underline: (Long) hair, Chocolate
   Circle: (gray) hair, chocolates
2. Sentences 1a and 2b are about individual items.
   Sentences 1b and 2a are about more general statements.

C1: Listening for Meaning and Use (p. 80)

		COUNT	NONCOUNT
2.	coffee	✓	
3.	glass		✓
4.	chocolate	✓	
5.	glass	✓	
6.	hair		✓
7.	basketball		✓
8.	paper	✓	

C2: Describing Classroom Objects (p. 81)

Answers will vary.

C3: Thinking About Count and Noncount Nouns (p. 81)

A. Count Nouns, Singular: building, jacket, pencil, sofa, telephone
Count Nouns, Regular Plural: boxes, car radios, computers, flowers, radios
Count Nouns, Irregular Plural: feet, mice, people, teeth, women
Noncount Nouns: furniture, jewelry, mathematics, music, weather

B. Answers will vary.

C4: Distinguishing Count and Noncount Nouns (p. 82)

A. 2. a. N   b. C   5. a. N   b. C
3. a. N   b. C   6. a. C   b. N
4. a. C   b. N

B. Answers will vary.

Think Critically About Meaning and Use (p. 83)

A. 2. a   3. b   4. b

B. 1. Answers will vary. When A uses a plural count noun, B's pronoun and verb need to change as well. For example, A: Where are the <u>flowers</u>? B: <u>They</u> <u>are</u> on the table.

2. B: Are earrings a good gift?

Edit (p. 83)

2. Comb your ~~hairs~~ *hair*.

3. correct

4. Mathematics ~~are~~ *is* easy.

5. correct

6. The furniture ~~are~~ *is* new.

7. ~~A football~~ *Football* is an exciting sport.

8. correct

Part 2 TEST (pp. 85–86)

1. A	5. a	9. NC	13. a	17. b
2. an	6. X	10. NC	14. c	18. b
3. a	7. C	11. C	12. b	19. a
4. X	8. NC	12. b	16. b	20. b

CHAPTER 6

A3: After You Read (p. 89)

Items to be checked:
2. ✓   4. ✓   6. ✓

Think Critically About Form (p. 90)

1. Underline: cars, collar, student, apartment
   Circle: small, red, serious, nice
2. a. Circle: black, red
      Underline: It, cat, collar
   b. Circle: black, red
      Underline: They, cats, collars

The nouns in sentence a are singular. The nouns in sentence b are plural. The form of the adjective does not change.

3. popular (favorites); great (condition); double (bed); nice (apartment); old (house); nice, inexpensive, sunny, quiet, perfect (apartment); serious (student); black (cat); long (tail); red (collar); black (backpack); two (textbooks); basic (Biology); advanced (Calculus);

B1: Listening for Form (p. 91)

	ADJECTIVE	NO ADJECTIVE
2.	✓	
3.	✓	
4.		✓
5.	✓	
6.		✓
7.	✓	
8.		✓

B2: Identifying Adjectives (p. 91)

2. The oatmeal cookies are delicious.
3. The students are intelligent.
4. Amsterdam is a pretty city.
5. The weather is cloudy and rainy.
6. He is a strong athlete.
7. Chocolate cake is on the menu.
8. We are tired and hungry sleepy.

B3: Forming Sentences with Adjectives (p. 92)

A. 2. He is an excellent student.
   3. Buy a new dress.
   4. Hiro is a famous writer.
   5. It is a small apartment.
   6. Don't use red ink.

B. 2. Don't buy an expensive car.
   3. Send them a wedding invitation.
   4. Tell us an interesting story.
   5. She's a university student.
   6. It's an unusual mistake.

Think Critically About Meaning and Use (p. 93)

1. Underline: red, Korean, young, interesting, small, round
2. Quality or opinion: interesting; size: small; age: young; color: red; origin: Korean; shape: round

C1: Listening for Meaning and Use (p. 94)

2. a   3. a   4. a   5. b   6. a

C2: Asking About Qualities and Opinions (p. 94)

Answers will vary. Some examples are:
2. A: How is the library?
   B: It's organized.
3. A: How are the teachers?
   B: They're serious.
4. A: How are the sports teams?
   B: They're fantastic.
5. A: How are the students?
   B: They're friendly.
6. A: How is the computer lab?
   B: It's high-tech.

C3: Understanding Adjectives (p. 95)

A. Quality/Opinion: beautiful, noisy, slow
   Size: large, small, tall
   Age: new, old, young
   Color: orange, red, yellow
   Origin: Brazilian, Italian, Spanish
   Shape: oval, round, square

B. Answers will vary.

C4: Understanding Nouns as Adjectives (p. 95)

A. 2. office   4. milk   6. seat
   3. chocolate   5. calculator

B. 2. gold earring   4. paper plate   6. coffee cup
   3. theater ticket   5. university student

C5: Writing Ads (p. 96)

A. Answers will vary. Some examples are:
   1. white/grey collar
      eyes are grey/small
   2. bright/cheap/quiet/big apartment
      bright/big bedrooms
      quiet students
   3. European/new sofa
      antique/European/low/new table
      antique/European/ classic/new chairs
      low prices
   4. long/yellow/green sweater
      round/yellow/green buttons
      long sleeves

B. Answers will vary.

C. Answers will vary.

Think Critically About Meaning and Use (p. 97)

A. 2. a   3. a   4. a

B. 1. 1. small = size; 2. hard = quality/opinion;
      4. small = size
   2. In 3, *school* is an adjective because it describes *bus*.

Edit (p. 97)

2. correct

3. Buy me a̲n̲ ~~a~~ expensive ring.

4. correct

5. The ~~girl~~ short g̲i̲r̲l̲ ∧ is my friend.

6. correct

7. Bring the b̲i̲g̲ ~~bigs~~ books.

8. Buy him a w̲o̲o̲l̲ ∧ sweater ~~wool~~.

CHAPTER 7

A3: After You Read (p. 101)

2. T   3. T   4. F   5. F   6. T

Think Critically About Form (p. 102)

1. Singular: roommate's
   Plural: roommates'

   The singular noun has an apostrophe + -s. The plural noun has an apostrophe.

2. Underline: brother, brother
   Circle: My, Their

B1: Listening for Form (p. 104)

	POSSESIVE NOUN	POSSESIVE ADJECTIVE	WHOSE
2.			✓
3.	✓		
4.		✓	
5.		✓	
6.		✓	
7.			✓
8.	✓		

B2: Working on Possessive Nouns (p. 104)

2. Brad and Jack's
3. Mr. Miller's
4. teachers'
5. Smiths'
6. children's
7. Tamika's
8. Sasha's

B3: Forming Questions with *Whose* (p. 105)

A. 2a. Whose car is new?
   2b. Whose is old?
   3a. Whose birthday is this month?
   3b. Whose is next month?
   4a. Whose family is large?
   4b. Whose is small?
   5a. Whose apartment is near school?
   5b. Whose is far?

B. Answers will vary.

B4: Working on Possessive Adjectives (p. 105)

2. his   4. our   6. her   8. our
3. Their 5. her   7. His   9. your

Think Critically About Form (p. 106)

1. Underline: My book, their cat
2. Circle: Mine, Theirs
   (*Mine* replaces "my book," and *theirs* replaces "their cat")

C1: Listening for Form (p. 107)

2. a   3. a   4. b   5. b   6. b

C2: Forming Sentences with Possessive Pronouns (p. 107)

2. The red coat is yours.
3. The tickets are his.
4. The chocolate is theirs.
5. The letter is ours.
6. The old newspapers are hers.

C3: Contrasting Possessive Pronouns and Possessive Adjectives (p. 107)

2. ours   4. Her   6. mine   8. yours
3. my   5. hers   7. yours

Think Critically About Meaning and Use (p. 108)

1. Underline: My, Keiko's, their, mine, Mary's, Her brother's
2. b ownership
   a a human relationship
   c a physical characteristic

D1: Listening for Meaning and Use (p. 109)

2. c   4. b   6. b   8. b
3. a   5. b   7. c

D2: Describing Physical Characteristics (p. 109)

Answers will vary.

D3: Identifying Ownership and Family Relationships (p. 110)

A. 2. mine   5. my   8. their   11. her
3. your   6. his   9. Jim and Diane's   12. our
4. Jim's   7. her   10. their

B. 2. Jim's   5. Jim and Diane's
3. Diane's   6. Juan's
4. Diane and Diego's

Think Critically About Form (p. 111)

1. *This* and *that* are singular because the nouns that follow them are singular.
   These and *those* are plural because the nouns that follow them are plural.
2. *This* and *these* are adjectives. *That* and *those* are pronouns. The adjectives come before nouns.
   The pronouns replace adjectives + nouns.

E1: Listening for Form (p. 112)

A. 2. Those   5. This
3. This   6. These
4. That

B. 2. adjective   5. pronoun
3. adjective   6. pronoun
4. pronoun

E2: Building Sentences (p. 112)

Answers will vary. Some examples are:
This cat is yours/small.
This building is yours/a dormitory/small.
That cat is young/yours/small.
That building is yours/a dormitory/small.
These children are young/yours/small.
These pictures are yours/small.
Those children are young/yours/small.
Those pictures are yours/small.

Think Critically About Meaning and Use (p. 113)

1. Underline: This, these, that, That('s), those
2. *This* and *these* refer to objects near the speaker.
   That and *those* refer to objects far from the speaker.

F1: Listening for Meaning and Use (p. 114)

	NEAR	FAR
2.		✓
3.	✓	
4.		✓
5.	✓	
6.	✓	

F2: Talking about Near and Far Objects (p. 114)

A. Answers will vary. Some examples are:
2. These glasses are expensive.
3. This window isn't broken.
4. This clock is silver.
5. These doors are open.
6. These books are thick.

Think Critically About Meaning and Use (p. 115)

A. 2. b   3. b   4. c

B. 1. *That* is used because it refers to an object far away from the speaker.

2. In 3, this would be used if the glass were close to the speaker. In 4, this would be used the apartment were close to the speaker, or if A and B were in the apartment.

Edit (p. 115)

2. Her ~~professors~~ professor's family is from Mexico.

3. correct

4. The records are ~~mines~~ mine.

5. Is this ~~your~~ yours or hers?

6. correct

7. ~~Who's~~ Whose house is this?

8. Wash these ~~dish~~ dishes. OR Wash ~~these~~ this dish.

Part 3 TEST (pp. 117–118)

1. a	5. c	9. a	13. a	17. d
2. a	6. c	10. a	14. a	18. c
3. c	7. b	11. b	15. b	19. a
4. c	8. a	12. c	16. c	20. b

CHAPTER 8

A3: After You Read (p. 121)

2. F   3. T   4. F   5. T   6. T

Think Critically About Form (p. 122)

1. The first part is a present form of the verb *be*. The second part is the base form of the verb + *–ing*.

2. Affirmative:
   line 1: is waking up
   line 2: 'm sitting
   line 5: 's complaining
   line 6: 's reading
   line 6: are sitting
   line 7: is wearing
   line 8: is wearing
   line 9: is standing
   line 9: are carrying and wearing
   line 11: Are they fighting?

3. Negative:
   line 5: isn't listening
   line 10: aren't talking
   line 11: aren't smiling

B1: Listening for Form (p. 124)

2. a   4. b   6. b   8. c
3. b   5. c   7. c

B2: Spelling the Present Continuous (p. 125)

2. am stopping
3. is hugging
4. are sitting
5. are coming
6. are studying
7. are exercising
8. is arguing

B3: Working with Affirmative and Negative Statements (p. 125)

2. It's not/It isn't snowing in Maine.
3. The children aren't playing outside.
4. Celia isn't exercising at the gym.
5. I'm not fixing the car.
6. We aren't/We're not studying.

B4: Writing *Yes/No* Questions (p. 126)

2. Is it raining?
3. Am I passing the course?
4. Are the kids playing outside?
5. Is she listening to a CD?
6. Are you studying Japanese?

B5: Writing Information Questions (p. 126)

2. Who is studying French?
3. Where is Naomi sitting?
4. What is Celia drinking?
5. How is Tom feeling?
6. What is John's father watching?

Think Critically About Meaning and Use (p. 127)

1. a
2. b

C1: Listening for Meaning and Use (p. 128)

	HAPPENING RIGHT NOW	NOT HAPPENING RIGHT NOW
2.		✓
3.	✓	
4.		✓
5.	✓	
6.		✓
7.		✓
8.	✓	

C2: Describing Activities in Progress (p. 128)

2. He's waiting for the bus.
3. He's playing baseball.
4. She's studying.
5. She's cooking.
6. He's playing the guitar.

C3: Talking About Activities in Progress but Not Right Now (p. 129)

A. Answers will vary.

B. Answers will vary

C4: Guessing Activities in Progress (p. 129)

Answers will vary.

C5: Combining Sentences with *And* (p. 130)

Dear Luisa,

Thank you for your letter. We're very busy, too. We're working hard and saving money. Celia is teaching piano at the local high school and giving private lessons on the weekends. I'm finishing my Ph.D. and writing my dissertation. At the moment, Celia is making dinner, and our daughter Lucy is helping her . . .

Think Critically About Meaning and Use (p. 131)

A. 2. b   3. a   4. b

B. 1. 3 and 4

2. Answers will vary.

Edit (p. 131)

Dear Gina,

I'm ~~Stand~~ standing in front of your apartment. Unfortunately, you're not at home, so I am writing you this note. My husband Dan and I are visiting our families. We're ~~live~~ living in San Diego now. Dan is working for a telecommunications company, and I'm looking for a job. What ~~you are~~ are you doing these days? Are you still ~~write~~ writing for the newspaper? Call me at my mother's house and please come visit us!

Miss you,

Holly

CHAPTER 9

A3: After You Read (p. 135)

2. F   Kyla lives alone.
3. F   Kyla 's family lives in Vermont.
4. T
5. T
6. T

Think Critically About Form (p. 136)

1. Circle: I, She, They
   Underline: come, comes, come

The verb form in sentence b ends in -*s*. The verbs in the other two sentences are base forms.

2. Circle: I, He, They
   2a: do not walk
   2b: does not walk
   2c: do not walk.

The negative verb form in 2b uses *does not*. Sentences 2a and 2c use *do not*.

3. Affirmative:
   line 5:   . . . she dances for Ballet Tech Company in New York City.
   line 10: I have ballet class from 10:30 to 12:00.
   line 11: Then we rehearse from 12:00 to 3:30 and 4:30 to 6:00.
   line 15: I go home and make dinner.
   line 16: Then I study or read and go to bed.
   line 19: I live alone.
   line 19: I have a tiny apartment in Manhattan.
   line 25: I have a lot of friends.
   line 26: They call or visit a lot.
   line 28: They come here, or I go home twice a month.
   line 32: I have a tutor for a couple of classes.
   line 33: For my other classes, I work by myself.
   line 33: But I communicate with students in my home high school on the telephone or on the computer.
   line 38: We have three weeks of vacation a year.
   line 39: I study a lot then, too.
   line 46: But I live in New York City, so it's not hard to find things to do.

   Negative:
   line 46: I don't have much free time.

B1: Listening for Form (p. 137)

2. a   4. b   6. a   8. b
3. c   5. b   7. b

B2: Working on Simple Present Affirmative Statements (p. 138)

2. lives   5. has   8. goes   11. watch
3. shares   6. fixes   9. exercises 12. make
4. drive   7. finish 10. drives

B3: Contrasting Simple Present Affirmative and Negative Statements (p. 138)

2. Trees don't lose their leaves in the summer. They lose their leaves in the fall.
3. The moon doesn't go around the sun. It goes around Earth.
4. Panda bears don't eat bananas. They eat bamboo.

5. An astronomer doesn't study the ocean. He/She studies the stars.
6. Water doesn't boil at 100° F. It boils at 212° F.

B4: Pronouncing the Third Person -s and -es (p. 139)

		/s/	/z/	/ɪz/
2.	smells		✓	
3.	washes			✓
4.	leaves		✓	
5.	notices			✓
6.	stops	✓		
7.	pays		✓	
8.	teaches			✓

Think Critically About Form (p. 140)

1. Circle: you, she, they
   A form of *do* (*do* or *does*) comes before each subject.
2. Sentence b uses the third-person singular form *Does*.
3. Underline: like, watch, have.

   No, we don't add an ending to the verb. It is the base form.

C1: Listening for Form (p. 141)

2. c   4. b   6. c   8. a
3. b   5. b   7. c

C2: Working on Simple Present *Yes/No* Questions (p. 141)

A. 2. Do   4. Do   6. Do   8. Does
   3. Do   5. Does   7. Does

B. Answers will vary.

C3: Asking and Answering *Yes/No* Questions (p. 142)

A. 2. Does   4. Does   6. Does   8. Does
   3. Do   5. Does   7. Do

B. 2. No, she doesn't.   6. No, he doesn't.
   3. Yes, they do.   7. No, they don't.
   4. No, it doesn't.   8. No, she doesn't.
   5. No, it doesn't.

Think Critically About Form (p. 143)

1. 1a and 2a are *Yes/No* questions. 1b and 2b are information questions.
2. *Yes/No* questions begin with *Do* or *Does*. Information questions begin with a *wh*-word.

D1: Listening for Form (p. 144)

2. Who   6. Who does
3. How do   7. When does
4. Where do   8. What
5. What do

D2: Working on Information Questions (p. 144)

A. 2. What does Lee's brother study?
   3. When do Lynn and Paulo begin work?
   4. How does Larry drive?
   5. Who drives his car to work?
   6. Why does Koji take a bus?

B. Answers will vary.

D3: Working on *Who/What* Questions (p. 145)

A. 1. e   2. f   3. a   4. b   5. c   6. d

B. Answers will vary. Some examples are:
   1. Who performs magic tricks?
   2. Who performs surgery?
      What does a surgeon do?
   3. Who repairs cars?
      What does an auto mechanic do?
   4. Who bakes cakes, cookies, and other sweets?
      What does a pastry chef bake?
   5. Who explains historic sites to tourists?
      What does a tour guide do?
   6. Who makes and sells eyeglasses?
      What does an optician do?

C. Answers will vary.

Think Critically About Meaning and Use (p. 146)

1. b   2. c   3. a   4. *makes*

E1: Listening for Meaning and Use (p. 147)

	HABITS AND ROUTINES	FACTUAL INFORMATION	FEELINGS AND SENSES
2.		✓	
3.	✓		
4.		✓	
5.			✓
6.		✓	
7.	✓		
8.			✓

E2: Describing Routines (p. 148)

A. 2. makes   5. corrects   8. eat   11. gives
   3. clean   6. go   9. call   12. watches
   4. shops   7. dance   10. take

B. Answers will vary. Some examples are:
   Saturday
   Who makes a list of all their weekend activities?
   When do Alex and Naomi clean the house?
   What does Alex do on Saturday afternoon?
   When does Alex shop for the week's groceries?
   What does Naomi do on Saturday afternoon?
   When does Naomi correct her students' homework?
   Where do they go on Saturday night?

   Sunday
   What do Alex and Naomi do on Sunday morning?
   When do they call their parents?
   What do they do on Sunday afternoon?
   When do they take a long walk in the park?
   What does Naomi do on Sunday evening?
   When does Alex watch a football game?

C. Answers will vary.

E3: Linking Ideas with Sequence Words (p. 149)

A. Answers will vary.

B. Answers will vary.

E4: Describing Routines (p. 150)

A. 2. What do they examine?
3. How do they dig?
4. Why is their job difficult?
5. Where do nautical archeologists work?
6. What do they use in their work?

B. Answers will vary.

E5: Writing a Description (p. 150)

A. 2. has   4. has   6. loves   8. feel
3. look   5. weighs   7. hate

B. Answers will vary.

Think Critically About Meaning and Use (p. 151)

A. 2. c   3. a   4. b

B. 1. 4 uses a stative verb: *owns*

2. Stative verbs express states and conditions; action verbs express actions.

Edit (p. 151)

goes
Sun-hee ~~go~~ to a college in Southern California. This is
seems
her freshman year, and everything ~~seem~~ new and exciting
has
to her. After three months at the college, she ~~have~~ many
doesn't   _gets_
friends and ~~don't~~ feel lonely. She works hard and ~~get~~ good
enjoys
grades, but she also ~~enjoy~~ life with her friends. On Thursday
study
mornings they ~~studies~~ together at the library, but in the
_do_
afternoons they take long walks or ~~doing~~ other outdoor
activities. Saturday morning is her favorite part of the
week. Her friends sleep late on Saturday, but Sun-hee
gets
~~get~~ up at 7:00 and goes horseback riding in a forest near
the college.

CHAPTER 10

A3: After You Read (p. 154)

2. F   3. T   4. F   5. T   6. T

Think Critically About Form (p. 156)

1. Underline: usually, always, often, rarely
2. In the sentences with *be*, the adverb of frequency is after the verb.
3. In the sentences with other verbs, the adverb of frequency is before the verb.

B1: Listening for Form (p. 158)

2. usually   5. generally
3. often   6. almost always
4. never   7. frequently

B2: Forming Sentences with Adverbs of Frequency (p. 158)

2. I don't usually watch TV.
3. She is always on time.
4. Rick rarely eats lunch.
5. Generally, we don't work late. OR We generally don't work late.
6. She never drinks coffee.

B3: Positioning Adverbs of Frequency (p. 159)

2. He always needs a lot of time to get ready.
3. He almost always spends 30 minutes in the shower.
4. He is never on time for work.
5. He usually stays out late with his friends. OR Usually, he stays out late with his friends.
6. He rarely goes to bed before 2:00 A.M.

B4: Forming *Yes/No* Questions with Adverbs of Frequency (p. 159)

A. 2. Do your friends always remember your birthday?
3. Do you almost always do your homework?
4. Are you generally in a good mood?
5. Do you usually take the bus to school?
6. Do you and your friends sometimes go to the movies?

B. Answers will vary.

Think Critically About Meaning and Use (p. 160)

1. Underline: usually, rarely, never, always
2. 100%   d. (always)
            a. (usually)
            b. (rarely)
   0%   c. (never)

C1: Listening for Meaning and Use (p. 161)

2. Mark   5. Erica
3. Mark   6. Erica
4. Mark

C2: Asking About Health Habits (p. 162)

A. Answers will vary.

B. Answers will vary.

C3: Expressing Opposites (p. 162)

Answers will vary. Some examples are:
2. It often/frequently rains in tropical areas of the world.
3. People rarely/seldom/almost never live for more than 100 years.
4. It is hardly ever hot in Canada in October.

C4: Asking Questions About Frequency (p. 163)

A. 2. How often do you go to a nightclub?
3. How often do you talk on your cell phone?
4. How often do you go to a bookstore?
5. How often do you study in the library?
6. How often do you visit your family?
7. How often do you take a bus?
8. How often do you do your laundry?

B. Answers will vary.

C5: Rephrasing Adverbs of Frequency (p. 164)

A. Answers will vary. Some examples are:
2. His co-workers never ask him to go to lunch.
3. He hardly ever/seldom talks to people in the office.
4. Alan rarely/almost never helps people.
5. Alan rarely remembers his coworkers' birthdays.
6. Alan's boss always likes his work.
7. Alan often cancels his vacation.
8. Alan always gets a big raise.

B. Answers will vary.

Think Critically About Meaning and Use (p. 165)

A. 2. a   3. b   4. c

B. 1. Answers will vary, *Some examples are: Yes, and he never complains about it. / Yes, he never does it late.*

2. Answers will vary. Some examples are: *Does your boss like this? / Why does this happen? / That's not good. What does your boss say?*

Edit (p. 165)

2. He ∧ gets up ~~rarely~~ on time. *(rarely inserted)*

3. correct

4. How often ∧ you call home? *(do inserted)*

5. I don't ~~never~~ study at night. OR I ~~don't~~ never study at night. *(ever inserted)*

6. You ~~always~~ aren't ∧ on time. *(always inserted)*

7. Do you ~~walk~~ usually ∧ to work? *(walk inserted)*

8. They ∧ almost always at home. OR They ∧ almost always at home. *('re / are inserted)*

Part 4 TEST (pp. 167–168)

1. b	7. a	13. is losing	17. b
2. b	8. c	14. are sitting	18. c
3. c	9. c	15. are studying	19. a
4. a	10. a		20. d
5. b	11. c	16. are having	
6. b	12. a		

CHAPTER 11

A3: After You Read (p. 171)

2. c   3. e   4. f   5. a   6. b

Think Critically About Form (p. 172)

1. They are affirmative. Subjects: pyramids (plural), temple (singular)
2. They are negative. The word *not* comes after the verb.
3. line 7: The pyramids were tombs for the pharaohs.
   line 9: The Egyptian temples were very special places, too.
   line 14: The six parts of a temple were : . . .
   line 18: The gate was the entrance at the front of the temple.
   line 20: The courtyard was a large open room . . .
   line 21: Many pictures . . . were on the walls of the courtyard.
   line 23: The temple courtyard was open to ordinary people only on special days.
   line 26: The first hall was a large, dark room.
   line 27: It was light only in the center aisle.
   line 27: This hall was full of columns . . .
   line 30: The second hall was full of columns, too.
   line 31: It was very dark.
   line 31: It was open only to priests and the pharaoh.
   line 33: The sanctuary was the most special . . .
   line 34: It was a dark and mysterious place.
   line 36: . . . this room was open only to priests and the pharaoh.
   line 37: A statue of the god was in the middle of the sanctuary.
   line 39: The sacred lake was a pool of water . . .
   line 40: The water from the sacred lake was important for special rituals.

B1: Listening for Form (p. 174)

B2: Working on Affirmative Statements (p. 174)

	WAS	WASN'T	WERE	WEREN'T
2.		✓		
3.				✓
4.			✓	
5.			✓	
6.	✓			
7.	✓			
8.		✓		

2. was   4. was   6. were   8. was
3. were   5. was   7. were

B3: Writing Affirmative and Negative Statements (p. 175)

2. Cleopatra wasn't a Persian general. She was an Egyptian queen.
3. Columbus wasn't a lawyer. He was an explorer.
4. Picasso and Rembrandt weren't astronomers. They were artists.
5. William Shakespeare wasn't a French writer. He was an English writer.
6. Cervantes wasn't an American inventor. He was a Spanish writer.
7. Marie Curie and Albert Einstein weren't philosophers. They were scientists.
8. Beethoven wasn't a German king. He was a composer.

B4: Forming *Yes/No* Questions (p. 176)

A. 2. Were you a good student?
3. Was your mother a housewife?
4. Was your hometown large?
5. Were your teachers friendly?
6. Was your home near a beach?

B. Answers will vary

B5: Forming Information Questions (p. 176)

A. 2. Who was Alexander the Great?
3. When was the American Revolution?
4. Where were the Mongols from?
5. Who were Marie Curie and Albert Einstein?
6. What were the pyramids?

B. 2. He was a Greek military leader.
   3. It was in the 18th century.
   4. They were from Mongolia.
   5. They were famous scientists.
   6. They were the tombs of pharaohs.

Think Critically About Meaning and Use (p. 177)

1. Situations that existed in the past: a, c, d, e, f
   Situations that exist in the present: b
2. c, d, e Underline: Yesterday (c.), Twenty years ago (d.), last year (e.)

C1: Listening for Meaning and Use (p. 178)

	PAST	PRESENT
2.		✓
3.	✓	
4.	✓	
5.		✓
6.	✓	

C2: Using Past Time Expressions with *Was/Were* (p. 178)

2. were/weren't   5. was/wasn't
3. was/wasn't   6. was/wasn't
4. was/wasn't

C3: Asking Questions About Frequency (p. 179)

See Appendix 12 of the Student Book.

C4: Guessing About the Past (p. 180)

Answers will vary.

C5: Talking About Your Past (p. 180)

A. Answers will vary.

B. Answers will vary.

C6: Describing Places in the Past (p. 180)

Answers will vary.

A. Think Critically About Meaning and Use (p. 181)

A. 2. a   3. b   4. b

B. 1. A's question is simple past. Answers B and C are simple present, so they don't answer A's question.)

   2. Answers will vary. Some examples are: *Maybe it wasn't Marta. / Maybe it was Marta in a wig! / Was it really Marta?*

Edit (p. 181)

My best friend in elementary school ~~is~~ ^{was} Hanna. We ~~was~~ ^{were} very close friends. Hanna ∧ ^{was} born in Seoul in 1984. Her parents ~~was~~ ^{were} teachers, and they ∧ ^{were} very kind people. Their house was very beautiful. Her grandparents were also very kind, but ~~they're~~ ^{they were} very old. Hanna's little brother was very funny. His toys ∧ ^{were} always on the living-room floor and his stuffed animal ∧ ^{was} always with him. He ~~not~~ ^{wasn't} naughty like my little brother.

CHAPTER 12

A3: After You Read (p. 184)

Think Critically About Form (p. 186)

1. *-d*

	EIGHTEENTH CENTURY (1700s)	NINETEENTH CENTURY (1800s)
2.	✓	
3.	✓	
4.		✓
5.		✓
6.	✓	

2. *-ed*
3. No, they don't.
4. line 26: *did not need*

A simple past negative form has three parts: *did*, the verb, and *not*.

B1: Listening for Form (p. 188)

2. a   4. b   6. b   8. a
3. b   5. b   7. a

B2: Working on Regular Simple Past Verbs (p. 188)

2. opened   7. lifted   12. smiled
3. walked   8. started   13. exclaimed
4. did not want 9. finished   14. handed
5. wanted   10. stopped
6. asked   11. looked

B3: Working on Irregular Simple Past Verbs (p. 189)

2. bought   5. spent   8. ate
3. took   6. saw   9. found
4. went   7. wore   10. met

B4: Contrasting Negative and Affirmative Simple Past Statements (p. 189)

2. In the 1700s upper-class men and women didn't cover their wigs with black powder. They covered them with white powder.
3. In the 1700s aristocratic French women did not have simple hairstyles. They had elaborate hairstyles.
4. French women did not use hairspray on their hair. They used paste.
5. Napoleon did not own hundreds of hats. He owned hundreds of gloves.

B5: Pronouncing Final *-ed* (p. 190)

A.

		/t/	/d/	/ɪd/
2.	stopped	✓		
3.	waited			✓
4.	knocked	✓		
5.	gained		✓	
6.	borrowed		✓	
7.	helped	✓		
8.	hated			✓

B. 2. /t/   6. /t/
3. /d/   7. /t/
4. /ɪd/   8. /ɪd/
5. /d/

B6: Changing the Simple Present to the Simple Past (p. 191)

A.   Teresa woke up at 7:00 and took a shower. Then she dried her hair and brushed her teeth. She cooked a light breakfast and drank a cup of coffee. She waited for her friend Eva on the corner, and they walked to the office together. On the way, they discussed their jobs and planned their day. At. 8:45 they arrived at the office and started their day. Teresa worked hard all day, and after work, she exercised and lifted weights at the gym. She got home at 7:00 and prepared a simple meal. After dinner, she relaxed and listened to music. Then she watched the evening news and went to bed.

B.

	REGULAR		IRREGULAR
/t/	/d/	/ɪd/	
brushed	dried	waited	took
cooked	planned	started	drank
walked	arrived	lifted	got
discussed	exercised		went
worked	prepared		
relaxed	listened		
watched			

Think Critically About Form (p. 192)

1. 1b and 2b. We know this because *Did* appears in the questions.
2. Sentence 2b. *Did* comes before the subject. The base form of the verb follows the subject.
3. Sentence 2a. Did comes between the *wh-* word and the subject. The base form of the verb follows the subject.

C1: Listening for Form (p. 193)

	DO	DOES	DID	Ø
2.				✓
3.			✓	
4.		✓		
5.			✓	
6.	✓			

C2: Forming Simple Past *Yes/No* Questions and Short Answers (p. 194)

A. 2. Did Carl buy a shirt yesterday? Yes, he did.
3. Did Rosa go to the hairdresser's? No, she went to a shoe store.
4. Did they eat burgers for lunch? No, they ate pizza.
5. Did they look at dolls? No, they looked at trucks.
6. Did they meet their friends? Yes, they did.

B. Answers will vary.

C. Answers will vary.

C3: Working on Information Questions (p. 195)

2. What did Carol make?
3. When did Carol graduate from college?
4. Who worked for a fashion designer?
5. Who taught her the latest fashions?
6. Who loved Carol's work?
7. What did Carol photograph?
8. When did Carol win a prize?

C4: Understanding Informal Speech (p. 196)

2. did you   4. Did he
3. did he   5. Did you

Think Critically About Meaning and Use (p. 197)

1. a
2. b

D1: Listening for Meaning and Use (p. 198)

	PAST	PRESENT
2.	✓	
3.	✓	
4.		✓
5.		✓
6.	✓	
7.	✓	
8.		✓

D2: Referring to Past Time Expressions (p. 198)

A. Answers will vary. Some examples are:
2. When did you see your friends?
3. When did you go to the movies?
4. When did you eat pizza?
5. When did you take a test?
6. When did you finish high school?

B. Answers will vary.

C. Answers will vary.

D3: Connecting Events in the Past (p. 199)

2. Then, she burned her shirt.
3. Next, she dropped the coffee pot.
4. Then, she missed the bus.
5. When she arrived at work, she saw a sign on the door.
6. When she told her story at work the next day, they laughed.

D4: Writing About Events in the Past (p. 200)

Answers will vary.

D5: Talking About the Past (p. 200)

A. Answers will vary. Some examples are:
2. Where did people work?
3. How long did people go to school?
4. What did people eat?
5. What did people wear?
6. How did families live?
7. How did people communicate?
8. What did people do for entertainment?

B. Answers will vary.

A. Think Critically About Meaning and Use (p. 201)

A. 2. a   3. c   4. a

B. 1. Choice "a" isn't the answer because it isn't logical: 10-year-old boys don't usually drive people to school.

2. 1. I drove my ten-year-old brother to school. 2. I did my homework.

Edit (p. 201)

I ~~graduate~~ *graduated* from high school in 1995. My high school years ~~are~~ *were* very difficult. For one thing, my school ~~were~~ *was* very far from my house, so I didn't ~~went~~ *go* out with my friends very often. In addition, my parents didn't like my friends. They worried about me, and they always ~~ask~~ *asked* me lots of questions. Where ∧*did* you ~~went~~ *go* last night? Who ∧*were* you with? What time did you get home? I hated all of those questions. Sometimes I didn't ~~told~~ *tell* the truth. To be honest, I ~~feeled~~ *felt* bad about lying.

CHAPTER 13

A3: After You Read (p. 205)

2. F The Chicago fire burned for three days.
3. F The fire destroyed 18,000 buildings.
4. F The hot sun heated the molasses and caused the explosion.
5. T
6. T

Think Critically About Form (p. 206)

1. The two words are *was/were* and the base form of the verb + *ing*.
2. line 12: was burning
   line 15: was burning
   line 23: was shining
   line 24: were enjoying
   line 27: was sitting
   line 33: was spreading
3. It has three words: *were, not,* and the base form of the verb + *-ing*.

B1: Listening for Form (p. 208)

2. b   3. c   4. c   5. b   6. b

B2: Forming Affirmative and Negative Past Continuous Statements (p. 208)

2. Marta and Derek were playing chess. They were not watching TV.
3. Jenny was studying for a history test. She was not planning Andre's party.
4. Toshio and Ana were sitting at home. They were not dining in a French restaurant
5. Robin was exercising at home. She was not jogging in the park.
6. Mark was texting his brother. He was not making dinner.

B3: Building Past Continuous *Yes/No* Questions (p. 209)

A. Answers will vary. Some examples are:
Was she studying yesterday/this morning?
Was she practicing at 5:00 P.M./yesterday/this morning?
Was it raining at 5:00 P.M./yesterday/this morning?
Were the children studying at 5:00 P.M./yesterday/this morning?
Were Susan and Victor studying at 5:00 P.M./ yesterday/this morning?
Were Susan and Victor practicing at 5:00 P.M./yesterday/this morning?
Were the children practicing at 5:00 P.M./yesterday/this morning?

B. Answers will vary.

B4: Working on Past Continuous Information Questions (p. 209)

2. was traveling
3. were you sitting
4. were you doing
5. were they acting
6. were they doing

Think Critically About Meaning and Use (p. 210)

1. a and b. The form of the verb is past continuous.
2. c. The form of the verb is simple past.

C1: Listening for Meaning and Use (p. 211)

	ACTIVITY IN PROGRESS	ACTION NOT IN PROGRESS
2.		✓
3.	✓	
4.		✓
5.	✓	
6.		✓

C2: Describing a Past Event (p. 212)

2. was raining
3. was blowing
4. began
5. started
6. were taking
7. was describing
8. noticed
9. saw
10. was burning
11. fell
12. hit
13. survived

C3: Describing Activities in Progress (p. 213)

A. First Story: was shining, were singing, was walking, was singing
Second Story: was blowing, were watching, was chasing, were running away, were screaming

B. Answers will vary. Some examples are:
The sun was shining and people were enjoying the good weather. Children were playing in the park. A street musician was playing the guitar.

C4: Writing about Simultaneous Activities (p. 214)

2. were playing basketball
3. was talking on the telephone
4. was studying in the library
5. were running/jogging
6. were taking a test

Think Critically About Meaning and Use (p. 215)

A. 2. a   3. c   4. a

B. 1. In 2, B uses the past continuous to describe an activity in progress at a specific time: *the sun was shining* [this morning]. In 4, B uses the past continuous to describe two activities in progress at the same time: [last night] *trying to study / playing loud music.*

2. Speaker A uses the simple past because "waking up" is not a continuous action. It happens at a specific time and does not continue.

Edit (p. 215)

2. correct

3. He ~~wasn't wanting~~ *didn't want* any food.

4. We looked up and they ~~are~~ *were* coming.

5. We were working while the children ~~are~~ *were* watching TV.

6. I didn't go because I ~~was having~~ *had* a bad cold.

Part 5 TEST (pp. 217–218)

1. c	7. a	12. was	15. c
2. a	8. b	talking	16. d
3. c	9. ran	13. were	17. b
4. c	10. started	living	18. a
5. b	11. read	14. was	19. c
6. a		looking	20. b

CHAPTER 14

A3: After You Read (p. 220)

2. T   3. T   4. F   5. F   6. T

Think Critically About Form (p. 222)

1. Underline: map, map, museum, taxis, drivers
Circle: art, food, food

2.

	A/AN	THE	Ø
before singular count nouns	✓	✓	
before plural count nouns		✓	✓
before noncount nouns		✓	✓

B1: Listening for Form (p. 223)

2. a   5. an   8. Ø
3. Ø   6. The   9. a
4. the   7. The   10. an

B2: Forming Sentences with *A/An* or No Article (p. 224)

2. I love Thai food.
3. He is working on a university degree.
4. Celia bought new furniture.
5. My friends rented a house in San Antonio.
6. Rosa met a wonderful man.
7. A guidebook is a book for tourists.
8. Keiko doesn't like museums.
9. Paris is a beautiful city.
10. New cars are expensive.

B3: Working with Indefinite and Definite Articles (p. 225)

2. a boy   7. a new store
3. X   8. a woman
4. an interesting book   9. a university
5. X   10. an expensive car
6. an answer

B4: Choosing the Correct Article (p. 225)

2. c   4. c   6. a   8. a, b
3. b, c   5. b, c   7. c

Think Critically About Meaning and Use (p. 226)

1. Underline: a (great) movie, The movie, an (English) soldier, The soldier
2. a and c
3. b and d

C1: Listening for Meaning and Use (p. 227)

		FIRST MENTION	SECOND MENTION
2.	trip	✓	
3.	tour	✓	
4.	tour		✓
5.	guide	✓	
6.	trip		✓
7.	accident	✓	
8.	park		✓

C2: Using Indefinite and Definite Articles (p. 228)

1. 2. a   4. The
   3. a   5. the
2. 1. the   3. an
   2. the
3. 1. Ø   3. a
   2. a   4. a

C3: Contrasting Indefinite and Definite Articles (p. 228)

A. 2. the   4. the
   3. a   5. The

B. 2. S   4. S
   3. NS   5. S

Think Critically About Meaning and Use (p. 229)

A. 2. a   3. c   4. c

B. 1. The word the completes B's sentence. We understand that one of the two gifts is a specific CD, so we need a definite article.

2. Because B is talking about a specific recipe: the recipe for A's eggs.

Edit (p. 229)

2. Prague is ~~the~~ *a* wonderful city.

3. Is ~~a~~ *the* telephone call for me?

4. correct

5. Museums are fun on ~~the~~ rainy days.

6. correct

CHAPTER 15

A3: After You Read (p. 232)

3. ✓ 4. ✓ 6. ✓

Think Critically About Form (p. 234)

1. Circle: communities, residents, money, stuff, traffic, work

2.

QUANTITY EXPRESSIONS	PLURAL COUNT NOUNS	NONCOUNT NOUNS
many	✓	
much		✓
a lot of	✓	✓
some	✓	✓
a little		✓
a few	✓	

B1: Listening for Form (p. 236)

2. no   5. a lot of
3. Many   6. a few
4. any

B2: Replacing *A Lot of* with *Much* and *Many* (p. 236)

On the street, you hear many languages. People here don't have much money, but they are very friendly. For example, Mr. Lee, the Chinese grocer, doesn't speak much Spanish, but he always says *buenos días* to his Spanish-speaking customers. The residents also celebrate many holidays. In February, many residents go to the Chinese New Year celebration. And no one does much work on *Cinco de Mayo*, a Mexican holiday. Come to my neighborhood and you can experience many different cultures in one afternoon.

B3: Working on Quantity Expressions (p. 237)

2. any   5. a lot of   8. much   11. much
3. no   6. any   9. no
4. some   7. many   10. a lot of

B4: Working on *A Few* and *A Little* (p. 237)

Conversation 1	*Conversation 2*
2. a little	1. a few
3. a few	2. a little
4. a few	3. a few
5. a few	4. a little
6. a little	

B5: Forming *Yes/No* Questions with Quantity Expressions (p. 238)

A. 2. Do sustainable communities have much crime?
3. Does a sustainable community have many fast food stores?
4. Do a lot of people in a sustainable community telecommute?
5. Do many people live in sustainable communities?
6. Do sustainable communities have much traffic?
7. Do some sustainable communities have a lot of bike paths?
8. Does this sustainable community have a lot of residents?

B. 2. b   4. a, b   6. a   8. b

3. a   5. a, b   7. a,b

B6: Asking Questions with *How Much* or *How Many* (p. 239)

A. 2. How many   6. How much
3. How much   7. How many
4. How much   8. How much
5. How many

B. Answers will vary. Some examples are:
How much public transportation does the town have?
How many shops does the neighborhood have?
How much traffic does the neighborhood have?

Think Critically About Meaning and Use (p. 240)

1. Underline: many, a lot of, a few, no, no, a lot of, much
2. large numbers or amounts: many, a lot of, much
   small numbers or amounts: a few, a little
3. The expression *no* means *none*.

C1: Listening for Meaning and Use (p. 241)

	LARGE QUANTITIES	SMALL QUANTITIES	NONE
2.	✓		
3.	✓		
4.			✓
5.	✓		
6.		✓	
7.	✓		
8.		✓	

C2: Expressing Opinions with Quantity Expressions (p. 242)

Answers will vary. Some examples are:
2. a lot of homework   6. a lot of creativity
3. a lot of patience   7. any trouble in their life
4. a lot of books   8. any parks
5. some repairs

C3: Asking and Answering Questions about Quantity (p. 242)

A. Answers will vary. Some examples are:
2. much/any/a lot of
3. much/any/a lot of
4. many/any/a lot of
5. much/a lot of

(*Note*: As everyone needs sleep, native speakers would not tend to ask *Do you need* <u>any</u> *sleep?*)
6. much/a lot of

(Note: Native speakers would not normally use *any* in this question. It is more common for them to ask *Do you drink coffee?*)
7. much/any/a lot of
8. much/a lot of/any

B. Answers will vary.

C4: Comparing Cities and Small Towns (p. 243)

Answers will vary. Some examples are:

BIG CITIES

Advantages:
Big cities have a lot of job opportunities.
Big cities have a lot of different cultures.
Big cities have many forms of public transportation.

Disadvantages:
Big cities have a lot of crime.
Big cities have a lot of residents.
Housing costs a lot of money in big cities.

SMALL TOWNS

Advantages:
Small towns have many friendly people.
Small towns don't have much crime.
Small towns have a lot of fresh air.

Disadvantages:
Small towns don't have many theaters or museums.
Small towns don't have a lot of different restaurants.
Small towns don't have a lot of job opportunities.

C5: Answering a Survey with Quantity Expressions (p. 244)

Answers will vary.

Think Critically About Meaning and Use (p. 245)

A. 2. a   3. c   4. a

B. 1. 1 and 3 refer to large quantities; 2 and 4 refer to small quantities.

  2. Answers will vary.

Edit (p. 245)

As a first-year university student, I had ~~much~~ *many* problems.
I didn't have ~~no~~ *any* friends and I was very lonely. I also didn't
speak a lot ∧*of* English then, so I had ~~a few~~ *a lot of* trouble
communicating. At the beginning ∧*a* lot of things were
strange, like the food and the subways. Luckily, I met a
~~little~~ *few* students from my country and they helped me. Today
I know ~~much~~ *many/a lot of* people. I also speak more English, so now I
don't have any problems.

CHAPTER 16

A3: After You Read (p. 249)

2. F   3. F   4. F   5. F   6. F

Think Critically About Form (p. 250)

1. Circle: (a new) painting, houses, stores, (a gray) circle
2. *There is* comes before a singular noun. *There are* comes before a plural noun.
3. line 11: There's no other painting
   line 15: There isn't enough security
   line 19: There are no houses
   line 20: There aren't any stores
   line 21: There are dark gray squares
   line 40: There are always many different opinions

B1: Listening for Form (p. 251)

2. b   3. b   4. a   5. a   6. b

B2: Writing Negative Statements with *There Is/There Are* (p. 252)

2. There aren't any stores on this street. There are no stores on this street.

3. There isn't a hospital in our town. There is no hospital in our town.
4. There isn't any crime in that neighborhood. There is no crime in that neighborhood.
5. There aren't any children in the park. There are no children in the park.
6. There isn't a jewelry store at the mall. There is no jewelry store at the mall.
7. There isn't a bus stop on my street. There is no bus stop on my street.
8. There aren't any noisy people in this neighborhood. There are no noisy people in this neighborhood.

B3: Working on *There Is/There Are* (p. 253)

Answers will vary. Some examples are:
2. There is a supermarket in picture A. There isn't a supermarket in picture B.
3. There is a stop sign in picture A. There isn't a stop sign in picture B.
4. There is a movie theater in picture B. There isn't a movie theater in picture A.
5. There is a drugstore in picture A. There isn't a drugstore in picture B.
6. There are some children in picture B. There aren't any children in picture A.
7. There is a bakery in picture B. There isn't a bakery in picture A.

B4: Writing *Yes/No* and Information Questions with *There Is/There Are* (p. 254)

2. Are there any public telephones in the library?
3. How many students are there at this school?
4. Is there a bank on Green Street?
5. Are there any expensive hotels downtown?
6. How many hours of homework are there every night?

B5: Writing Statements and Questions with *There Is/There Are* (p. 254)

A. Answers will vary. Some examples are:
  2. There are a lot of children in my neighborhood.
  3. There aren't a lot of interesting shows on TV tonight.
  4. There is a good article in the newspaper today.

B. Answers will vary.

Think Critically About Meaning and Use (p. 255)

1. Sentence a. It introduces the noun *patient* with the indefinite article *a*.
2. Sentence b. It refers to a specific patient and uses the definite article *the*.

C1: Listening for Meaning and Use (p. 256)

	INTRODUCES A NOUN (*THERE IS/ARE*)	EXPRESSES POSSESSION (*THEIR*)	POINTS TO A NOUN (ADVERB *THERE*)
2.	✓		
3.	✓		
4.			✓
5.		✓	
6.			✓

C2: Writing Facts (p. 256)

2. There is one month with 28 days.
3. There are 24 hours in a day.
4. There are nine planets in the solar system.
5. There is one sunrise every day.
6. There is one full moon every month.
7. There are 100 pennies in a dollar.
8. There are 50 states in the Unites States.

C3: Describing a Picture (p. 257)

Answers will vary.

C4: Describing a Neighborhood (p. 258)

A. Answers will vary.

C5: Combining Sentences with *But* (p. 259)

There's a new student in our class. Her first name is Ana, but I don't know her last name. Her English seems pretty good, but she never says much in class. She's from South America. There are four students in my class from Venezuela, but Ana is the only one from Argentina.

Think Critically About Meaning and Use (p. 260)

A. 2. a   3. b   4. c   5.a   6.c

B. 1. B says "No, there aren't.

2. The word *it* completes B's sentence. It refers back to "their car."

Edit (p. 261)

2. correct

3. ~~Is~~ Are there any oranges in the kitchen?

4. Are there any English ~~class~~ classes in the morning?/ ~~Are~~ Is there ~~any~~ an English class in the morning?

5. correct

6. correct

7. There are some books here.

8. There aren't ~~no~~ any chairs./There ~~aren't~~ are no chairs.

9. ~~There are~~ Are there any students in the hall?

10. Look in the refrigerator. Are there any sandwiches?

Part 6 TEST (pp. 263–264)

1. c	5. a	9. b	13. a	17. c
2. b	6. b	10. a	14. an	18. b
3. b	7. c	11. b	15. the	19. d
4. b	8. a	12. a	16. The	20. e

CHAPTER 17

A3: After You Read (p. 267)

2. T   3. F   4. F   5. T   6. T

Think Critically About Form (p. 268)

1. Singular: Holy Jones is going to be . . .
Plural: The New Jersey Diamonds are going to play . . .
The base form of the verb follows *to*.

2. line 4:   aren't going to win
line 14:   isn't going to play
line 17:   'm not going to lie
We add *not* after the verb *be*.

B1: Listening for Form (p. 270)

2. a   3. a   4. b   5. a   6. a

B2: Working on Affirmative and Negative Statements with *Be Going To* (p. 270)

A. *Conversation 1*
2. are going to have

Conversation 2
1. is going to help
2. 's going to give
3. are going to enjoy
4. 's going to be

B. 2. People aren't going to live on the moon in the next ten years.
3. I'm not going to meet the president.
4. The population of the world isn't going to decrease by 2010.
5. Scientists aren't going to discover life on Mars.
6. It's not going to/It isn't going to snow next August.

B3: Understanding Informal Speech (p. 271)

2. are going to be
3. are going to watch
4. is not going to play
5. are going to win
6. is going to be
7. is going to be
8. are going to go

B4: Working on *Yes/No* Questions (p. 272)

2. Are you going to attend the games?
3. Is it going to rain tomorrow?
4. Are the Tigers going to lose?
5. Are we going to have practice tonight?
6. Are we going to win the championship?

B5: Forming Information Questions (p. 272)

2. Where are you going to play next year?
3. Why are you going to change teams?
4. What are you going to do after you retire?
4. When is your team going to win a championship?
5. Who is going to be your new coach next season?

Think Critically About Meaning and Use (p. 273)

1. a
2. b

C1: Listening For Meaning and Use (p. 274)

	PLANS	PREDICTIONS
2.	✓	
3.		✓
4.		✓
5.	✓	
6.		✓
7.	✓	
8.	✓	

C2: Talking About Future Plans (p. 274)

A. Answers will vary.

C3: Using Future Time Expressions (p. 275)

A. Answers will vary.

C4: Making Predictions (p. 276)

Answers will vary. Some examples are:
2. She's going to skate.
3. They're going to eat.
4. The children are going to cross the road.
5. The children are going to go to school.
6. He's going to hit a homerun.

Think Critically About Meaning and Use (p. 277)

A. 2. c   3. a   4. b

B. 1. In 1, it's used to talk about a future plan. In 2 and 4, it's used to ask about a future plan. In 3, it's used to make a prediction.

2. It makes the meaning of B's answer more certain. When B says, "It's *probably* going to rain," it suggests that B is not 100% sure. There is still room for doubt.

Edit (p. 277)

2. Where are you going ∧ᵗᵒ be tomorrow?

3. Are they going to ∧ᵇᵉ happy?

4. correct

5. Who is going to ~~being~~ ᵇᵉ your coach?

6. Carl is ∧ⁿᵒᵗ going to ~~not~~ be a great player.

CHAPTER 18

A3: After You Read (p. 280)

2. F   3. F   4. T   5. T   6. T

Think Critically About Form (p. 282)

Underline: You, We
The form of *will* stays the same with different subjects.

B1: Listening for Form (p. 284)

	SIMPLE PRESENT	FUTURE WITH WILL	FUTURE WITH BE GOING TO
2.		✓	
3.		✓	
4.		✓	
5.			✓
6.	✓		

B2: Working on Affirmative and Negative Statements with *Will* (p. 284)

2. won't be   4. will fly
3. 'll look   5. won't forget

B3: Forming Questions with *Will* (p. 284)

2. When will dinner be ready?
3. Where will your best friend be in five years?
4. Who will you marry?
5. What will you wear tomorrow?
6. How will she get home?

B4: Understanding Informal Speech (p. 285)

2. friends will   5. Who will
3. What will   6. teeth will
4. weather will

Think Critically About Meaning and Use (p. 286)

1. c   2. b   3. a

C1: Listening for Meaning and Use (p. 287)

	PREDICTION	PROMISE	QUICK DECISION
2.	✓		
3.			✓
4.	✓		
5.	✓		
6.		✓	
7.			✓
8.		✓	

C2: Making Predictions (p. 287)

Answers will vary. Some examples are:
2. I'll clean the apartment tomorrow.
3. I'll buy you a new dress.
4. I won't fall asleep at work again.
5. I'll wash the dishes tomorrow night.
6. I won't speed again.

C3: Making Predictions (p. 288)

Answers will vary. Some examples are;
2. Children won't go to school. They'll communicate with their teachers by email.
3. Most people will work only four hours a day.
4. Computers will be very cheap.
5. People won't travel by car. They'll use public transportation.
6. Car won't use gas. They'll use hydrogen gas.
7. People will still eat three meals a day.
8. People will still watch TV for relaxation. Interactive TV programs will be very popular.

C4: Expressing Quick Decisions (p. 288)

Answers will vary. Some examples are:
2. I'll buy two tickets for the 9:50 train.
3. I'll buy a blue one.
4. I'll take section B.
5. I'll take the one on the fifth floor.
6. I'll come on Thursday.

Think Critically About Meaning and Use (p. 289)

A. 2. b   3. c   4. a

B. 1. In 2, speaker A uses *will* to make a prediction.
2. In 3, speaker B uses *will* to make a quick decision.

Edit (p. 289)

2. correct

3. I'll ~~to~~ wait for you right here.

4. We ~~will~~ᵂᵒⁿ'ᵗ be home tonight.

5. correct

6. Who will ~~goes~~ go to the library with her?

7. Will he ~~be~~ at work next week?

8. They won't come ~~not~~.

Part 7 TEST (pp. 291–292)

1. c	6. c	11. c	16. c
2. c	7. d	12. a	17. b
3. b	8. b	13. a	18. d
4. c	9. b	14. d	19. a
5. d	10. a	15. d	20. b

CHAPTER 19

A3: After You Read (p. 295)

	OPTIMIST	PESSIMIST
2.		✓
3.	✓	
4.		✓
5.	✓	
6.	✓	

Think Critically About Form (p. 296)

1. Circle: We, It, It, They, I

May and *might* do not have different forms with different subjects.

The base form of the verb follows *may* and *might*.

2. line 6: might not talk
line 8: might not pass
line 12: may not listen

B1: Listening for Form (p. 297)

	MAY	MIGHT	NO MODAL
2.			✓
3.	✓		
4.			✓
5.	✓		
6.		✓	
7.			✓
8.		✓	

B2: Forming Affirmative and Negative Statements (p. 298)

2. We may go to Taiwan next week.
3. Claudia might be in a meeting.
4. He might not take the job.
5. The governor may not win the election.
6. They might not have any money.

B3: Asking and Answering Questions (p. 298)

Answers will vary.

Think Critically About Meaning and Use (p. 299)

1. 1a refers to a possibility in the future. 2a refers to a possibility at the present time.
2. 1b and 2b

C1: Listening for Meaning and Use (p. 300)

	POSSIBILITY	CERTAINTY
2.	✓	
3.		✓
4.		✓
5.	✓	
6.		✓
7.		✓
8.	✓	

C2: Talking About Possibility and Certainty (p. 300)

2. might	4. will	6. might	8. might
3. might	5. will	7. might	

C3: Expressing Possibility and Certainty (p. 301)

Answers will vary. Some examples are:
2. He might fall and hurt himself.
3. He might be late for the exam.
4. He may get into an accident.
5. You may win a lot of money!

C4: Talking About Possibility and Certainty (p. 301)

Answers will vary.

C5: Expressing Possibility and Certainty (p. 302)

2. He's going to drop the boxes. He might frighten the child. The child may cry.
3. The box is going to hit the car. It may cause a lot of damage. The movers may lose their jobs.
4. The child is going to pop the balloon. The noise might frighten the woman. She may drop the tray and spill all the drinks.

Think Critically About Meaning and Use (p. 303)

A. 2. a 3. a 4. a

B. 1. B's first sentence shows uncertainty, so *will* is incorrect.

2. Answers will vary. Example: *"She's finally decided. She'll stay with me."*

Edit (p. 303)

2. We might ~~to~~ leave at noon.

3. Dan may ~~sees~~ see him today.

4. correct

5. correct

6. What might ~~happens~~ happen tomorrow?

7. They might ~~probably~~ take the train tomorrow.

8. There is someone at the door. It may ~~be~~ Jenna.

CHAPTER 20

A3: After You Read (p. 306)

2. F	3. F	4. F	5. T	6. F

Think Critically About Form (p. 308)

1. Circle: Jacob, He, the children, Child prodigies

Can and *could* do not have different forms with different subjects.

The base form of the verb follows *can* and *could*.

2. line 17: couldn't read or write
   line 31: couldn't tie
   line 37: can't (really) be
   line 39: can't play
   line 40: can't be

We add *not*. The negative of *can* is *cannot*, the negative of *could* is *could not*.

B1: Listening for Form (p. 310)

2. can	5. can't	8. couldn't
3. could	6. can	9. could
4. could	7. can't	10. couldn't

B2: Forming Sentences with *Can* and *Can't* (p. 310)

2. Teresa can't speak Spanish.
3. Irina cannot swim very well.
4. Julie can play the piano and the guitar.
5. The baby can't eat solid food.
6. Tomek can't run very fast.

B3: Forming Questions with *Can* (p. 311)

2. Can you speak many languages?
3. Can Hanna play any instruments?
4. Can you ride a bicycle?
5. What can Alex cook?
6. Who can beat me at tennis?

B4: Working on *Could* and *Couldn't* (p. 311)

A. 2. Eva couldn't roller skate.
3. Eva couldn't tie her shoes.
4. Eva could draw beautiful pictures.
5. Eva couldn't ride a bicycle.
6. Eva could play the piano.
7. Eva couldn't play tennis.
8. Eva could write simple poetry.

B. 2. A: Could Eva roller skate?
   B: No, she couldn't.
3. A: Could Eva tie her shoes?
   B: No, she couldn't.
4. A: Could Eva draw beautiful pictures?
   B: Yes, she could.
5. A: Could Eva ride a bicycle?
   B: No, she couldn't.
6. A: Could Eva play the piano?
   B: Yes, she could.
7. A: Could Eva play tennis?
   B: No, she couldn't.
8. A: Could Eva write simple poetry?
   B: Yes, she could.

Think Critically About Meaning and Use (p. 312)

1. a, c   2. b, d

C1: Listening for Meaning and Use (p. 313)

2. a	4. a	6. a	8. b
3. b	5. b	7. a	

C2: Talking About Present Abilities (p. 313)

A. Answers will vary.

C3: Talking About Past Ability (p. 314)

Answers will vary. Some examples are:

A. 2. I could play basketball.
3. I couldn't run a mile.
4. I could read very fast.
5. I couldn't talk to anyone.
6. I could read and write.

B. Answers will vary.

C4: Contrasting Past and Present Ability (p. 314)

2. couldn't	4. can	6. can	8. couldn't
3. couldn't	5. can't	7. couldn't	

Think Critically About Meaning and Use (p. 315)

A. 2. b   3. a   4. b

B. 1. Both question and answer refer to past ability, so *could* is used.

2. b

Edit (p. 315)

2. They can ~~to~~ see in the dark.
3. She can ~~runs~~ run very quickly.
4. correct
5. Could he ~~spoke~~ speak German?
6. What ~~you can~~ can you cook?
7. She ~~cans~~ can sing and dance.
8. Greg is bilingual. He ~~can't~~ can speak two languages.

CHAPTER 21

A3: After You Read (p. 319)

2. AS   3. AG   4. AS   5. UN   6. AS

Think Critically About Form (p. 320)

1. **Modals of request:** *Can, Could, Would, Will*

The common subject is *you*. The modal comes before the subject.

2. **Modals of permission:** *Could, May*

The common subject is *I*. The modal comes before the subject.

B1: Listening for Form (p. 322)

	CAN	COULD	MAY	WILL	WOULD
2.	✓				
3.					✓
4.			✓		
5.	✓				
6.	✓				
7.		✓			
8.				✓	

B2: Forming Statements and Questions (p. 322)

A. 2. You can't park your car here.
3. You may not leave early.

4. They may borrow my computer.
5. You can't talk to him now.

B. 2. Can you give us a ride?
3. Would you please close the door? (OR Would you close the door, please?)
4. Could I please have more time? (OR Could I have more time, please?)
5. When can I call him?

B3: Working on Short Answers (p. 323)

2. I will	5. you can	8. I can't, you can
3. I can't	6. you can	9. I can
4. you can	7. I will	10. I can't

Think Critically About Meaning and Use (p. 324)

1. b, e, f
2. a, c, d

C1: Listening for Meaning and Use (p. 326)

	PERMISSION	REQUEST
2.		✓
3.	✓	
4.	✓	
5.		✓
6.	✓	

C2: Making and Responding to Requests (p. 326)

Answers will vary. Some examples are:

Conversation 2
Could
No, I can't. There are no tables available near the window.

Conversation 3
Would
No, I won't. I don't want to share my answers. It's a test!

Conversation 4
Would
Sure, I can. Do you know the address?

Conversation 5
Could
Of course, I will. I know it's your favorite meal.

C3: Asking for Permission (p. 327)

A. Answers will vary. Some examples are:
2. Excuse me. Could I borrow your pen, please?
3. May I take this empty chair please?
4. Hello, Mr. Gomez. May I please speak to Rosa?
5. John, can I use your computer tonight?
6. Marcus, I have a date tonight. Can I use your car, please/?

B. Answers will vary.

C4: Making Requests and Asking for Permission (p. 328)

Answers will vary. Some examples are:
2. A: Could you get my kite for me, please?
   B: Of course, I can!
3. A: Would you please help me with these groceries?
   B: Sure. Let me have them.
4. A: Mom, can I go to the mall this weekend? They're having a great sale!

B: I'm sorry, you can't. You went last weekend and spent $100 dollars!
5. A: May I ask a question, please?
   B: Of course, you may.
6. A: Could we sit at that table by the window?
   B: I'm sorry, we're saving it for someone.

Think Critically About Meaning and Use (p. 329)

A. 2. b   3. a   4. b

B. 1. *May* and *please*

2. This conversation seems to take place between family members. That means they know each other well, so they don't need to be so polite with each other.

Edit (p. 329)

2. No, you ~~mayn't~~ *may not* smoke here.

3. correct

4. ~~Would~~ *Could/Can/May* I leave now?

5. ~~May~~ *Can/Could/Will* you help me?

6. Would ~~please~~ you ∧*please* help me? OR Would ~~please~~ you help me ∧*,please*?

7. correct

8. ~~Sure,~~ *Sorry,* I can't help you now. I'm busy.

CHAPTER 22

A3: After You Read (p. 333)

Answers will vary.

Think Critically About Form (p. 334)

1. Subjects: people, A person, (Every) car, Students
Should and *must* do not have different forms with different subjects.
2. Subjects: We, The car, You
Have to has different forms with different subjects: we use *has to* with third-person singular subjects and *have to* with subjects in all other persons.
The base form of the verb follows *have to*.

B1: Listening for Form (p. 336)

	(DON'T) HAVE TO	MUST (NOT)	SHOULD (NOT)
2.			✓
3.	✓		
4.		✓	
5.	✓		
6.			✓

B2: Building Sentences with *Should, Must,* and *Have To* (p. 336)

Answers will vary. Some examples are:

Affirmative Sentences:
I must make a speech.
I should take the test.

I have to go by plane.
You must take the test.
You have to take the test.
You have to go by plane.
The other students must go by plane.
The other students should make a speech.
The other students should study tonight.
Susan must take the test.
Susan should make a speech.
Susan has to go by plane.

Negative Sentences:
I don't have to take the test.
I must not make a speech.
I should not go by plane.
You don't have to take the test.
You must not make a speech.
You should not study tonight.
The other students don't have to go by plane.
The other students must not take the test.
The other students should not study tonight.
Susan doesn't have to go by plane.
Susan must not take the test.
Susan should not make a speech.

B3: Forming *Yes/No* Questions with *Should* and *Have To* (p. 337)

2. Do you have to go to class tomorrow?
3. Does your friend have to study chemistry next year?
4. Should we have homework on the weekends?
5. Should the school library be open all night?

B4: Writing Information Questions with *Should* and *Have To* (p. 337)

Answers will vary. Some examples are:
2. What do we have to read for tomorrow?
3. Who should check the deposits?
4. How long do I have to wait for the test results?
5. When do Julie and Mark have to leave?

Think Critically About Meaning and Use (p. 338)

1. a   2. c   3. b and d; d is more formal.

C1: Listening for Meaning and Use (p. 339)

2. necessity   6. prohibition
3. opinion   7. necessity
4. lack of necessity   8. lack of necessity
5. advice

C2: Giving Advice (p. 339)

Answers will vary.

C3: Describing Rules and Requirements (p. 340)

A. Answers will vary.

B. Answers will vary. Some examples are:
2. Students don't have to wear a uniform.
3. Students don't have to buy a dictionary.
4. Students must not smoke in the classroom.
5. Students must not eat in the computer lab.
6. Students must do homework.
7. Students don't have to carry a student ID.
8. Students must pay school fees.

Think Critically About Meaning and Use (p. 341)

A. 2. b   3. a   4. c

B. 1. Choice "a" is correct; we would use it if the sign says something like "Visitors cannot park here." We might use choice "b" if the first speaker says something like, "We have to park here. Look at that sign." We can use choice "c" if there is a choice of places to park and the first speaker says something like, "We don't have to park here. We can park in another place. Look at that sign."

2. b = necessity; a = prohibition; c = lack of necessity

Edit (p. 341)

2. correct

3. correct

4. U.S. voters ~~should~~ *must* be at least 18 years old.

5. You must ~~to~~ finish before 6:00.

6. Does she ~~has~~ *have* to leave immediately?

7. You should not ~~studying~~ *study* every night.

8. Didn't you see the sign? You ~~don't have to~~ *must not* smoke here.

Part 8 TEST (pp. 343–344)

1. b	5. a	9. b	13. a	17. f
2. c	6. d	10. c	14. d	18. a
3. d	7. a	11. a	15. c	19. g
4. b	8. d	12. d	16. a	20. d

CHAPTER 23

A3: After You Read (p. 347)

2. Shichi Go-San   6. Boxing Day
3. Day of the Dead   7. Loy Krathong
4. Loy Krathong   8. Shichi Go-San
5. Boxing Day

Think Critically About Form (p. 348)

1. Underline: Mrs. Allen, her, the manager, him
2. Nouns: Mrs. Allen, the manager, pronouns: her, him

B1: Listening for Form (p. 349)

	ME	HIM	HER	IT	US	THEM
2.					✓	
3.				✓		
4.			✓			
5.		✓				
6.	✓					

B2: Working with Object Pronouns (p. 349)

2. them   4. me   6. her
3. it   5. us

B3: Using Subject and Object Pronouns (p. 349)

2. it   4. I   6. She   8. We
3. them   5. I   7. us

Think Critically About Form (p. 350)

1. Underline: sang, sang, sang
   Circle: a folk song, it, a folk song
2. Double underline: the children

C1: Listening for Form (p. 352)

A. 2. their friends and family
3. their guests
4. Christmas cookies
5. their homes
6. toys

B. 2. IO
3. IO
4. DO
5. DO
6. DO

C2: Identifying Direct Objects (p. 352)

2. X
3. his friends and family
4. a letter
5. an important question
6. X
7. a wife
8. a career
9. an answer
10. a letter

C3: Identifying Direct Objects and Indirect Objects (p. 353)

3. DO
4. DO
5. DO
6. IO
7. DO
8. DO
9. DO
10. IO
11. IO
12. DO

C4: Forming Sentences with Direct and Indirect Objects (p. 353)

2. I bought him a present yesterday.
3. We gave her a birthday cake.
4. Mrs. Johnson got a glass of water for him.
5. She wrote an essay for the school newspaper.
6. They are showing us their photos.

Think Critically About Meaning and Use (p. 354)

1. Underline: a book, his retirement
   Circle: his teacher, everyone
2. Greg bought a book. Greg's teacher received his gift.
3. The boss announced his retirement. The boss made the announcement to everyone.

D1: Listening for Meaning and Use (p. 355)

	DIRECT OBJECT	INDIRECT OBJECT
2.		✓
3.		✓
4.	✓	
5.	✓	
6.		✓
7.	✓	
8.		✓

D2: Using Direct Objects (p. 356)

Answers will vary. Some examples are:
2. a mall
3. new clothes
4. a car
5. a new puppy
6. ethnic food

D3: Using Indirect Objects (p. 356)

Answers will vary. Some examples are:
2. Alex mailed the guests the invitations last week.
3. Alex gave directions to Amy's parents.
4. Alex baked Amy a chocolate cake yesterday.
5. Alex bought Amy a birthday gift at the mall.
6. Alex wrote a short speech for Amy.

D4: Talking About Holidays (p. 356)

A. Answers will vary.

Think Critically About Meaning and Use (p. 357)

A. 2. c　　3. a　　4. c

B. 1. They owe a lot of money to the bank.

2. A: you = indirect object; German = direct object B: me = indirect object

Edit (p. 357)

2. I made ~~for you~~ a cake ∧ for you. OR I made ~~for~~ for you a cake.

3. He sends ~~to us~~ an email ∧ to us every year. OR He sends ~~to~~ us an email every month.

4. correct

5. We bought a bicycle ∧ for my daughter. OR We bought ~~a bicycle~~ my daughter ∧ a bicycle.

6. correct

7. They said ~~me~~ good-bye ∧ to me.

8. Let me tell ~~she~~ her the answer.

CHAPTER 24

A3: After You Read (p. 360)

Mistake: 4 and 6
Not a Mistake: 2, 3, and 5

Think Critically About Form (p. 362)

1. line 6:　like to talk
   line 7:　prefer to read
   line 8:　learn to say
   line 12: begin to improve
2. to + the base form of a verb
3. line 22: enjoy celebrating
   line 29: don't like discussing
   line 30: prefer beginning
   line 31: avoid using
4. base form of verb + -ing

B1: Listening for Form (p. 363)

	INFINITIVE	GERUND
2.	✓	
3.	✓	
4.		✓
5.		✓
6.	✓	
7.		✓
8.		✓

B2: Identifying Infinitives and Gerunds (p. 364)

2. X　4. I　6. G　8. G
3. I　5. I　7. X

B3: Building Sentences with Infinitives and Gerunds (p. 364)

A. Answers will vary. Some examples are:

Affirmative Infinitive:
The students want to speak Chinese.
The students need to pass this course.
Her boss needs to sign the contract.
Her boss plans to move to California.
Our teacher needs to sign the contract.
Our teacher is learning to speak Chinese.
His parents are planning to sign the contract.
His parents are planning to move to California.

Negative Infinitive:
The students don't want to pass this course.
The students are not learning to speak Chinese.
Her boss doesn't need to sign the contract.
Her boss isn't planning to move to California.
Our teacher doesn't want to speak Chinese.
Our teacher isn't planning to sign the contract.
His parents aren't planning to move to California.

B. Answers will vary. Some examples are:

Affirmative Gerund:
Most of my friends enjoy speaking in front of a large audience.
Most of my friends kept taking piano lessons last year.
My cousin and I enjoyed taking piano lessons last year.
My cousin and I kept taking piano lessons last year.
Philip keeps making mistakes.
Philip discussed taking piano lessons last year.
I enjoyed taking piano lessons last year.
I avoid making mistakes.

Negative Gerund:
Most of my friends didn't enjoy taking piano lessons last year.
Most of my friends don't enjoy making mistakes.
My cousin and I don't enjoy making mistakes.
My cousin and I are discussing opening a business together.
Philip doesn't enjoy making mistakes.
Philip keeps making mistakes.
I enjoyed speaking in front of a large audience.
I don't enjoy making mistakes.

B4: Forming Questions Infinitives and Gerunds (p. 365)

A. 2. What do you want to do this summer?
3. Where do your friends enjoy going on weekends?
4. What kinds of films do you avoid watching?
5. What do you hope to do in the future?
6. Where do you expect to live in ten years?

B. Answers will vary.

B5: Choosing the Infinitive or the Gerund (p. 365)

2. b   4. a, b   6. a, b   8. a, b
3. a   5. a   7. b

Think Critically About Meaning and Use (p. 366)

1. Sentences b and c talk about an activity. Sentence a does not.
2. b and c

C1: Listening for Meaning and Use (p. 367)

2. b   3. b   4. a   5. b   6. a

C2: Talking About Activities and States (p. 367)

A. Answers will vary. Some examples are:
2. eating red meat
3. to take a vacation
4. jogging in the park
5. cleaning my room
6. to borrow money
7. studying for exams
8. to be a vegetarian

B. 1. 2, 4, 5, 7
2. 3, 6, 8
3. 1

C3: Expressing Likes and Dislikes (p. 368)

A. Answers will vary.

Think Critically About Meaning and Use (p. 369)

A. 2. b   3. a   4. c

B. 1. No, the meaning stays the same.
2. No, we can't replace the gerund with an infinitive because dislike only takes a gerund.

Edit (p. 369)

Keisha plans ~~going~~ *to go* to college next year so she is starting ∧ *to* apply to different schools. She wants to go to a school in Chicago because she wants ∧ *to* live at home. In this way, she'll avoid ~~to~~ spending a lot of money on room and board. She enjoys ~~to study~~ *studying* biology and chemistry, and she likes ~~help~~ *helping/to help* people. She wants to ~~becoming~~ *become* a nurse. Her grades are good so she expects ∧ *to* get into several schools in the area.

Part 9 TEST (pp. 371–372)

1. c	5. b	9. a	13. b	17. e
2. d	6. a	10. d	14. c	18. c
3. a	7. d	11. c	15. d	19. b
4. d	8. b	12. c	16. f	20. g

CHAPTER 25

A3: After You Read (p. 374)

	FEATURE PHONE	SMARTPHONE
2.	✓	
3.		✓
4.		✓
5.		✓
6.	✓	

Think Critically About Form (p. 376)

1.
Adjectives	Adverbs
weaker	harder
older	faster

We add *-er* to the adjective or adverb.

2.
Adjectives	Adverb
more popular	more slowly
more efficient	

We use *more* + adjective or adverb.

B1: Listening for Form (p. 378)

	REGULAR FORM WITH *-ER*	REGULAR FORM WITH *MORE*	IRREGULAR FORM
2.	✓		
3.	✓		
4.		✓	
5.			✓
6.		✓	
7.	✓		
8.	✓		

B2: Forming Comparatives (p. 378)

A.
Adjectives	Adverbs
2. easier	5. faster
3. more intelligent	6. more happily
4. more expensive	7. more quietly
	8. more carefully

B.
Adjectives	Adverbs
2. nice	5. badly
3. tall	6. well
4. pretty	7. slowly
	8. efficiently

B3: Making Comparative Statements (p. 379)

2. faster than
3. more quickly than
4. better than, cheaper than
5. more convenient than, more reliable than
6. faster, more accurately than

B4: Working on Comparative Adjectives and Adverbs (p. 379)

Conversation 1
2. shorter
3. more violent

Conversation 2
1. harder
2. more effectively
3. friendlier/more friendly
4. more popular
5. better

Think Critically About Meaning and Use (p. 380)

1. a 2. c 3. b

C1: Listening for Meaning and Use (p. 381)

2. a 4. b 6. a 8. a
3. a 5. b 7. a

C2: Making Comparisons (p. 381)

Answers will vary. Some examples are:
1b. A motorcycle is more dangerous than a bicycle.
2a. A football player is stronger than a basketball player.
2b. A basketball player jumps higher than a football player.
3a. A bird is more beautiful than a cat.
3b. A cat is quieter than a bird.

C3: Expressing Similarities and Differences(p. 382)

A. Answers will vary.

C4: Expressing Opinions (p. 382)

A. Answers will vary.

B. Answers will vary.

Think Critically About Meaning and Use (p. 383)

A. 2. a 3. a 4. a

B. 1. a. less; b. better

2. c. "That's great!"

Edit (p. 383)

2. Davis High School is ~~large~~ larger than Union High School.
3. Who is ~~more tall~~ taller?
4. Ling sings ⋀more beautifully than Sam.
5. correct
6. Erica is friendlier ~~from~~ than Luiz.
7. My computers are ~~more~~ newer than yours.
8. correct

CHAPTER 26

A3: After You Read (p. 386)

2. Barbie doll
3. ATM
4. computer
5. liquid paper
6. satellite technology

Think Critically About Form (p. 388)

1.
Adjective	Adverb
the greatest	the fastest

To form the superlative of these words, we use *the* + adjective/adverb + *-est*.

2. the most popular   the most efficient
the most useful

To form the superlative of these words, we use *the most* + adjective/adverb.

B1: Listening for Form (p. 390)

	COMPARATIVE	SUPERLATIVE
2.	✓	
3.		✓
4.	✓	
5.		✓
6.	✓	
7.	✓	
8.		✓

B2: Forming Superlatives (p. 390)

A. Adjectives
2. the easiest
3. the most intelligent
4. the newest

Adverbs
5. the most happily
6. the most gracefully
7. the most fluently
8. the most carefully

B. Adjectives
2. pretty
3. thin
4. happy

Adverbs
5. fast
6. badly
7. quickly
8. well

B3: Working with Superlative Adjectives and Adverbs (p. 391)

Conversation 1
2. the highest
3. the hardest

Conversation 2
1. the most careless
2. the best
3. the most efficiently

Conversation 3
1. the worst
2. the most carefully

Conversation 4
1. the longest
2. the largest

Think Critically About Meaning and Use (p. 392)

1. a   2. b   3. c

C1: Listening for Meaning and Use (p. 393)

	LIGHTHOUSE UNIVERSITY	WESTBROOK COLLEGE	CRANBERRY UNIVERSITY
2.			✓
3.			✓
4.			✓
5.			✓
6.	✓		
7.		✓	
8.		✓	

C2: Expressing Opinions (p. 393)

A. Answers will vary.

C3: Making Comparisons (p. 394)

A. 2. bar-headed goose
3. anaconda
4. cheetah
5. blue whale
6. sea wasp jellyfish
7. sea turtle
8. peregrine falcon

C. Answers will vary. Some examples are:
2. The bar-headed goose can dive the fastest of all other animals.
3. The anaconda is the longest snake in the world.
4. The cheetah is the fastest animal in the world.
5. The blue whale is the heaviest animal in the world.
6. The sea wasp jellyfish is the most dangerous sea animal.
7. The sea turtle lives the longest of all sea animals.
8. The peregrine falcon can fly the highest of all animals.

C4: Expressing Opinions (p. 394)

Answers will vary.

Think Critically About Meaning and Use (p. 395)

A. 2. a   3. a   4. c

B. 1. a

2. Answers will vary. Some examples are: B: Yes, in a few years it's going to be the most useful language for business. / C: I don't think so. It's the most difficult of all the languages at our school.

Edit (p. 395)

2. correct
3. He's ~~an~~ *the* oldest person in the class.
4. correct
5. This restaurant is not the ~~cheaper~~ *cheapest* one in the city.
6. This is the ~~most~~ slowest bus in this town.
7. She is the smartest ~~than~~ *of* all.
8. They're the ~~carefullest~~ *most careful* students.

Part 10 TEST (pp. 397–398)

1. d
2. a
3. a
4. d
5. c
6. d
7. c
8. d
9. c
10. c
11. d
12. e
13. a
14. c
15. easier
16. better
17. worse
18. faster
19. more accurately
20. more convenient